TAKING
FUND RAISING
SERIOUSLY

Dwight F. Burlingame
Lamont J. Hulse,
Editors

Foreword by Eugene Dorsey

TAKING
FUND RAISING
SERIOUSLY

Advancing
the Profession and
Practice of
Raising Money

 Jossey-Bass Publishers
San Francisco   •   Oxford   •   1991

TAKING FUND RAISING SERIOUSLY
Advancing the Profession and Practice of Raising Money
by Dwight F. Burlingame and Lamont J. Hulse, Editors

Copyright © 1991 by: Jossey-Bass Inc., Publishers
350 Sansome Street
San Francisco, California 94104

&

Jossey-Bass Limited
Headington Hill Hall
Oxford OX3 0BW

Library of Congress Cataloging-in-Publication Data

Taking fund raising seriously : advancing the profession and practice
   of raising money / Dwight F. Burlingame and Lamont J. Hulse,
   editors.
        p.   cm.—(Jossey-Bass nonprofit sector series)
   Includes bibliographical references and index.
   ISBN 1-55542-388-4
   1. Fund raising—United States.   2. Corporations, Nonprofit—
United States—Finance.   I. Burlingame, Dwight.   II. Hulse, Lamont
J.   III. Series.
HG177.5.U6T34   1991
658.15′224—dc 20   91-18232
                                                                CIP

Manufactured in the United States of America

The paper in this book meets the guidelines for
permanence and durability of the Committee on
Production Guidelines for Book Longevity of the
Council on Library Resources.

JACKET DESIGN BY WILLI BAUM

FIRST EDITION

Code 9191

The Jossey-Bass
Nonprofit Sector Series

Contents

Foreword   xiii
by Eugene Dorsey

Preface   xxi

Contributors   xxix

Part One: The Field of Fund Raising   1

1.   Toward a Philosophy of Fund Raising   3
     Robert L. Payton, Henry A. Rosso,
     Eugene R. Tempel

2.   The Evolution of Professional Fund Raising: 1890–1990   18
     Jeanne Harrah-Conforth, John Borsos

3.   Metaphors Fund Raisers Live By: Language and
     Reality in Fund Raising   37
     Richard C. Turner

     Part Two: The Moral Dimension of Fund Raising   51

4.   A Historical and Moral Analysis of Religious
     Fund Raising   53
     Thomas H. Jeavons

5.   What Counts as Deception in Higher Education
     Development   73
     Deni Elliott

6.   Conflicts of Interest Between Nonprofits and
     Corporate Donors   83
     Barbara J. Lombardo

     Part Three: The Professionalization of Fund Raising   101

7.   Fund Raising in Transition: Strategies for
     Professionalization   103
     Harland G. Bloland, Rita Bornstein

8.   Effective Business Practices in Fund Raising   124
     Margaret A. Duronio, Bruce A. Loessin

9.   The Feminization of Fund Raising   144
     Julie C. Conry

     Part Four: Improving Fund Raising Practice   171

10. My Sixteen Rules for a Successful Volunteer-Based
     Capital Campaign   173
     Alex Carroll

11. Can We Throw Away the Tin Cup?   184
     Kay Sprinkel Grace

12.   What Fund Raisers Should Know About the Law   200
        Betsy Hills Bush

13.   Contemporary Trends in Black Philanthropy:
        Challenging the Myths   219
        Emmett D. Carson

14.   The Economics of Fund Raising   239
        Richard Steinberg

15.   Investing More Money in Fund Raising—Wisely   257
        Wilson C. Levis

16.   Taking Fund Raising Seriously: An Agenda   272
        Robert L. Payton, Henry A. Rosso,
        Eugene R. Tempel

        Index   283

Foreword

A member of a national board on which I serve recently wrote a blistering letter to the board's president because she had been asked to participate in a membership campaign. She indicated quite sharply that she had not assumed a board position to engage in fund raising; it was demeaning and something she did not do. She implied that such involvement was hazardous to her health and her reputation.

Leaving aside the question of whether or not seeking new members is fund raising, her reaction quite startled me. I have for well over thirty years been both a willing and an unwilling participant in fund-raising campaigns. I share the ambivalence that seizes many volunteer campaigners when they are asked to call their friends on behalf of another capital or endowment campaign. I have never found fund raising as exhilarating or demoralizing as a game of golf, but I have never doubted its importance or disputed its vital place among the factors that undergird the philanthropic sector. However, I have to admit that through the years, I have observed developments and attitudes associated with raising funds that are somewhat unsettling even as others are very reassuring. I will comment on them and put them into perspective, at least into my perspective, warped though it may be.

Sensitizing Fund Raisers and Donors to Mission

Curious ironies, estrangements, and shifting relationships have
punctuated the fund-raising drama. This is not to say that fund
raising has a monopoly on such characteristics, but I think about
the success of skilled fund raisers who perform brilliantly for just
causes but have insufficient awareness of the real impact such causes
have on people's lives. I think about the success of certain fund
raisers who know how to exploit the generous motives of good
people for personal gain. I think about the selfless, dedicated
individuals whose existence is almost entirely consumed by their
commitment to helping others, yet who cannot mount successful
fund-raising efforts. I also think about and applaud the work of
professional and volunteer fund raisers who are able to bring their
hearts and their skills together to achieve enormously significant
results with a full and rich appreciation for the sector they serve and
the lives they improve.

I have long reflected on the mechanical quality of many campaigns to raise funds: the competition among divisions in a United
Way drive, the emphasis on reaching goals, and the technical clarity
of the steps to success in selling a cause. Does the end become
forgotten as the execution of the solicitation, rather than the need
for the funds, drives the outcome?

How can we better sensitize fund raisers, both professional
and volunteer, to the real mission of the organizations they are
serving? How can we make them feel, not just understand, the
plight of those for whom the funds are being raised—how the recipients live and what has created the circumstances they are in?

The motives of volunteer solicitors vary. Some seek recognition and career advantages from their roles. There is nothing wrong
with that. But this nation can benefit from a widespread visceral
involvement on the part of volunteers in the frustration, despair,
and hopelessness of millions of Americans who are the beneficiaries
of philanthropy.

Impersonalization is encouraged by some campaign methods. What used to be called slick, boiler-room operations are now dubbed "telemarketing," a new triumph in the use of euphemisms. If the approach were limited to the selling of circus tickets to benefit handicapped children, I could tolerate it, despite the abuses. But now that telemarketing has fallen into the hands of stockbrokers, there is no way to achieve your daily minimum requirement of broccoli at your evening meal because of the phone calls. The method has spread and many reputable organizations now rely on telephone solicitation.

To go beyond this impersonal approach, we need to evoke the compassion and understanding necessary to create a healing environment that penetrates government as well as the private sector. A challenge exists, I believe, to bring the seekers and the served more closely together. Methods can include tours of troubled sections of our cities; close-up conversations with the disadvantaged; and use of videos depicting the needs of social agencies, museums, and shelters for the homeless.

I wonder how many board members of nonprofit organizations have ever seen the areas served by their group, or been inside the agencies, or met with a recipient of aid. One of the most effective tools employed by the Rochester United Way was a tour of the inner city for board members and key leaders in its campaign. I know that as a board member I identified much more emotionally and rationally with the effort because I had seen into the lives of many who were receiving benefits from United Way agencies. I am sure that such a procedure has become more common, but numberless fund-raising efforts still fail to make that vital link between the solicitors and those served.

Council on Foundations president James Joseph has spent considerable time examining the giving patterns and the motives of philanthropists in various cultures. He has pointed out that active altruism is usually sparked when a person becomes aware of his or her interconnectedness. In *The Charitable Impulse* (1989), he writes, "The growth of philanthropy may be measured by the extent to which the notion of community came to include outsiders (the poor, slaves, even enemies) whose fate was previously a matter of little or no concern" (p. 150). It is that sense of community that I believe must be developed among fund raisers, funders, and those who benefit from the funds.

Training Fund Raisers

The struggle of small nonprofits to raise funds is especially troubling as the pipeline of government support continues to diminish. Many small organizations are fortunately brought into the fold of the United Way, but many are not. Even those that are part of it still face special campaign requirements for capital needs, emergencies, and other costs. Can more support be received from corporations and foundations to teach fund-raising skills to those who have needs but lack knowledge? I think it can be done, even recognizing that those with small budgets and limited staff may not have the time to learn and execute those skills. There will always be a place for the retired professional fund raiser to provide, on a voluntary basis, his or her expert knowledge for the task of getting a small organization to the point where it can support an on-staff development person.

More foundations and corporations must concentrate on leveraging their grants and supporting projects that enable nonprofits to raise more funds from individuals. There are a number of ways to do that, including general technical and management assistance, but certainly the area of fund raising offers one of the most productive avenues.

While I was president of the Gannett Foundation, we made a number of grants, particularly to new community foundations, that were aimed at assisting nonprofits in the initial funding of a development executive. Some other organizations, such as human service agencies, have received similar Gannett Foundation assistance. Another approach has been to experiment with fund-raising workshops for nonprofit executives. Although teaching some of the fundamentals of raising funds is not as effective as providing a fund-raising professional to an organization, it at least sets an organization on a course toward attracting resources. Fund raisers may be quite skilled and professionally qualified, but if the organization they are working for is not fulfilling its mission, is poorly managed, or is not serving its clients, their efforts will soon become less successful.

In Chapter Eleven, Kay Sprinkel Grace poses the question "Can we throw away the tin cup?" One of the answers, she says, depends on educating donors about the nonprofit sector—the way it operates, its needs, its position, and its potential. Until that happens, there will be an expectation of tin cup fund raising. She notes that "to replace the notion of 'needy' organizations with the idea of organizations that are meeting community needs will require diligence and patience on the part of those who are shaping our sector for the future. It will also require an increased sense of partnership with the media, with legislators, and with the court system to help them become aware of what this sector is truly about—that fund raising is not begging." She's right. This is a remarkable sector that has experienced unusual growth and yet has been taken for granted. And despite the challenges it faces, it may be operating in a new social environment that could encourage a higher level of generosity. Successful fund raising is dependent on many factors, not just the execution of the practice itself.

Growth of the Sector

During the past fifty years, the sector has grown at an astounding rate. In 1946, Internal Revenue Service reports were filed by just under 100,000 tax-exempt organizations. By 1963, that number had risen to between 400,000 and 500,000 groups—an increase of more than 400 percent—and since that time, the number has doubled. Approximately 72 percent of the groups currently on IRS rolls were granted exempt status after 1960.

The Exploratory Project on Financing the Nonprofit Sector, conducted by the Institute for Public Policy and Administration, emphasized in its October 1988 report that the sector is the major service provider in most, if not all, of the areas in which it operates. The report noted that during the past fifty years the United States has increasingly relied on nonprofit organizations to provide needed public benefits, such as delivering services funded by tax monies; representing the public interest to both government and business; attending to arts, culture, education, and other enrichment activities; and providing opportunities for self-help, charitable pursuits, and improvement in the quality of life. The report said: "A deeper assessment of the role of the nonprofit sector, however, must recognize nonprofits as a key feature of our democratic, pluralistic society; they are important even beyond the services they provide. The independent, nonprofit sector embodies the American tradition of encouraging any person or group to take the initiative to speak, act, or organize for the public good" (Institute for Public Policy and Administration, 1988, p. 2).

The prominence of the nonprofit sector is very much an American phenomenon, the report reminded us. And it is true that although some European countries have voluntary sectors, they tend to be considerably smaller and less important than their American counterpart.

Raising Time and Money from Individuals

Federal support for the sector was reduced significantly during the 1980s. Although expenditures for Medicare and Medicaid increased, reductions occurred in all other program areas, according to studies by Lester Salamon of Johns Hopkins University and Alan Abramson of the Urban Institute. The inflation-adjusted value of federal spending in the nonprofit fields of employment and training, social services, health services (excluding Medicare and Medicaid), community development, higher education, and international affairs declined by $120 billion during the period between fiscal year 1982 and fiscal year 1990.

The Urban Institute has studied human service nonprofits and found that they were not able to offset their government funding cuts with increased charitable contributions. Whatever recovery they achieved was the result of increased fees, which accounted for 70 percent of the replacement income. Increased fees, of course, can reduce the number of needy people able to benefit from the services. The Exploratory Project on Financing the Nonprofit Sector concluded that "private funding cannot expand indefinitely, and there is evidence that it may be topping out now" (Institute for Public Policy and Administration, 1988, p. 2).

I am more sanguine than that about the prospects for in-

creased private giving. For three years I served as chairman of IN-
DEPENDENT SECTOR's "Give Five" campaign, a project aimed
at imprinting on the public's mind a standard or guideline for
giving and volunteering. "Give Five" means five percent of income
and five hours of volunteer time a week to charitable organizations.

The landmark 1988 survey of giving and volunteering conducted by the Gallup organization for INDEPENDENT SECTOR
revealed that 71 percent of respondents gave to charity and almost
50 percent volunteered. Seventy-five percent said they believed Americans should volunteer, yet half of those who espoused voluntarism
did not give of their own time. Three-fourths said they believed they
should give to charity, but 27 percent declined to back up this belief
with donations. And as had been revealed in other studies, many
individuals reported they did not know how much they should give
or how much time they should volunteer but felt they should do
more (Hodgkinson and Weitzman, 1988, p. 2). I believe the potential
for expanding the financial support of the nonprofit sector is enormous. But it will require strong, well-managed nonprofits that communicate effectively about their activities and employ professional,
ethical fund raisers to solicit their prospects.

Across the land, there is a growing awareness of the stagger-
ing size and influence of America's philanthropic sector. Many signals indicate that we may be on the threshold of a new era of social
consciousness. Historian Arthur Schlesinger wrote that "the nation
turns at 30-year intervals—the span of a generation—to public purpose, idealism, and affirmative government" (1989, p. 18). Since the
beginning of this country, foreign visitors have commented on the
surprising persistence of Americans in forming voluntary organizations and developing nongovernmental institutions to solve community problems. INDEPENDENT SECTOR has pointed to the
incredible variety of American institutions that have emerged from
this impulse: libraries, museums, civic organizations, universities,
the United Way, symphony orchestras—the list is almost endless.

In this decade, as many people seek to put more meaning
into their lives, fund raisers must relate what their organizations are
doing as part of this splendorous, pluralistic ballet that is our democracy. Sometimes wild heavings and dislocations occur in this
sector, but, as a heart continues to beat although it may occasionally

be interrupted by unexpected palpitations, the nonprofit sector keeps pumping the lifeblood of our republic. And it is in this independent sector that is found not just the heart of our country but its soul. May the raisers of funds always be conscious of their responsibilities to preserve and strengthen this organ so vital to sustaining American life.

When we look out over the vista of rushing cities, with millions mired in poverty and illiteracy, children weak from hunger, arts organizations closing their doors, libraries crumbling, illegal drugs sold on street corners, and babies born with AIDS, there is so much yet to be done. Arthur Dobrin said: "Whatever good there is in the world I inherit from the courage and work of those who went before me. I, in turn, have a responsibility to make things better for those who will inherit the earth from me" (*Giving Is Caring*, July 12, 1988). Those are words to ponder as we take fund raising seriously.

Rochester, New York   Eugene Dorsey
August 1991

References

Giving Is Caring calendar, July 12, 1988. New York: Workman, 1988.

Hodgkinson, V., and Weitzman, M. *Giving and Volunteering in the United States: Summary of Findings from a National Survey.* Conducted by the Gallup Organization. Washington, D.C.: INDEPENDENT SECTOR, 1988.

Institute for Public Policy and Administration. *Part of the Solution: Innovative Approaches to Nonprofit Funding.* Washington, D.C.: Union for Experimenting Colleges and Universities, 1988.

Joseph, J. *The Charitable Impulse.* New York: Foundation Center, 1989.

Schlesinger, A., Jr. "America, the Arts and the Future." First annual Nancy Hanks lecture on arts and public policy, Washington, D.C.: Gannett Foundation, 1989.

Preface

The March 1990 edition of the *NonProfit Times* reported the results of a survey which found that only 37 percent of Americans felt that fund raisers were "trustworthy" ("Less Than Half . . . ," 1990). According to this survey, the American public trusts fund raisers more than lawyers (30 percent), politicians (7 percent), and car salespersons (5 percent). However, Americans place more trust in television news anchorpersons (54 percent) and doctors (71 percent) than in those whose profession it is to raise money for charitable causes.

This poor public image is particularly disturbing to fund raisers entrusted with this vital function in the operation of third-sector organizations. Recent years have seen a growth in the demands placed on nonprofit agencies for programs and services. At the same time, those agencies must now work harder to secure the resources necessary to present programs and services. Faced with declining governmental support and competition for private monies in an era of increasing costs, nonprofit organizations are taking the need for fund raising very seriously.

The urgent need for money and the immediate challenges of raising funds leave practicing fund raisers little time to seriously consider important questions about fund raising as a profession or examine different perspectives on the field. The most effective practicing fund raisers are very busy people. Asking for money from foundations, corporations, or individuals is itself a complex and time-consuming process, but that task is only one that fund raisers must perform. They stand at a critical intersection between their organization and the communities it serves, thereby providing a link between the mission of the organization and the means necessary to implement the mission. In executing that linkage, a fund raiser often must balance competing, sometimes conflicting, demands and expectations of staff, colleagues, volunteers, trustees, and donors. To reconcile all of these reasonable demands takes statesmanship, and statesmanship takes time.

The demands of fund raising allow too little time for training and even less for considered reflection on professional matters not of immediate concern. Time may be allocated to read the latest journals and periodicals or to attend professional meetings, because these efforts provide information about new techniques or technological advancements—knowledge immediately translatable into productivity. Few fund raisers, however, provide themselves the opportunity to reflect and philosophize. This is particularly true with the new recruits to fund raising who have been moved immediately into the front lines with little formal training and no access to the apprenticeship tradition that educated earlier generations of fund raisers.

All fund raisers should have the requisite technical knowledge, but the most effective are those working from a base of both knowledge and wisdom. They adjust to changing times and conditions because they have a sense of who they are as professionals, appreciate the role of fund raising in their organization, and understand that what they do is important to the philanthropic sector and to society as a whole. Those who take fund raising seriously seek new perspectives on the profession to better understand their craft and enrich their professional lives. Only by addressing fundamental issues about fund raising and its role in a democratic society will the disparity between its negative public image and its importance

to the third sector be reconciled. That is a basic assumption behind
Taking Fund Raising Seriously.

Audience

Fund raisers who are only looking for a few helpul hints will find
this book useful. However, *Taking Fund Raising Seriously* will be
most meaningful to those practitioners who seek a deeper understanding of the wisdom, tradition, and purpose behind fund raising. The time they give themselves to read and consider these essays
will be repaid. The marginal increase in their productivity may not
be immediately apparent, but the long-term rewards should be
significant.

    Taking Fund Raising Seriously will interest many scholars
of the third sector. Philanthropy is now being studied from many
disciplines, including economics, history, sociology, anthropology,
English, philosophy, religion, women's studies, and American and
African-American studies. Staff and faculty in professional schools
of business, public administration, arts administration, and social
work, and from emerging programs in philanthropic studies and
nonprofit management also may find value here. Practitioners in
related fields such as public relations, advertising, and marketing
could also read these essays for a better understanding of an allied
field.

    Practicing fund raisers are obviously interested in taking
their profession seriously. They will argue strongly that their paid
and volunteer colleagues at nonprofit agencies should also understand fund raising better, and some may choose to present this book
as a gift to directors and trustees who demonstrate a need to consider
fund raising and fund raisers more seriously.

    It is important to remember that philanthropy involves not
only asking but giving. Foundation staff members, corporate giving
officers, and individuals who give are already serious about fund
raising and will have a natural interest in this book. The authors
hope that these essays might encourage those who do not yet participate in the philanthropic process to be more sympathetic to the
importance of fund raising.

Overview of the Contents

The genesis of this book was a collection of papers prepared for a symposium hosted by the Indiana University Center on Philanthropy at Indiana University–Purdue University at Indianapolis in the spring of 1990. The chapters build on the discussions at the symposium and represent the beginning of a concerted effort to study fund raising seriously. As pioneers in a new field of study, the editors and authors have the privilege and responsibility of mapping a course through largely uncharted scholarly territory. The four parts of this book represent the editors' attempt to define general topical areas relevant to a serious discussion of fund raising.

The chapters in Part One introduce the field of fund raising with a discussion of its theory, history, and professional language. Robert L. Payton, Henry A. Rosso, and Eugene R. Tempel open by sharing their efforts to move "Toward a Philosophy of Fund Raising." By articulating their beliefs about the importance of fund raising to philanthropy and of philanthropy to a democracy, they establish for fund raisers a clear rationale as to the importance of their social role.

Fund raising is a new profession, and many working senior fund raisers learned their craft from the founders of the field. Jeanne Harrah-Conforth and John Borsos interviewed a number of the leaders in the second generation of fund raisers and use these oral histories to discuss the development of the profession. The traditions of fund raising are directly reflected in the language practitioners use as they talk with each other. Richard C. Turner examines some of that language in "Metaphors Fund Raisers Live By" and argues that unintended messages may be carried by these metaphors. Turner also cautions fund raisers that metaphoric shorthand may limit or direct their thinking and practice.

If many people do not take fund raising seriously, it is because of their perception that there is something morally incorrect about asking for money. A few flagrant ethical violations in recent history have left a more vivid impression than have the efforts of thousands of fund raisers who adhere to professional standards of ethics. In Part Two, a group of authors explores the moral dimension of fund raising. In "A Historical and Moral Analysis of Religious Fundraising," Thomas H. Jeavons examines the theological foundation for fund raising in the Western world.

Two other authors in Part Two demonstrate that those who attempt to raise funds ethically face a challenging and complex set of issues. Deni Elliott, drawing from the efforts of journalists to define professional ethical standards, argues that fund raisers must consider the implications of both withholding information and telling deliberate untruths. On the other hand, some gifts carry with them potential conflicts of interest. In her study, Barbara J. Lombardo looks at how some nonprofit organizations balance "Conflicts of Interest Between Nonprofits and Corporate Donors." In most cases, Lombardo finds, fund-raising strategy is formulated to ensure adherence to the mission of the nonprofit.

Is fund raising a profession? This is the theme of Part Three and the question asked by Harland G. Bloland and Rita Bornstein. Bloland and Bornstein review the literature on professionalization and question how well fund raising measures up against accepted definitions of professionalism. One barrier to its acceptance as a profession stems from the fact that fund raisers draw from the experience of so many occupations. Margaret A. Duronio and Bruce A. Loessin see this eclecticism as a strength of effective fund raisers, who should be "rigorously professional," use the skills of the manager and the marketer, and act as entrepreneurs as they perform good works. In recent years, more women have entered the field of fund raising and are assuming positions of greater responsibility in nonprofit organizations. Julie C. Conry documents this demographic shift and speculates on what it means now and for the future, to women fund raisers and fund raising as a profession.

The skills of fund raising have been traditionally transmitted orally, but some scholars and practitioners are recording their observations and research in order to improve the practice of fund raising. The chapters in Part Four present an overview of some of these approaches. Alex Carroll's "My Sixteen Rules for a Successful Volunteer-Based Capital Campaign" is a statement of common-sense principles that are often overlooked in the pursuit of more exotic techniques. Its inclusion here affirms the important role that volunteers can and should play in fund raising. In "Can We Throw Away the Tin Cup?," Kay Sprinkel Grace views fund raising as an ongoing relationship between the contributor and the community that goes beyond the single contribution. The donor supports the organization because it meets distinct community needs, not just because it is "needy."

Fund raisers must understand the political, social, and economic environment in which they and their organizations operate. Betsy Hills Bush tells us some of "What Fund Raisers Should Know About the Law," particularly as legislatures impose new constraints on operations. In our increasingly multicultural society, fund raisers must learn to address donors from a variety of heritages. African-American fund raisers may have observed some of the "Contemporary Trends in Black Philanthropy" identified by Emmett D. Carson, but this chapter is offered here for the particular illumination of professionals of Anglo-European heritage.

One of the popular methods to gauge the effectiveness of fund-raising programs is the "fund-raising share," the ratio of money spent on fund raising against the net gain provided by the donation. Richard Steinberg uses economic analysis to argue that this is not a fair measure, either of ethics or of effectiveness. In a similar vein, Wilson C. Levis highlights the direct relationship between dollars spent on fund raising and dollars earned in donations, offering some useful guidelines on "Investing More Money in Fund Raising—Wisely."

Finally, Robert L. Payton, Henry A. Rosso, and Eugene R. Tempel return to translate their philosophy of fund raising into a definition of what fund-raising practice should be.

Acknowledgments

Many people and organizations have contributed to making this work possible. The planning committee of the third annual symposium sponsored by the Indiana University Center on Philanthropy and the symposium support committee deserve special mention, as does the Lilly Endowment, which cosponsored the symposium and gave it major support. In addition, the word processing support and staff assistance of the Center on Philanthropy are most appreciated.

Finally, the editors wish to thank the authors for being understanding and always attentive to suggestions for revision of their essays. The authors represent a variety of backgrounds, viewpoints, specialties, and orientations. Neither the editors nor the contributors intend the individual chapters to represent a consensus of opinion. However, a collection such as this does not become a whole without important give and take for a common theme—in our case, taking fund raising seriously.

Indianapolis, Indiana   Dwight F. Burlingame
August 1991   Lamont J. Hulse

Reference

"Less Than Half of Americans Rate Fundraisers Trustworthy." *NonProfit Times,* Mar. 1990, pp. 1, 17.

Contributors

Harland G. Bloland is professor of higher education at the University of Miami. He received his B.S. degree (1951) from the University of Wisconsin in education, his M.A. degree (1955) from the University of Connecticut in government and international relations, and his Ph.D. degree (1968) from the University of California, Berkeley, in social foundations. He is the author of *Higher Education Associations in a Decentralized Educational System* (1969), *Associations in Action: The Washington Higher Education Community* (1985), and (with Sue M. Bloland) *American Learned Societies in Transition* (1974). His interests include higher education administration, sociology and politics of higher education, independent sector analysis, and qualitative research methods and philosophy.

Rita Bornstein is president and professor of education at Rollins College in Winter Park, Florida. Bornstein earned her B.A. (1970) and M.A. (1971) degrees from Florida Atlantic University in English literature. In 1975, she received her Ph.D. degree in educational leadership and instruction from the University of Miami. Before becoming president of Rollins, Bornstein served as vice president for development at the University of Miami. Her publications include "The Capital Campaign," in *The President and Fund Raising* (1989); "Adding It Up: Capital Campaigns Are Not Created Equal," in CASE *Currents* (1989); "Career Development for the Foundation Relations Professional," in *Cultivating Foundation Support for Education* (1989); "Ambiguity as Opportunity and Constraint: Evolution of a Federal Sex Equity Education Program," in *Educational Evaluation Definitions, Distinctions, Costs and Benefits* (1981); and *Freedom or Order: Must We Choose?* (1976).

John Borsos earned a B.A. degree (1985) from Wallace College and an M.A. degree (1987) from the University of South Carolina, both in history. He is currently a Ph.D. candidate in history at Indiana University. His research interest is the history of the American working class, including class politics and philanthropy.

Dwight F. Burlingame is associate director for academic programs and research at the Indiana University Center on Philanthropy and visiting professor of philanthropic studies, Indiana University-Purdue University at Indianapolis. Prior to joining the center, Burlingame served for six years as vice president for university relations and professor at Bowling Green State University. He holds a B.S. degree (1965) from Moorhead State University in business and political science, an M.S. degree (1967) from the University of Illinois in library science, a post-master's degree from the University of Minnesota in higher education, and a Ph.D. degree (1974) from Florida State University in library science. He became a certified fund-raising executive of the National Society of Fund Raising Executives in 1989. Burlingame is a frequent speaker, consultant, and author on topics relating to philanthropy, libraries, and development.

Betsy Hills Bush is government affairs specialist with the law firm of Perlman & Perlman in New York City. Prior to joining the firm, she served several years as director of governmental affairs for the American Association of Fund-Raising Counsel. She received her B.F.A. degree (1982) from New York University's Tisch School of the Arts. In 1988 she received an M.A. degree from the Liberal Studies Department of New York University's Graduate School of Arts and Sciences. She is the author of numerous articles on fund-raising regulation and other topics on philanthropy. Her column on state fund-raising regulation appears monthly in *NonProfit Times*.

Alex Carroll is senior vice president of Prudential-Bache Securities in Indianapolis, Indiana. He earned his credentials in philanthropy and fund raising through decades of experience as an enthusiastic advocate, volunteer, and director for a number of cultural, professional, and civic organizations. Carroll earned a B.A. degree (1939) in political science/economics from Williams College in Williamstown, Massachusetts.

Emmett D. Carson is a program officer in the Human Rights and Social Justice Program of the Ford Foundation. Prior to joining the Foundation, Carson directed a three-year national study at the Joint Center for Political Studies on the charitable giving and volunteer behavior of blacks and whites. He is the author of two books and numerous articles on black philanthropic activity. Carson received his B.S. degree (1980) in economics from Morehouse College, and his M.P.A. (1983) and Ph.D. degrees from Princeton University in public and international affairs.

Julie C. Conry is director of external affairs and development for The Ohio State University Graduate School. She obtained a B.A. degree (1979) from Oberlin College in history and communications and an M.A. degree (1982) from Ohio State University in journalism. In 1981–1982 she received the Carl Dipman Alumni Fellowship from Oberlin College and was a Kiplinger Fellow in public affairs reporting in the school of journalism at Ohio State. Conry has developed and presented seminars and workshops on proposal writing and fund raising for many nonprofit organizations. Current research interests include the impact of technology in philanthropy, the role of mentoring in career success, leadership development, and gender issues in the work force.

Eugene Dorsey is chairperson of INDEPENDENT SECTOR, the Washington, D.C.-based coalition of 815 foundations, nonprofit organizations, and corporations with national interest and impact in philanthropy and voluntary action. Dorsey received a B.S. degree (1949) from the University of Illinois in journalism and holds an honorary doctor of law degree from the College of Idaho and an honorary doctorate of humane letters from Keuka College, Penn Yan, New York. He has been a board member of INDEPENDENT SECTOR since 1985 and is the former national chairperson for the Give Five campaign. He received a Private Sector Initiatives award from President Reagan in 1988 on behalf of the Give Five campaign. He is a member of the Dartmouth/Council for the Advancement and Support of Education (CASE) task force on ethics and philanthropy in higher education and has delivered numerous speeches and lectures on philanthropy, volunteerism, and communications. Dorsey has formed Dorsey Consulting Services, which specializes in non-profit communications, foundation evaluations, corporate philanthropy, and management of voluntary organizations.

Margaret A. Duronio is director of administrative services in the office of the vice president of university relations and development at the University of Pittsburgh. She received her B.A. degree (1969) from Pennsylvania State University in English, her M.S.W. degree (1973) from the University of Pittsburgh, and her Ph.D. degree (1985) from the University of Pittsburgh in higher education. Duronio has directed three national studies on fund-raising effectiveness and has worked as a management development consultant and a marriage and family therapist.

Deni Elliott is director of the Institute for the Study of Applied and Professional Ethics at Dartmouth College and an adjunct professor of philosophy. She holds a B.A. degree (1974) from the University of Maryland in communication and an M.A. degree (1982) from Wayne State University in philosophy. Her doctoral degree (1984) from Harvard University was interdisciplinary, with work in policy, law, philosophy, and education. Prior to joining Dartmouth College, Elliott served as an ethics consultant/reporter for the *Philadelphia Inquirer,* the *Louisville Courier-Journal,* and WCSH-TV in Portland, Maine. She collected and edited *Responsible Journalism,* a collection of original essays, which was published in 1986.

Kay Sprinkel Grace is western regional director of The Fund Raising School, Indiana University Center on Philanthropy, in San Francisco. She holds B.A. (1959) and M.A. (1975) degrees from Stanford University in communications, and journalism and education, respectively, and in 1979 she received Stanford's highest volunteer award, the Gold Spike. Grace has been a presenter at Fund-Raising Days in San Francisco, San Jose, Monterey, Sacramento, and Oklahoma City and a featured speaker for the Australasian Institute of Fund Raising, the Western Alliance of Arts Administrators, and the National Association for Hospital Development. Her writings include chapters in two books scheduled for publication in 1991, and articles for Prentice-Hall Charitable Solicitation publications and *Fund Raising Management*.

Jeanne Harrah-Conforth is a research specialist and oral historian for the Indiana University, Bloomington campus, Oral History Research Center, and a Ph.D. candidate at the Folklore Institute, IU Bloomington. She received a B.A. degree (1978) from the University of California, Berkeley in cultural anthropology, and an M.A. degree (1983) from the Folklore Institute, Indiana University, Bloomington in folklore. She completed the Educational Research and Its Applications Graduate Program in Education at the University of California, Berkeley in 1979. At present her professional and academic interests are in research and publication in philanthropy and in interpretations of social and cultural events and traditions.

Lamont J. Hulse is senior associate at POLIS: The Research Center for Indianapolis at Indiana University-Purdue University in Indianapolis, where he combines duties as a practicing fund raiser and historian. His degrees include a B.A. degree (1972) from DePauw University in history and an M.A. degree (1987) in history, with a certificate in museum studies, from the University of Delaware, where he was a Hagley Fellow. Hulse was also awarded a public management certificate from Indiana University (1982).

Thomas H. Jeavons is associate director of programs for the Association of American Colleges (AAC) and an adjunct professor of organizational theory and management at Seton Hall University. Jeavons is currently a doctoral candidate in management and cultural studies at the Union Institute. He received his B.A. degree (1974) from the University of Colorado in philosophy and dance and his M.A. degree (1978) with honors from the Earlham School of Religion in theology. He received a graduate certificate in business management from Georgetown University in 1987. His current research focuses on the history, place, and management of religious service organizations as essential contributors to and components of the nonprofit sector. Jeavons is also exploring ways in which theological tenets, historical traditions, and societal expectations shape the philosophies and practices of management of religious organizations.

Wilson C. Levis is a senior research associate with the Nonprofit Management Group at Baruch College/CUNY in New York City. He received his B.S. degree (1953) from the University of Delaware in mechanical engineering. He is currently involved with several research projects that address funding fund raising, fund-raising productivity, and the quality of nonprofit financial reporting. In 1987 he conducted an analysis of campaign productivity at the United Way Strategic Institute, United Way of America. In 1989 he completed the Funding Fund Raising Research Project. Mr. Levis was also project director for INDEPENDENT SECTOR's Average Gift Size Study and the National Society of Fund Raising Executives' Fund-Raising Cost Study. He has published numerous articles and papers on fund-raising costs and productivity.

Bruce A. Loessin is vice president for university relations and development at the University of Pittsburgh. He received his B.A. degree (1965) from the University of Southern California in political science and his M.A. degree (1967) from the University of Wisconsin in political science. After more than twenty years' experience in fund raising, more than half at the level of vice president, Loessin was responsible for managing the University of Pittsburgh's recently completed $225 million campaign. In addition to fund-raising and research activities, he serves as chairperson for the CASE Committee on Research and has lectured in England and the United States on fund-raising effectiveness.

Barbara J. Lombardo is currently a senior consultant with KPMG Peat Marwick, San Francisco, specializing in management consulting for nonprofit institutions. She received her B.A. degree (1983) from Lafayette College in economics and business; her M.B.A. degree (1987) from the University of California, Berkeley; and her Ph.D. degree (1990) from the University of California, Berkeley, in business and public policy. In 1989 Lombardo was awarded a dissertation fellowship from the American Association of University Women. She has presented her research at conferences of the Indiana University Center on Philanthropy and INDEPENDENT SECTOR. Her current research interests include corporate philanthropy as well as strategic planning and managerial ethics in the nonprofit sector.

Robert L. Payton is director of the Indiana University Center on Philanthropy and professor of philanthropic studies at Indiana University-Purdue University at Indianapolis. Before becoming director of the center, Payton was scholar-in-residence at the University of Virginia, served ten years as president of Exxon Education Foundation, and was president of C. W. Post College and Hofstra University. He holds a master's degree from the University of Chicago in history. In 1988 the University of Chicago awarded him its Alumni Medal. Among his many writings in philanthropy and education is his 1988 book *Philanthropy: Voluntary Action for the Public Good.* He serves on the national advisory boards of the Mandel Center for Nonprofit Organizations at Case Western Reserve University and the Program on Law and Philanthropy at New York University, among many others.

Henry A. Rosso, director emeritus of The Fund Raising School, Indiana University Center on Philanthropy, presents fund-raising courses and lectures extensively throughout the United States and abroad. Rosso founded The Fund Raising School in San Francisco in 1974, and in 1988 it was incorporated into Indiana University. Prior to founding the school, he was a senior vice president and member of the board of directors, G. A. Brakeley and Company. Rosso was the first independent consultant elected as an associate member of the prestigious American Association of Fund-Raising Counsel. He is a magna cum laude graduate of Syracuse University, from which he received his B.A. degree (1949) in English and journalism, and a member of Phi Beta Kappa Society. He received the Outstanding Fund-Raising Executive Award at the 1985 international conference of the National Society of Fund-Raising Executives. In 1990, Indiana University created the Henry A. Rosso Award for lifetime achievement in ethical fund raising, and he became its first recipient.

Richard Steinberg is associate professor of economics at Indiana University-Purdue University at Indianapolis. Steinberg earned a B.S. degree (1977) from the Massachusetts Institute of Technology and a Ph.D. degree (1984) from the University of Pennsylvania, both in economics. His research interests center on the economics of the nonprofit sector, including the regulation of fund raising, the relation between government social service spending and charitable donations, tax treatment of personal donations, unfair competition with for-profits, and antitrust suits against nonprofit organizations.

Eugene R. Tempel, vice chancellor for external affairs at Indiana University-Purdue University at Indianapolis, has been active in the fields of fund raising and administration management for higher education. He played a key role in establishing the university's Center on Philanthropy, located at Indiana University's Indianapolis campus, and conducts research and teaching programs on voluntary giving. Tempel holds an M.A. degree (1973) in English and an Ed.D. degree (1985) from Indiana University. His professional service activities include consulting, chairing committees, and speaking before regional and national organizations in education and philanthropy. Before assuming his current post, he served as vice president of the Indiana University Foundation and executive director of the foundation office in Indianapolis.

Richard C. Turner is professor and chairman of the English department at Indiana University-Purdue University at Indianapolis. He received an A.B. degree (1966) from Boston College in classics and M.A. (1968) and Ph.D. (1972) degrees from Emory University in English. He has published articles on Milton, Swift, literary theory, and the teaching of literature. He is currently working on issues in literature and science and in literature and philanthropy.

TAKING
FUND RAISING
SERIOUSLY

PART ONE

THE FIELD
OF FUND RAISING

Chapter 1

Toward a Philosophy
of Fund Raising

Robert L. Payton
Henry A. Rosso
Eugene R. Tempel

This chapter opens a continuing discussion about the underlying assumptions and organizing principles of fund raising. We believe that a philosophy of fund raising is not an empty exercise but has a serious practical purpose. We believe that a philosophy of fund raising must reflect what fund raisers themselves say and do. If pursued seriously, discussions of such a philosophy will improve both understanding and practice.

It will be obvious that we write as "reflective practitioners," not as professional philosophers. We offer what follows for revision—even rejection—by those better qualified. We offer no apology, however, for our purpose. We believe strongly that fund raising needs a philosophy to guide its practice. Fund raisers have tended to leave such discussion to others, especially when the discussion seems to lead beyond immediate concerns.

It is also true that scholars, even those interested in philanthropy, have neglected fund raising. There is widespread academic bias against fund raising and fund raisers but very little solid argument to justify the prejudice.

3

We believe that fund raising is an essential part of American philanthropy; in turn, philanthropy—as voluntary action for the public good—is essential to American democracy. And so we align ourselves with others who believe that it is time to take fund raising seriously.

We say *toward* a philosophy of fund raising because we hope this chapter serves as a stimulus to discussion about the subject; it does not presume to provide definitive answers. (In fact, we are convinced there are no definitive answers.) We say *a* philosophy of fund raising, therefore, because we believe that there could be other philosophies that might be advanced or that exist implicitly in practice.

When we use the word "philosophy" here, we mean it in the sense of a rational and practical guide to conduct. We address questions of "why" as well as of "what," "how," and "how-to." We try to summarize some basic assumptions on which decisions can be made and actions taken: We want to develop principles that should guide action. To use the word philosophy at all means that we should give reasons and arguments that are clear and consistent, that reflect experience and practice. A workable philosophy should be generally applicable to particular cases. People have to be able to understand a philosophy if they are to be guided by it in their practice.

We use the term "fund raising" more broadly than it is commonly used because we see it as a convenient entry into the whole scope and purpose of voluntary action for the public good. Fund raising does not take place in a vacuum; it is one of the central elements of a larger system of philanthropy and is best seen in its role as the servant of philanthropy. We believe that fund raising can be understood only through studying the full range of philanthropic purposes, values, techniques, and resources. Professional fund raising often focuses almost exclusively on gathering financial resources and, as a consequence, neglects or even betrays its own larger purposes. Philanthropy is misunderstood when it is reduced to any one of its elements; therefore, fund raising is not the whole of philanthropy and is about more than money, being inextricably tied to philanthropic values, purposes, and methods. Fund raisers exist because fund raising is necessary; it is not justified because fund raisers need employment.

Although we hope some of the things we say will be useful elsewhere in the world, we are primarily concerned with what we know best—putting forward a philosophy that makes sense in the context of the United States in the last decade of the twentieth century. We will not attempt to argue the case here, but we believe that the United States is a free, open, and democratic society, that pluralism in the form of voluntary association is an essential aspect of democracy in the United States.

Our underlying argument can be summarized in an old-fashioned syllogism:

1. Major premise: Philanthropy is necessary in a democratic society.
2. Minor premise: Fund raising is necessary to philanthropy.
3. Conclusion: Fund raising is necessary to a democratic society.

That is, fund raising is too important to be left entirely to fund raisers.

A Philosophy of Fund Raising

Ethical fund raising is often about the conflict of goods and rights, rather than choices between good and evil, right and wrong. Sometimes it is the choice between the lesser of two unpleasant outcomes. Even causes advanced with the highest moral purpose come into conflict and competition. One painfully well-known example is the abortion controversy, but many others are equally familiar: environmental issues such as toxic waste disposal; animal rights claims against medical research; human rights issues in Africa and Latin America.

There is nothing wrong with conflict; controversy, disagreement, and debate are healthy in a democratic society. Fund raisers are sometimes caught in the middle. They are sometimes asked to take positions that they do not wholly share; they are sometimes criticized for being too partisan and at other times for avoiding commitment and controversy. The fund raiser as much as anyone else involved with these issues must be alert to the limits on conflict. As a recent marketing newsletter puts it: "Many manipulative techniques that a marketer might find questionable in another context can seem perfectly justified 'in a good cause'" (Andreasan, 1989, p. 4).

Knowing about the larger environment within which fund raising for specific purposes takes place is important to fund raisers if they are to have a balanced and enlightened perspective on their work. In what follows, we will draw examples from the ephemeral literature of fund raising; we will borrow also from relatively ancient sources such as the Federalist papers and from relatively recent philosophers like John Dewey. We believe it is useful to examine current practice in the light of its development in tradition and social thought.

Mission. Mission comes first. Philanthropy is justified because its first goal is to serve others. The mission of philanthropy as a tradition is based on three very simple and powerful premises: (1) Things go wrong; (2) things could always be better; and (3) voluntary initiatives are often appropriate responses to either or both of the first two.

Mission justifies fund raising. Organizations of the independent sector come into being to respond to some form of human or social need. The need, or the opportunity for service, becomes the reason for existence of the not-for-profit entity. Philanthropic organizations exist because society values its children, values knowledge, values its past, and believes in the possibility of a better life for all. The act of asking for funds is legitimate when an organization fulfills a need based on the shared values of the society or of a subsector of the society. The first question the fund raiser must be prepared to answer for the organization, then, is Why do we exist?

Making the Case. The case empowers fund raising by summarizing the full range of reasons why the organization merits support. The organization justifies itself in terms of the merits of its case, its ability to translate the social values and beliefs of its mission into an action program—goals and objectives that can be used in the measurement of results. The case answers the question What is distinctive about us? and other questions, such as What is it specifically that we seek to accomplish? How do we propose to go about it? How can we hold ourselves accountable to those who provide support? The case links aspiration to method, what we want to achieve to what we need to reach the goal. The case defines programs and processes for addressing the needs identified in the mission statement. The case projects the costs for personnel, equipment, and facilities to carry out the program. The case provides the rationale for the budget.

Governance. Mission is entrusted to the governing board, and governance entails stewardship. The question of governance is Who owns us? Governance is the exercise of authority and control derived from and in behalf of public ownership, and because philanthropic organizations serve public purposes, governance is a continuing call for allegiance to the mission. It acknowledges the sacredness of the trust to those immediately served and beyond that constituency to the larger community. Trustees are the primary stewards of philanthropy. They hold the nonprofit organization in trust in the public interest to ensure that it functions according to its statement of mission. Governing boards must then manifest the values and beliefs of the mission and case and accept responsibility for developing the organization's resources, both of talent and money, and directing them toward its goals and objectives. The acceptance of accountability means that the governing board must also assess the effectiveness of the organization in achieving its goals and objectives.

The trust that donors invest in nonprofit organizations rests ultimately with the conscientiousness of the trustees. When that trust is justified, as it usually is, the fact goes unremarked. When trustees fail to be conscientious and vigilant, the resulting scandals can become headline news. For example, the Covenant House board of directors recently had to explain to contributors that mistakes had been made in the operation, while at the same time requesting their continued support. Mistakes in turn subtly influence the public attitude toward other organizations whose trustees have served them faithfully and well. In the vocabulary of the ethical fund raiser, "trustworthiness" is a powerful, omnipresent word.

Fund raising thus begins with the governing board. Fund raising is the lengthened shadow of the organization, wearing the mantle of dignity, pride of accomplishment, and commitment to service. Fund raising by itself has no substance in the eyes of the contributor—the credible connection between the organization and its mission is the governing board. Organizations with good trustees are especially fortunate, if Alexander Hamilton was right: "Hence it is that there can be but few men in the society, who will have sufficient skill in the laws to qualify them for the station of judges. And making the proper deductions for the ordinary depravity of human nature, the number must be smaller still of those who unite the requisite integrity with the requisite knowledge" (Hamilton, 1961c, pp. 529–530).

The Cause. The cause is more important than the organization. Whether it be shelter for the homeless or a program for young artists, the cause itself comes before the narrow interests of the organization created to meet the needs of the cause. Intrasystem goals should not come first, although they often do. To quote Hamilton again: "It is a known fact of human nature that its affections are commonly weak in proportion to the distance or diffuseness of the object. Upon the same principle that a man is more attached to his family than to his neighborhood, to his neighborhood than to the community at large . . . " (Hamilton, 1961a, p. 107). That is, fund raisers are tempted to give priority to their own organizations and not to give too much time or attention to the public interest. Some libertarians argue that that is the way things should be. Without attempting to pursue the debate, we simply assert our opinion that the public interest has a claim on us. The public interest, to modify an ancient Jewish metaphor, is a fence around self-interest.

Fund Raising as Moral Action

Philanthropy seeks funds and other resources that could be used for other purposes. Philanthropy is about stewardship; good works entail accountability. Accountability is often no more than simply giving reasons for what we have done in ways that allow others to judge impartially whether we have acted responsibly. Throughout

this paper we argue that making the case is the way the fund raiser
spells out goals and objectives that make later accountability possible. Fund-raising practice as it becomes more professional becomes
more open, more candid, more accountable to those who have given
their money and other resources to advance the organization. That
broader form of accountability is much more important to donors
than are the narrow reports required by the Internal Revenue
Service.

For these and other reasons, *fund raising is moral action.* We
believe that fund raising for social purposes engages fund raisers in
the lives of other people for their benefit or for some larger public
benefit as well as for the benefit of the fund raisers themselves.
Intervening in the lives of others for their benefit is a moral action.
How do we "intervene" in the lives of others? Consider the curriculum of the Hartford Early Learning Program (a program sponsored by the University of Hartford and The Travelers that works
with the Hartford, Connecticut, public schools). The curriculum
includes the use of computers and hands-on activities designed to
develop problem-solving skills in the young pupils and to build a
sense of accomplishment and an interest in school activities.

In the words of the Southern Education Foundation's chairman, Norman C. Francis, "Nothing is more exciting and gratifying
than to see the impact that our efforts have on individuals" (Southern Education Foundation, 1989, p. 9). (The Southern Education
Foundation was created in 1937 in a merger of four grant-making
foundations. It recently changed its status to that of a public charity
and now raises funds as well as makes grants. Both in grant making
and fund raising the goal is to have an impact on individuals.)

Like it or not, then, we contend that fund raising is moral
action—applied ethics. (We accept the useful distinction between
"morals" as having to do with behavior and"ethics" as systematic
reflection on that behavior. When we examine what fund raisers do,
we focus on the morals of fund raising; when we discuss why one
fund-raising practice is better than another, we focus on the ethics
of fund raising.) The ethics of fund-raising practice proposed here
is based on three elements: (1) an ethics of competence, (2) an ethics
of rhetoric, and (3) an ethics of relationships. We believe that the

most fruitful search is for an ethics of responsibility in fund raising that balances the three elements.

The first principle of philanthropy is akin to the first principle of medicine: Do no harm. Implicit in what was said earlier, intervention in the lives of others for their benefit presumes an ability to achieve that benefit. Competence thus becomes a central part of the ethics of philanthropy. With all our talk about the importance of a fund-raising philosophy, it remains idle and even harmful talk if fund-raising practice is slipshod. Ethical fund raising must be competent.

Competence, however, is not enough. In order to avoid doing harm and in the hope of doing good, it is necessary to begin by asking the first ethical question: What is going on? (Niebuhr, 1963, p. 60). The first question may be aimed at determining what need the organization seeks to meet. It may also require reflection on the consequences of what is done; if our work engages us in interventions in the lives of other people for their benefit, we have to think carefully about the effect that our work has on individuals. A recent United Way report contains this observation: "United Ways are also learning that moving people toward self-sufficiency is a complex process—requiring more than single solutions or 'one-shot' treatments" (United Way of America, 1989, p. 1).

A Theory of Human Nature

Everyone has a working theory of human nature; ours is that we assume that human beings are responsible agents. People are free to act as they choose, and yet they are in some ways predictable because of their genetic makeup and cultural circumstances. We assume that people sometimes act voluntarily with the well-being of others primarily in mind, sacrificing for others without prospect of any external benefit, even gratitude or appreciation. We assume that altruism complements and balances egoism but does not replace it. Altruism can be a powerful force in human affairs, but it is a less reliable force than egoism most of the time. As Alexander Hamilton put it: "The best security for the fidelity of mankind is to make their interest coincide with their duty" (1961b, p. 488). That is why philanthropy—like all other forms of moral action—must be taught and learned. We assume that human beings have a legitimate self-interest and a concern for others at the same time. Fund raising thus uses self-interest to help people go beyond self-interest. People must come to learn that voluntary action for others is a rational and desirable way to behave.

People may also make their decisions and choices on the basis of their analysis of the pros and cons of a particular action. We accept the principle that a human being is an autonomous self, but that the self exists in society. One of the most noble development activities is to assist others in self-help. People who strive to take themselves out of poverty demonstrate a commitment and concept of self-worth whereby they take ownership of their accomplishments. When external aid is needed and applied in a sensitive manner, partnerships with self-help initiatives will produce effective results.

Our underlying assumptions about human nature (usually unexamined) have great influence on how and why we act philanthropically. The Founding Fathers warned us that our preferences and other personal considerations are so strong that we have to keep them in check. They also understood that we strongly prefer the things we do voluntarily to those that we are required to do.

We accept the argument that collections of individuals can take on the character of individuals (for example, that a corporation can have a conscience). These assumptions permit us to resolve the tensions and conflicts between individualism and the values of community that we espouse. The good works of individuals working together in organizations are proposed as a model intended to advance the good life for the individual and the good society for all the organizations' members. Experience suggests that individuals are more impulsive and emotional, less systematic in cost-benefit analysis, than are complex organizations whose decisions reflect consensus among many individuals.

People benefit from serving others. The most important benefits are satisfactions: spiritual, moral, and psychological. We accept the psychological evidence that voluntary service in behalf of others enhances self-esteem and self-worth. The secret seems to lie in the liberation of the self from its own preoccupations by sympathy for and empathy with others. We believe that the arguments for philanthropy and fund raising are therefore more rational than are the arguments for misanthropy and selfishness.

We believe that service to others is a virtue, an important word in philosophy these days. We turn to the philosophy of John Dewey in looking for a guide to virtuous behavior. Dewey said that virtue has three basic characteristics: It is wholehearted, persistent, and impartial (Dewey and Tufts, 1932). Mentioning the notion of *wholeheartedness* raises the familiar question of conflicts of interest. Fund raisers frequently face the question Who is my client? *Persistence* is fundamental to good works—"more than single solutions or 'one-shot' treatments," as quoted by the United Way earlier. Benefits of persistence are gained by the person who persists in service as well as by the person who is served. *Impartiality* is a word of special moment to organizations reaching out to serve those in need—AIDS victims, for example.

The debates about the different characteristics and preferences of men and women are of great consequence for philanthropy. We assume that tough-mindedness and tender-mindedness are both essential to fund raising. We assume that people are subject to emotion as well as to reason. Fund raising makes appeals to both: Reason without emotion often fails to lead to action; emotion without reason often leads to wrong action. Effective and ethical fund raising would seem necessarily to balance both elements. We assume that other fundamental beliefs are at work in voluntary action, even though they cannot be neatly integrated into a calculus of motives or of results. The traditional virtues and their modern variants are advocated as values to sustain us through periods of doubt, confusion, and adversity.

The need for praise is a powerful but immeasurable motivator; envy appears to be similarly important. Fund raisers sometimes act as stewards of organizational resources of praise and other forms of public recognition. Fund raisers, unfortunately, sometimes crudely manipulate envy and the promise of praise to win support. George Washington is said to have been guided by a strong sense of "honor," described as "that principle of action which operates out of desire for 'the esteem of wise and good men'" (see McDonald, 1985). The indiscriminate allocation of praise can cheapen its value and reduce its motivation.

Essentials in Successful Fund Raising

A Team Activity. Philanthropy is about relationships. There is a fundamental ethics of relations that should protect all concerned: the donor, the recipient, the organization, the manager, the fund raiser, the volunteer, and the public. A philosophy of ethical fund raising returns again and again to the notion of trust and trustworthiness. The professional fund raiser is expected to be reliable in using the tools and techniques of the field. Professional fund raisers are expected to give higher priority to their client's interests than to their own. Professional fund raisers are expected to be trustworthy in their use of the language. Professional fund raisers are expected to act as evenhandedly and wholeheartedly for one client as for another. Winning the praise and trust of the wise and good men and women of the society is perhaps the best measure of success in a field where quantifiable results are often difficult to measure.

People cannot do very much alone. Fund raising is one of many techniques that enable people to act together to accomplish purposes that they could not accomplish acting as single individuals, assuming voluntary associations of individuals working together in an organization toward some common goal. Isolated and individual acts of benevolence are of great importance, but they are not the focus of organized philanthropy.

Fund raisers are often facilitators rather than solicitors; success is therefore a group achievement. They very often have to minimize their own compensated contribution—they are more often charged with overstating it—to encourage those whose gifts are entirely voluntary.

Organization. Organization requires entrepreneurship, leadership, and management. As a good cause does not just appear without being discovered by someone with a moral outlook, a good cause does not win support without organization. Complex not-for-profit organization entails the same problems of efficiency and effectiveness that are confronted by government agencies and for-profit corporations. And, as Peter Drucker points out, not-for-profit managers, by definition, have to do more with less (Drucker, 1989).

Philanthropy is about leadership. Because philanthropy is about voluntary action and not about what we are required to do, and about public goods rather than private ones, greater leadership—deeper and more sustained commitment and response—is always needed.

Positive Thinking. Fund raising calls for pride and not apology. This is a psychological perspective: We feel differently about ourselves when we are positive and confident rather than negative and uncertain. As with the benefits gained from voluntarily serving others, the benefits of a philosophy of positive thinking seem to be empirically supported. Others insist that confidence is based on a firm grasp of what is going on and what one is doing about it: Competence underlies the confidence that is trust-engendering in others.

When the fund-raising process is undergirded by an examination of the organization's mission and case, it is a task that can be carried out with dignity. The person seeking the gift should never demean the request by clothing it in apology, robbing the gift of its dignity. Apology seems to imply that we are ashamed, that we are begging, that the cause has no merit, no meaning. The fund raiser working with volunteers is helping the volunteer gain confidence and overcome a feeling of inferiority. If the fund raiser shares those feelings of inferiority or lacks commitment, the volunteer will pay the price.

The process of asking for a gift begins with informing potential contributors of the social need being met by the organization, moves on to involve them in the work of the organization, and ends with an invitation to invest financially in that work. Gift making is based on voluntary exchange: The contributor offers something of value to the organization without any expectation of a material or pecuniary return. The reasons for making a gift are manifold. The organization, in its turn, responds with nonmaterial rewards to the contributor: recognition, satisfaction in supporting a worthy cause, a feeling of making a difference in the resolution of a problem, a sense of "ownership" in a program that serves the public good.

Truthfulness. Truth-telling is essential to ethical fund raising. Deception of self can be as harmful as deception of others. Hopefulness sustains philanthropy; wishful thinking betrays it. Fund raising is normative and rhetorical and always vulnerable to "showing the false and hiding the real" (Bowyer, 1982). The passion of the case statement must reflect a case that is empirically grounded in reality. An article in the marketing newsletter *Nonprofit Issues and Opportunities* argues: "Marketing is merely a set of techniques and a philosophy designed to change the behavior of target audiences for the benefit of the marketer, the target audience, and the general society . . . the 'price' for a blood donation is a lot different from the 'price' for a gourmet meal at a fancy restaurant. It takes imagination to see the differences. But it is all marketing" (Andreasan, 1989, p. 1). Marketing may be value-neutral; philanthropy and fund raising are not. Fund raising is always more than marketing.

Passion and urgency are the principal strains on truth-telling, but fund raising requires a sense of urgency as well as a sense of purpose. Amid the myriad causes and appeals, the fund raiser must be able to evoke some sense of priority and immediacy. Making the case for priority and urgency is the best test of the importance of the case itself.

Volunteers. Volunteers are essential to the voluntary tradition, and we decry the tendency for professional fund raisers to displace them. We believe that the fund raiser's primary role is as facilitator. As stated earlier, the volunteer is also the first test of an organization's credibility. The volunteer is proof that there is a cause that goes beyond the self-interest of the people who, like the fund raiser, are employed by the organization.

The scarcest human resource is time: When volunteers give time and personal service, they reveal their most important values. Fund raising focuses on money too often to the exclusion of consideration of gifts of time. Money is often more important to the organization than volunteer time, but the priorities are often reversed for the volunteer. If there is merit to the philanthropic maxim that the highest form of giving is to give of oneself, then a fund-raising philosophy must keep time and money in proportion, and treasure the volunteer.

Serial Reciprocity. We repay the benefits we receive from others who have no direct or formal responsibility for our welfare by the good works we perform in turn for those who have no direct or formal claim on us. We must also remember that misanthropy produces perversions of the principle: I will do nothing for others because others have done nothing for me; others harmed me in the past and I am going to harm others in turn.

Responsibility. Fund raising is a "responsibility system," ethical at its base and tied to a larger complex of authority, control, and responsibility. Honesty, openness, and accountability are therefore essential to the integrity and credibility of fund raisers. The professional fund raiser is ethical and virtuous as well: wholehearted, persistent, and impartial.

In this chapter we devoted considerable attention to our assumptions about human nature. We remind the reader that our assumptions are like those of the authors of the Federalist papers (James Madison this time): "As there is a degree of depravity in mankind which requires a certain degree of circumspection and distrust: So there are other qualities in human nature, which justify a certain portion of esteem and confidence" (Madison, 1961, p. 378).

References

Andreasan, A. R. "Communicating by Listening," *Nonprofit Issues and Opportunities,* Aug. 1989, *1* (5), 1-4.

Bowyer, J. B. *Cheating.* New York: St. Martin's Press, 1982.

Carnegie, A. "The Gospel of Wealth." In E. C. Kirkland (ed.), *The Gospel of Wealth and Other Timely Essays.* Cambridge, Mass.: Harvard University Press, 1962.

Dewey, J., and Tufts, J. H. *Ethics.* New York: Holt, Rinehart & Winston, 1932.

Drucker, P. F. "What Business Can Learn from Nonprofits." *Harvard Business Review,* July/Aug. 1989, 88-93.

Hamilton, A. "The Federalist No. 17." In J. E. Cooke (ed.), *The Federalist.* Middletown, Conn.: Wesleyan University Press, 1961a.

Hamilton, A. "The Federalist No. 72." In J. E. Cooke (ed.), *The Federalist.* Middletown, Conn.: Wesleyan University Press, 1961b.

Hamilton, A. "The Federalist No. 78." In J. E. Cooke (ed.), *The Federalist.* Middletown, Conn.: Wesleyan University Press, 1961c.

McDonald, F. *Novus Ordo Seclorum.* Lawrence: University Press of Kansas, 1985.

Madison, J. "The Federalist No. 55." In J. E. Cooke (ed.), *The Federalist.* Middletown, Conn.: Wesleyan University Press, 1961.

Niebuhr, H. R. *The Responsible Self: An Essay in Christian Moral Philosophy.* New York: HarperCollins, 1963.

Southern Education Foundation. *Annual Report: 1988–89.* Atlanta, Ga.: Southern Education Foundation, 1989.

United Way of America. *Community,* Winter 1989, *8* (3), 1.

Chapter 2

The Evolution
of Professional Fund Raising:
1890–1990

Jeanne Harrah-Conforth
John Borsos

In April 1989, the board of directors of the National Society of Fund
Raising Executives (NSFRE) met behind closed doors and decided
to eliminate a ban on commissions from the NSFRE ethical code.
The commission clause prevented members from accepting as a form
of payment a percentage of the funds they had raised, in effect en-
suring that remuneration would be received only in the form of a
fixed salary or a flat fee. Its elimination followed a similar move two
years earlier by the American Association of Fund-Raising Counsel
(AAFRC). The AAFRC position was framed largely around a legal
argument, that the retention of such a clause might make the organization more vulnerable to antitrust legislation; the NSFRE's stance
was explained succinctly by Marianne G. Briscoe, chairperson of the
organization's ethics committee: "We are dropping the clause because we simply don't feel it is enforceable." Although both organizations went on the record as favoring a fixed salary as the preferred
method of payment, the simple fact that the clause was changed
reveals that there are at least some involved in the fund-raising
profession who feel otherwise. As Steven Ast, an NSFRE member,

observed, "The conventional wisdom of the leadership says it's un-ethical to take a percentage. This sounds like the leadership has caved in to pressure to liberalize an attitude which already exists" (Melillo, 1989, p. 10).

Ast's reference to conventional wisdom and the commission issue in general provide a framework for placing this recent controversy into the larger history of professional fund raising. At its heart, the debate reflects a tension, inherent in the fund-raising profession, between the profession's position in a larger American philanthropic tradition and the fact that this position is where an ever-increasing number of individuals make their living. In short, professional fund raising contains elements of being both a ministry—a calling in which service to humankind provides the fundamental motivation—and a job—a career whose personnel are found mainly through default and who apply marketing and "people" skills to persuade potential donors. A closer look reveals that this tension, between fund raising as a calling and fund raising as a business, dates its origins to the earliest days of the profession.

Our study is a generational view of the fund-raising profession based on a combination of written documents and oral histories. For the earliest generation, the pioneers, our study was based almost exclusively on written texts, although some of our older interviewees had worked directly under one or another of the founders and therefore were able to provide some personal insights into these figures and the profession in its formative years. For the second grouping of fund raisers, the "over-sixty" generation, the analysis is based primarily upon oral histories and complemented by what written sources we could find, such as the various publications of Arnaud Marts and Wolcott Street's *A Beacon for Philanthropy* (1985). Like the second, the interpretation of the third grouping of fund raisers, the "under-sixty" generation, was developed largely through oral histories, again complemented by pertinent written sources. Here the *Chronicle of Philanthropy* yielded considerable insight, not only into contemporary developments in the field but also on occasion into significant information on the more recent past. Scott Cutlip's *Fund Raising in the United States: Its Role in American Philanthropy* (1965) remained an absolutely priceless source for essential factual information on all three generations and should be consulted by any interested student of the field.

To say that the questions we addressed and the historical information we gathered delineate distinct generational differences among fund raisers would be misleading. As our title suggests, the profession was marked by change *and* continuity. Indeed, much of the profession, beginning with the central tension in the field and carrying down to some of fund raising's more technical aspects, has remained remarkably constant through the generations. Moreover, among fund raisers there are many overlapping opinions and approaches that cross generations, and the generations themselves are not as age-specific as one would like in order to extract an "ideal" study profile. The over-sixty generation, in fact, has members who hold professional positions and share values of the under-sixty generation, and vice versa. But differences remain, and for the sake of argument, we have emphasized generational boundaries. What we have discovered and what we present are tendencies and evidence suggestive of generational differences.

The Pioneers

Most historians would date (somewhat arbitrarily) the emergence of organized philanthropy in the United States to 1889—the year in which Andrew Carnegie advanced his "Gospel of Wealth" and Jane Addams and her benefactors established Hull House in Chicago. Although in the next few decades organized philanthropy would strengthen its organizational structure through the emergence of foundations and federations, in general the field remained highly chaotic right through the period of World War I. In large measure, philanthropic giving was the exclusive reserve of a select group of America's wealthiest citizens and, not surprisingly, fund raising reflected this trend. Driven by a need to rationalize and make more efficient the donation process, however, the newly emerging federated agencies began to pool resources in order to cut down on the number of requests made to wealthy benefactors. The federated fund-raising agencies, led by pioneer William J. Norton, consolidated the number of requests made to America's affluent. But from one perspective things changed very little: The number of individuals contacted remained extremely small (Bremner, 1988; Cutlip, 1965; Allen, 1912).

The emergence of what historians have labeled the Progressive Movement at the turn of the century, however, began to produce fundamental changes among fund raisers. As social welfare and various public agencies proliferated in the epoch, the number of individuals involved in philanthropic activities likewise extended the purview of those citizens asked to contribute to these organizations. To reach more individuals, fund raisers (still amateurs at this point) were forced to create more innovative techniques. Their solution—the campaign method—was, as Scott Cutlip observed, "to change profoundly the nature of social welfare, health, and educational institutions in the United States by making philanthropy a broad public enterprise and not just a hobby of the very rich" (Cutlip, 1965, p. 26). Unless otherwise noted, the basic information for this historical overview has been drawn from Cutlip and, to a lesser extent, from Marts (1961).

For practitioners in the field of fund raising today, it is worth remembering that many of the contemporary standard methods of fund raising were at one time highly innovative developments. In short, they had to be invented. Such is the case of the campaign method—a practice that called for the setting of a particular monetary amount to be raised in a defined period of time and was characterized by heavily publicized competition among teams of volunteers. The campaign method and other techniques that define professional fund raising were developed at the Young Men's Christian Association (YMCA) at the turn of the century by two highly motivated individuals, Charles Sumner Ward and Lyman Pierce. Considering the bourgeois purpose of the YMCA, to inspire values of Protestant Christianity as an avenue of individualistic social uplift, one can see traces of the fundamental tension in fund raising.

Charles S. Ward was born in 1858 in Danville, Connecticut, to an old-line New England Congregational family. After prep school in Vermont and matriculation at Dartmouth, where he graduated in 1881, Ward took a job with the YMCA as the general secretary, serving in various posts throughout the Midwest. While at Grand Rapids in 1892, Ward turned his attention to more highly organized methods of fund raising, in his words, "to get the agony over quickly" (Cutlip, 1965, p. 41). Realizing that businessmen and other high-profile volunteers had only a limited amount of time they were willing to devote to fund raising, Ward hit on the idea of compressing the fund-raising calendar into a shorter, much more intensive fund-raising campaign. The success of Ward's innovation captured the attention of many within the YMCA, perhaps none more than Lyman Pierce.

Like Ward, Lyman Pierce, an 1892 graduate of the University of Minnesota, had also come around to the idea of the short, intensive fund-raising campaign because he, too, wanted free time to pursue other things. By 1901, he had risen through the YMCA ranks to become the general secretary in Washington, D.C., where he enlisted Ward's aid in the 1905 campaign to raise $300,000 for the YMCA building in the nation's capital. The YMCA's Washington campaign of 1905 stands as a watershed in professional fund raising's history, for it was here that most of the ingredients of the campaign method first began to coalesce. Limiting themselves to twenty-seven days to raise the final $80,000 needed for the project, Ward and Pierce put into place many features that today have become obligatory campaign practices, as summarized by Cutlip: "careful organization, picked volunteers spurred by team competition, prestige leaders, powerful publicity, a large gift to be matched by public donations, careful records, report meetings, and a definite time limit" (Cutlip, 1965, p. 44).

Before the outbreak of the World War I, however, these innovations in fund raising remained largely within the fold of the YMCA. Fund raising under the tutelage of Ward and Pierce became not only a source for gathering enormous sums of money but also a breeding ground in which one sector of the first generation of professional fund raisers received their training, including Arnaud C. Marts and Carlton Ketchum. Above all, the "YMCA school" was grounded in a Christian philanthropic tradition, so much so that John Price Jones referred to them as "the Christers" (Cutlip, 1965, p. 43). Both Ward and Pierce were driven by a missionary fervor and generally considered their fund raising as an expression of moral stewardship. Ward described fund raisers as "engineers of movement in the service of other men" and was often heard to remark, "I would leave this work immediately if I thought I were merely raising money. It is raising men that appeals to me" (Cutlip, 1965, p. 43). John D. Rockefeller's conception of moral stewardship, like the mission of the YMCA in general, involved the inculcation of values and sobriety, thrift, individualism, and social mobility. And yet, as Scott Cutlip has observed, "this [religious] motivation did not make them immune to quest for power and profit" (Cutlip, 1965, p. 164).

This other side of the YMCA school was best expressed in the person of Frederick Courtney Barber. A former newspaperman and free-lance writer, Barber became aware of the YMCA and its fund raisers through his work in a hospital campaign in Salem, Ohio. Realizing the commercial potential of an effective fund-raising organization, Barber established in 1913 what in many ways should be considered the first professional fund-raising firm, Barber and Associates. Specializing in fund raising for hospitals, Barber was among the first to take the potent Ward-Pierce plan outside the fold of the YMCA. But Barber added another dimension as well: He adopted a high-profile scheme both in terms of heavily publicizing the campaign (through modern marketing techniques) and publicizing himself. As Ward and Pierce intimate Arnaud Marts observed: "Instead of the quiet, behind-the-scenes counselling position which Mr. Ward and Mr. Pierce always assumed, [Barber] took personal charge with fireworks and ballyhoo" (Marts, 1961, p. 36). In later years, Barber drew further scorn for his policy of calculating his salary on a percentage (anywhere from 5 to 15 percent) basis. Despite Marts's later attempts to draw clear-cut distinctions between Barber and the YMCA men, however, clippings in the Pierce scrapbooks at the University of Wisconsin reveal evidence of carnival-like, fund-raiser–centered campaigns with cartoons and pictures of Pierce featured prominently in local campaign coverage (Pierce *Scrapbooks*). Moreover, on occasion Ward at least was not above taking a commission as his form of payment. Although it is certainly true that in later years Pierce and Ward set a standard for fund-raising counsel to remain out of the limelight of campaigns, their ambivalence in earlier years and Barber's overt choice to use the field as a pathway to a successful business career only accentuates the tension that has reverberated in professional fund raising ever since these formative years.

This tension is also central to the second major impulse behind the creation of fund raising as a profession, the John Price Jones school. Born in 1877 in Latrobe, Pennsylvania, John Price Jones attended Phillips Exeter Academy and then graduated from Harvard in 1902. Employed as a journalist, Jones worked at several newspapers, including the *Washington Post,* before landing a job at the H. K. McCann advertising company. In 1916, Jones began working on the $10 million endowment campaign at Harvard, and here he gained his first experience in a major fund-raising drive. From there he combined his background in journalism, advertising, and fund raising in his work on behalf of the war effort. Educated in the power of public persuasion by the work of the U.S. government's Committee on Public Information, Jones applied the methods of public relations to the nascent fund-raising profession after the war. Considered by his contemporaries to be virtually inarticulate and a martinet, Jones had three great loyalties, according to one observer: "Exeter, Harvard, and the Republican Party" (Cutlip, 1965, p. 182). In contrast to the YMCA men, as Jones's "Christers" epithet reveals, he was decidedly areligious. Contributing a penchant for thorough research and organization as well as a strong reliance on the publicity techniques developed during World War I, John Price Jones personified a businesslike, commercial, secular strain in the fund-raising field that combined with the YMCA men's vision of religion-based moral stewardship to form the ideological foundation of fund raising as a profession at the conclusion of the war.

Prior experience in fund raising coupled with the pioneers' intensified instruction in public relations during the First World War resulted in the realization that there was sufficient demand for the services that fund raisers could offer. This demand warranted the establishment of businesses whose primary function was to raise capital for philanthropic causes. Not surprisingly, Charles Ward, Lyman Pierce, and John Price Jones were instrumental in the creation of what Arnaud Marts described as "a new calling—that of the professional fund raising counsel" (Marts, 1961, p. 35). Indeed, most of the individuals and fund-raising firms that went on to prominence in the field in its formative years originate out of the firms of one of these three pioneers.

After Barber and Associates in the early 1910s, the next professional fund-raising firm was Ward & Hill (with Ward of course being Charles S. Ward), established in May 1919. In September of the same year, Lyman Pierce and a business associate joined the firm, which then became Ward, Hill, Pierce & Wells. And, as Cutlip has observed, "There was no lack of business. Ward's fame, and to a lesser extent Hill's and Pierce's, was widely acclaimed in philanthropic circles" (Cutlip, 1965, p. 159). The healthy business climate enabled the firm to expand its staff, hiring junior partners Christian Dreshman, Olaf Gates, and Arnaud Marts, along with a staff that included George Lundy, George Tamblyn, Bayard Hedrick, and Howard Beaver, a virtual "who's who" among the first generation of fund-raising counsel. The common occupational background of these men as executives either in the YMCA or in the wartime Red Cross campaign (and in some cases both), along with a personal and professional association, reveal the way they entered the profession. These men (and it is important to emphasize that this was entirely a profession of white males) did not become fund raisers through a specified academic training or a rigidly defined apprenticeship. Their entry into the field was predicated upon a loose and ill-defined experience in raising money, which brought them into contact with one of the field's pioneers. A similar trend occurred in the Jones sector of organized philanthropy.

Like Ward and the others, John Price Jones recognized, after the First World War, the enormous potential for a business devoted to counseling others in raising money. With the encouragement of Thomas Lamount, a partner in the House of Morgan, John Price Jones was incorporated in New York in November 1919. With a board of directors that included Jones, Robert F. Duncan, and George Brakeley, Sr., among others, the John Price Jones company began to recruit a professional staff headed by Harold "Si" Seymour and Chester E. Tucker. If activity in the YMCA or Red Cross was prerequisite for being hired at Ward, Hill, Pierce & Wells, a prep school education (preferably at Phillips Exeter), a Harvard degree, and newspaper experience were the standards at John Price Jones. And although the backgrounds of the Jones staff differed dramatically from those of the first generation of YMCA men, the homogeneity of the staff and the relatively informal manner in which they were recruited were shared characteristics. Professional training per se had little to do with becoming a fund-raising counsel.

By the mid-1920s, the Jones and YMCA schools began to merge to define, informally and perhaps unconsciously, the field of professional fund raising. The YMCA group provided a respectability generally accredited to the moral stewardship of the YMCA. Foremost in this agenda was the elimination of commissions as an acceptable form of compensation. By the end of the decade, the fixed fee had become a professional dogma, which, as Arnaud Marts recalled, was fundamental to his and George Lundy's goal of "making our fund raising more dignified and worthy of respect" (Marts, 1961, p. 35). The Jones school developed many of fund raising's most essential technical aspects, codified by Si Seymour in the John Price Jones company's two-volume *Standard Practices* guide. As Donald Kersting, an early associate at John Price Jones, observed, Seymour "was a theoretician" (Kersting, p. 8).

According to Wolcott Street, who joined the Jones firm in 1929, it was Seymour who developed fund raising's "classic" tenet of the Rule of Thirds: "You get one-third of capital from the top ten givers, another third from the next hundred, and the final third from the prospects who give" (Street, 1985, pp. 11–12). In 1935, the two groups, along with fund raisers centered around the American City Bureau, merged more formally in the creation of the American Association of Fund-Raising Counsel (AAFRC).

According to Wolcott Street, whose *Beacon for Philanthropy* (1985) provides all of the essential data for the AAFRC from its founding in 1935 to 1985, the establishment of the organization formalized a previously informal information exchange network among fund raisers of both the YMCA and Jones traditions as well as the American City Bureau. But the establishment of the AAFRC did not merely signify the cross-fertilization of the divergent traditions; it fulfilled the goal defined by Arnaud Marts to make "our fund raising more dignified and worthy of respect." Like other members of occupations that strove toward professionalism, such as doctors, lawyers, and even historians, the professionalization of fund raising was a demand for respect in an otherwise suspicious world, as well as an attempt to further the interests of the profession in a market economy (Haskell, 1984). For fund raisers of the pioneer generation, it was doubly significant because it served as their final statement on the mission/business tension endemic in the field.

The pioneers identified their profession as being in the service of philanthropy, even if they and their firms also derived wealth from advertising and public relations—activities in no way associated with philanthropic causes. They tried to create an image of fund raising as primarily a philanthropic enterprise, an ideological and moral endeavor that also made excellent business sense. To philanthropic organizations searching for experienced fund raisers whose expressed purpose was to promote philanthropic causes, a "professional" fund-raising firm would logically be a more attractive organization to hire than one whose sole expressed purpose was to make a profit—even if their skill and experience were exactly the same. In short, the professionalization of fund raising not only failed to eliminate the tension between fund raising as a business and fund raising as a mission but embedded that tension into the very center of the profession. This was the legacy passed on by the pioneer generation.

The Over-Sixty Generation

The over-sixty generation of fund-raising managers includes names with which most fund raisers will be familiar, among them, George A. Brakeley, Jr., John J. Schwartz, Maurice Gurin, Melvin Brewer, and E. Burr Gibson. Like their predecessors, this generation is made up almost solely of white males—a sociological stratification not unlike other growing professions in this country. The homogeneous composition of fund raising's practitioners and professional organizations (AAFRC, NSFRE, Council for the Advancement and Support of Education [CASE]) consolidated a proverbial "old-boys network." This network assisted in securing jobs in both lateral and upwardly mobile shifts and was a way to share information about clientele and colleagues.

In the over-sixty generation, there were two primary ways of finding employment in fund raising. From the earliest generation of fund-raising managers came a small group of men who inherited fund-raising firms. Among them are George Brakeley and Donald Kersting, and more recently Dave Ketchum and Martin Grenzebach.

In the third generation of leadership, this means of advancing toward leadership and ownership will likely become more commonplace. However, the primary method by which members of the over-sixty generation entered the profession and began the path toward leadership as a consultant or CEO was initially through what can only be called default. As George Brakeley put it, "I'd say that 50 percent of the men—if not more—get into the business by default. They failed at something else. They don't know what else to do with themselves. It looks like an easy way to make a living. I think my percentage is low. They fall into it. I doubt that 10 to 15 percent of them have a goal—conscious goal—going through college" (George A. Brakeley, Jr., audio interview, Nov. 23, 1987).

A profession that was not "chosen," but rather one into which its members "fall," would appear to lack professional substance. Yet, this means of "finding" philanthropy is in keeping with the pioneer generation. A field whose members may have found their careers because they "could not make it in another field," or had an unexpected opportunity presented to them in fund raising, is not entirely negative. There is a fortuitous aspect of such a default career. Elitism or professional snobbery has remained in large measure out of reach of even the highest echelons of fund-raising leaders. First, the fund raiser's professional objectives—working for causes to assist those in need—serve as a constant reminder of one's position and privileges in life. Second, the requirements, including specialized education and professional training, to "join the club" are fewer in fund raising than for most professions, and there is a greater potential to attract a truly diverse cadre of professionals.

On the other hand, this lack of standards is a serious drawback. The image of fund raising has suffered immensely for a variety of reasons. Public perception of fund raisers as amateurs is sustained because there are so few formalized professional requirements for entry into the field. There is a dearth of public knowledge about the approaches and standards in the profession. The image of the transient fund raiser, whose career is based on a life-style of travel and constantly changing campaigns, compounds the negative public perception.

The very essence of fund raising—being asked for money by

someone making his or her own living through this act—challenges acceptable American middle-class values. For many people, the charitable impulse is very American, yet so is financial privacy and independence, so that a profession whose essential denominator is asking for money, usually for those in need (who can be interpreted as dependent and unreliable), is antithetical to the very nature of what it means to be "American." There is a disturbing imbalance between the altruistic goals imbued in the profession (goals consistent with the intent of many people) and the deeply ingrained value Americans attribute to self-reliance and free enterprise.

Additionally, the public's feeling about professional fund raising may be one of sympathy with the cause yet irreverence toward the fund raiser. Because so few people know about philanthropic fund raising, the profession has lagged behind others in attaining status with the outside world. Professional standards demand that fund raisers hide themselves in order to shift the focus of acknowledgment and interest toward the cause and the donors; therefore, fund raising remains a behind-the-scenes career. Thus, the profession has a limited ability to join the ranks of similar professions and businesses, such as public relations or advertising, at least in the public's eye. J. Patrick Ryan summarizes the problem nicely:

> It is not a high visibility thing that we do, and if we become high visibility, we have probably lost some of our effectiveness. I don't need anyone to know who my firm is or who I am, nor does any member of our firm need to be known as to who they are, except by the president of the institution, the chair of the board, some of the key volunteers we're working directly with, and staff members who know we are helping them. But in the same respect, the staff members who are working in an agency have that same low visibility. When the appeal for funds goes out, it's Danny Thomas or it's the chair of the board whose name is put forward. It is not the fund raising executive. So there is nothing we do, or should do, that brings attention to us or, therefore, our career. So, it's a behind-

the-scenes function. Most people don't even think about it. And, ideally, I would much rather you be interested in giving to Harvard because you love the school, you're impressed with the programs it's going to try to develop to improve education or society or mankind, than to know that there are people out there who have figured that if we print these cards in yellow instead of green, we'll get a five-tenths of one percent improved response. And that I've somehow been influenced by that person. Who cares about that? That's not what inspires anybody. It's our job as facilitators. It is to help match up a cause that is caring for people and that wants to do a better job with people who care about that cause and want to see that cause succeed. All we're doing is facilitating that. Who cares about us in the middle? Nobody should (J. Patrick Ryan, audio interview, Apr. 10, 1989).

The days of resident (or field) managers who headed a program for a few years and then relocated are quickly fading. In-house development offices have generally taken the place of external fund-raising firms at universities and hospitals. The predominant responsibility of fund-raising firms is consultation, rather than providing resident campaign direction. Maurice Gurin discussed this shift from resident life to consultation and the increase in development offices. His firm (Bowen and Gurin, Inc.) was one of the first to give up resident campaign direction and focus on consulting. "We were the only one that took that position, and the others stayed with resident campaign direction. Now that was in the 1960s. Since then, over half of the members of the member firms of the association (AAFRC) provide counseling in addition to resident management" (Maurice Gurin, audio interview, Dec. 6, 1989). It was in large part the resident life that gave fund raisers such a poor reputation. The instability and transience (sometimes in image only, sometimes in actuality) that characterized resident management undermined the image that could have been created through the exhaustive efforts demanded by these positions.

Many fund raisers defended their dedication to philanthropic values by pointing to the long working days, time away from family and friends, constant motivational leadership, and (until recently) mediocre remuneration given to resident managers. Fund raisers sought their own rewards from personal satisfaction rather than external benefits. For interviewees, their dedication in spite of these professional hardships demonstrated their commitment to the field and is the primary evidence of their adherence to true philanthropic values.

Fund raising can be seen as a continuum extending between philanthropic values and the mere notion of having a job. Professional fund raisers fall everywhere in between these two poles. It is here that the newest generation of fund-raising directors, managers, and consultants comes into play. In fact, the primary impetus for the research on which this chapter is based was derived from the differences between the over- and under-sixty generations, which mirror the tension between fund raising as philanthropy and fund raising as business.

Repeatedly, interviewees expressed concern that abrupt expansion and changes in fund raising have jeopardized traditional philanthropic values. In the interviews with many of the over-sixty generation, a fear surfaced that the very elements that are enhancing the public image of fund raising and promoting its professionalism are also eroding its underlying values. For example, the motivations and goals for entering and remaining in a field such as fund raising may well be changing. With the slow establishment of a relatively higher profile through special fund-raising events, the reemergence of environmental and social issues, and accelerated salary levels for development positions, fund raising is no longer rewarded solely by personal inner satisfactions but has begun to shape itself into a profession whose participants can reap monetary and stature gains. In certain respects, fund raising in its new-found professional glory is becoming indistinguishable from business, advertising, or public relations.

The concern of such leaders as John J. Schwartz, Harold Treash, and Melvin Brewer has brought this discrepancy to light. They and many of their colleagues believe that fund raising is, or should be, backed by a philosophy deeper than merely meeting financial goals. Most in this generation claim a sense of commitment to the field as a means of service and a calling. The over-sixty generation instigated and welcomes positive changes in the field, for themselves and for the sake of the profession and its image. These professional improvements have indeed led to higher salaries. The newest generation of fund-raising professionals is attracted to opportunities in this quickly changing and growing field, does not hesitate to switch jobs and commitments, and can rationalize commission income. The field then has made a shift in its external values—for example, a rise in all of the appropriate professional qualifiers. There is a profound fear among the second-generation members, therefore, that the internal values are making a shift as well.

Through our readings and interviews, we encountered a middle ground that, although not a resolution of the tension between fund raising as a mission and fund raising as a job, does illuminate some of the details present in this tension. As George A. Brakeley, Jr. indicated in his interview, fund raising is a business. One may very well see the benefits others get from it and feel good about that, but it is equally a job and a business. Fund raising is a perfect example of the chicken and egg debate. Which comes first: a sense of mission and altruism or the job (with the value-laden benefits being recognized later)?

Harold Treash and Ralph Chamberlain—from the over-sixty generation—expressed that the sense of service they received from their work has continued to sustain their motivation and given them deep satisfaction. However, they felt motivated initially to enter the profession because of their individual backgrounds and life histories, which included strong religious impulses and charitable values. Interviewees of the over-sixty generation spoke of the personal rewards they felt after a campaign goal was met. Many of these people, like the younger generation, work day to day without personal altruistic objectives but after achieving success in a project feel a sense of satisfaction and accomplishment money does not bring.

The Under-Sixty Generation

The under-sixty generation shares the mixed perceptions of fund raising as business and as altruism. Patrick Ryan spoke of fund raising as a profession and a business, yet made a strong statement that there were few other careers where one could see the impact of his or her work on so many people. Other under-sixty heads of firms, such as Toni Goodale, Jane Geever, and Franklyn Cook, all believe in their missions and yet have an interest in fund raising as a business and as a career. The tension between the sets of values is thus well represented by the newest generation of fund raisers.

The career possibilities in fund raising no doubt attract many young people who do not have strong service-oriented values but who, like their predecessors, find their way into the field by default, or at least through the relative ease with which one can enter the ranks and advance. If this is the comparative method by which the outgoing leadership views the values of its professional offspring, then there is room for concern and some validity to the fear that fund raising is becoming merely the business of raising money. It is only through the historical record that any form of perspective can be gained regarding the values of generations of fund-raising leaders.

It would be impossible to prove a shift from philanthropic to self-interested motivations between the second and third generation of fund raisers. The default method of entry into the profession obscures the importance of deeper philanthropic values to both under- and over-sixty fund raisers. The tension between self-interest and philanthropy transcends generational change.

 The two major developments over recent decades have been the innovative implementation of technology, such as using computers for telemarketing and donor profiles, and the striking increase of women in the profession.

Technology has streamlined (to an extent) the methods and practices of fund raising, making it akin to a business more than ever before. Computer-related management has transformed people into numbers and "potential profiles" and helped increase the competitiveness of fund-raising firms and consultants. The goals of campaigns based on these methods may be seriously philanthropic, however, and the process does not question the values of the person pushing the keys, the case, or the cause.

Social, economic, and other historical changes all mounted to affect the demographics of the fund-raising profession. The impact of the social movements of the 1960s, especially the women's movement, and the influence of other professions' acceptance of women has had a profound effect. Although the highest ranks of the profession are still occupied primarily by males, these ranks no longer comprise gender autonomy, and the "old-boys network" is being dismantled and replaced by something yet to be defined.

In fund raising overall, women make up over 50 percent of organizational and development placement. To use an age-old but highly accurate phrase, "fund raising," as Diane Carlson says, "is one of the few professions in which a woman can make the world her oyster" (Diane Carlson, audio interview, Apr. 28, 1989). What make this profession so unique and appealing to women are the factors already addressed in this study. Since specific educational or professional training is not necessary, women can enter the profession without fear of discrimination once they have raised their families (after being away from the job or academic environment) and can be relatively assured of quicker results from their efforts than in other competitive career environments. The field in general is expanding rapidly and requires more personnel than previously; therefore, it offers multiple opportunities. Further, women have traditionally been responsible for positions that involve service and interpersonal skills (for example, teaching and nursing), and fund raising fits well into the framework for a career having similar dimensions. Women have been active participants and leaders of volunteerism. And lastly, women have become accustomed to major roles in tasks that lack visibility and gratitude. These variables all make fund raising a dynamic target for women to find familiarity and career possibilities.

The dramatic increase of women in the fund-raising field was verbally supported by every interviewee and through nearly all other sources of information. This support seems to stem from the premise that fund raising is a profession requiring sensitivity and intuition. Whether or not it is true that women share these attributes more than men does not seem to matter. What does matter is the *belief* that women have these attributes and that this belief is held by both men and women in hiring, collegial, and donor positions.

The newest generation of fund raisers, then, is made up in

large proportion of women; to a lesser extent, minorities are becoming more visible. This generation has a different public image and a set of different prospects compared to those of even ten years ago. Overall, they will be well paid and will work in interesting jobs. They will have the security of knowing that women as well as men, and, with luck, minorities of either gender, can become owners, CEOs, and consultants. But will they know the meaning of giving and the importance of identifying with the cause or community of people? Will the values that the outgoing generation advocates and the very definition of philanthropy be submerged beneath the expansion, technology, and professionalism itself?

As witness to the diversity of these values, at the NSFRE meetings in Orlando, Florida, Reverend Paul C. Reinert gave a succinct and well-organized presentation on the topic "The Art of Fund Raising in the 1990s." One of his major points was that philanthropy, and in particular fund raising, breeds a form of satisfaction and reward that is unequaled nearly anywhere else. The ramifications of such efforts can be far reaching. The point he tagged onto this message, however, was that fund raising should be experienced much differently than a job; that in fact, fund raising can be likened to a ministry. His presentation was not simply support, or a report of such a philosophy, but was meant to be persuasive. His real agenda appeared to be to convince the people in his audience of the importance of this form of dedication, for not only would one be better as a fund raiser (more convincing), but the genuine message of philanthropy could be carried beyond the business and marketing strategies (Reinert, 1990).

His hope and attempts are not unlike those of many to whom we have spoken. For better or worse, however, one does not have to search far for opposing viewpoints. At this same conference, we overheard a large number of people skeptically criticizing these approaches to "putting the philanthropy back into fund raising." One person specifically stated that fund raising is merely marketing and accounting, and that discussion of topics dealing with fund raising as service to humankind, or a calling, are all fringe and pomp—a way of enabling the profession to distinguish itself and raise its professional self-esteem, which has languished for so long. In short,

Reverend Reinert's paper and the rections to it merely illustrate the persistence of the tension between fund raising as a calling and fund raising as a job—a conflict endemic in the profession from its very beginning.

References

Allen, W. H. *Modern Philanthropy: A Study of Efficient Appealing and Giving*. New York: Dodd, Mead, 1912.

Bremner, R. H. *American Philanthropy*. (2nd ed.) Chicago: University of Chicago Press, 1988.

Cutlip. S. M. *Fund Raising in the United States: Its Role in America's Philanthropy*. New Brunswick, N.J.: Rutgers University Press, 1965.

Haskell, T., ed. *The Authority of Experts: Studies in History and Theory*. Bloomington: Indiana University Press, 1984.

Marts, A. *Man's Concern for His Fellow Man*. Geneva, N.Y.: W. F. Humphrey Press, 1961.

Melillo, W. "Fund Raisers Drop Ban on Commissions from Ethics Code." *Chronicle of Philanthropy*, Apr. 18, 1989, pp. 1, 10.

Pierce, L. *How to Raise Money*. New York: Harper Collins, 1932.

Pierce, L. *Scrapbooks*. Madison: State Historical Society of Wisconsin, n.d.

Reinert, P. C. "The Art of Fund Raising in the 1990s." Paper delivered at NSFRE Conference, Orlando, Fla, 1990.

Street, W. D. *A Beacon for Philanthropy: The American Association of Fund-Raising Counsel Through Fifty Years: 1935-1985*. New York: American Association of Fund-Raising Counsel, 1985.

Chapter 3

Metaphors
Fund Raisers Live By:
Language and Reality
in Fund Raising

Richard C. Turner

In *Metaphors We Live By*, George Lakoff and Mark Johnson (1980) take a serious look at the way metaphors reflect and shape the experiences that we embed in our language. They point out, for instance, how our habits of talking about argument are undergirded by metaphors of war and how such a connection not only shapes the kind of thinking we do about argument but often prevents our thinking of other forms of argumentation. Given this fact, Lakoff and Johnson argue, language users can no longer treat metaphor as an ornament on language that is otherwise clear and straightforward. They suggest that an awareness of metaphoric systems is necessary for a more accurate sense of how we connect with our worlds: "Metaphor is for most people a device of the poetic imagination and the rhetorical flourish—a matter of extraordinary rather than ordinary language. Moreover, metaphor is typically viewed as characteristic of language alone, a matter of words rather than thought or action. For this reason, most people think they can get along perfectly well without metaphor. We have found, on the contrary, that metaphor is pervasive in everyday life, not just in language but in thought and action. Our ordinary conceptual system, in terms of which we both think and act, is fundamentally metaphorical in nature" (Lakoff and Johnson, 1980, p. 3).

Although most people tend to think of language as a transparent conduit for meaning, Lakoff and Johnson, and other linguists, have established the fact that language and meaning are socially constructed systems that deserve special attention, including attention to the common metaphor that language is a conduit.

This chapter looks at the metaphors that fund raisers use when they talk about their work and describes the figures that recur in the texts fund raisers write and read. Publications include fund-raising training materials, issues of *The Journal, Fund Raising Management,* and books that established practitioners have written. The chapter focuses on fund raisers discussing fund raising, rather than on aspects of their work that might borrow terminology from other areas of discourse as a regular procedure. For instance, if a fund raiser uses business metaphors in a piece on organizing accounting procedures, the presence of those business metaphors is readily understandable in terms of the ordinary voice and vocabulary of the subject matter. But when a fund raiser uses a business metaphor in a discussion of the future of fund raising or the need for different training experiences for colleagues, the presence of the metaphor suggests an orientation of values and perceptions of reality that are significant and worthy of comment.

A look at the term "fund raiser" itself might help to set the direction for this discussion of metaphor. The *Random House Dictionary* points out that "fund raiser" is a relatively new term in the language, citing its appearance in Vance Packard's *Hidden Persuaders* (1957) as the first printed use of the term. "Fund raising" goes back to the late 1930s. But what is of present interest is the ways in which the terms create meaning and how they convey what their users hope to convey.

"Fund," the *Random House Dictionary* tells us, comes from the same word that creates "foundation" and originally meant a solid pile of something. By a series of applications since its origin in Latin, "fund" has taken on more liquid properties ("funds for . . . ") and can now be seen as a collection of individual units ("adding to the fund"). "Raise," you will not be surprised to hear, has over twenty distinct meanings listed, ranging from increased physical elevation to increasing amounts of any kind, especially in a gambling context. What is interesting to note is that fund raisers characteristically operate with a number of these different senses. It is the job of most fund raisers to create that solid pile that every organization needs to operate comfortably, usually called an endowment. Going about increasing that pile requires that "funds" be seen as existing in smaller units that can be garnered from donors and added to the pile.

"Raise" originates in a distinctly physical context, but the meaning that refers to assembling or collecting is the sixteenth meaning listed, a good bit of etymological distance from its origins. Yet "raising" as an act of physical accumulation stays with the meaning of the word even as it refers to assembling discrete units. Even though associates and acquaintances understand that fund raisers solicit and collect money for an organization, fund raisers are apt to become fixed in their minds as persons involved in a physical, somewhat Herculean, labor of changing the shape of this solid, more or less huge pile.

One of the primary meanings of "raise" has to do with building a framework for something so that the lifting is tied in with building of some sort. This sense of building accompanies some of the meanings that are more remote from the first meaning so that raising funds carries with it a sense of purpose. I would suggest that the term "fund raiser" carries with it some aspects of the usage seen in "barn raising," an activity that fulfills a goal and also incorporates the elements of voluntarism, public spiritedness, and cooperation that arise from the popular image of barn raisings.

So "fund raiser" carries with it a host of meanings that arise from its etymological origins and its cultural history. The point is that the phrase "fund raiser" refers not only to a person who solicits and collects for a reason but also to a specific image of that activity, an image that acts as a metaphor for that activity. The point that Lakoff and Johnson make in *Metaphors We Live By* is that this complex of meanings that surrounds most of the terms we use is metaphorical and that these metaphors embody the way we think about and react to our world. Looking closely at the meanings that surround "fund raiser" is not merely a curious activity for bookish sorts or English professors who have a stake in manufacturing meanings. The impulse to look that closely at the metaphors embedded in language use arises from a sense of how much such metaphors are central to our definitions of selves and to how a person presents herself or himself to others. This sense of the importance of metaphor in understanding language is part of a larger revision of how language and thought interact. It is this change in attitudes toward language that ought to motivate all discourse communities, including fund raisers, to look more closely at the metaphors they live by.

It is likely that fund raisers will recognize themselves in the following definition of traditional expectations about how language and metaphors work: "There is what might be called the *classical* view [of metaphor], which sees metaphor as 'detachable' from language; a device that may be imported into language in order to achieve specific, prejudged effects. These aid language to achieve what is seen as its major goal, the revelation of the 'reality' of a world that lies, unchanging, beyond it" (Hawkes, 1982, p. 90).

Most people regard language as being primarily in the business of communicating information about independent realities, and so simplicity and clarity are the qualities most sought and valued. The description Hawkes offers suggests how attitudes toward specific language uses are shaped by the overall conception of language as a conduit for meaning. Within that framework, metaphors can be effective additions to a message, but they are not essential, and the message can be sent without the metaphor attached. Under that rubric, the kind of attention I have been paying to metaphor seems precious at best and of interest only to specialists who have the time for such convoluted considerations.

What justifies such attenuated considerations of how metaphors work is a redefinition of how language works. Hawkes adds a description of a "modern" view of metaphor, one that sees language as essentially metaphorical and the action of metaphor as that of creating a "new" reality when it is deliberately invoked. The metaphor depicts something that had not been anticipated and could not be described (that is, could not be sent as a message) without the metaphor. Part of this newer understanding includes a recognition that the reality metaphors embody amounts to a reinforcement and restatement of an older reality that our total way of life presupposes. Our language use reflects the values and conceptions that we have inherited from our culture and/or incorporated into our outlook from personal experiences.

Lakoff and Johnson in *Metaphors We Live By* and Lakoff in *Women, Fire, and Dangerous Things* suggest that metaphors have to be taken seriously as a part of how language users experience the meanings they acquire. These books suggest that, because meanings are rooted in physical and emotional experience, the understanding of how they create meaning requires that those physical and emotional contexts be recognized. The classical view of metaphor assumes that thinking is a matter of manipulating abstract symbols, and so messages remain untouched and unaffected by their use. More recent treatments of language and metaphor argue that the thinking we do and the conclusions we draw about our world are rooted in the values and experiences that shape our perspectives even as we are unaware of the influence.

Metaphors We Live By addresses directly the ways in which metaphors shape what we know, rather than embellishing preexisting articulations of thought. Lakoff and Johnson identify a number of the metaphors that inform the way modern Americans see their world. Their point that war is an argument was mentioned previously. They point out how commonly the metaphor *argument is war* appears in ordinary conversation (Lakoff and Johnson, 1980, p. 4):

> Your claims are indefensible.
> He attacked every point in my argument.
> The criticisms were right on target.
> I demolished his argument.
> If you use that strategy, he'll wipe you out.
> He shot down my argument.

The pattern emerges clearly that argument is equated with war, not only in the language choices but also in the way speakers position themselves and behave. The understanding of argument is embedded in experiences of war, whether or not the speaker has been in an actual war.

The same pattern can be seen in statements that work meta-
phorically, such as the following, in which time is equated with
money (Lakoff and Johnson, 1980, p. 8):

> I don't have the time to give you.
> How do you spend your time these days?
> That flat tire cost me an hour.
> I've invested a lot of time in her.
> You're running out of time.
> Is that worth your while?
> He's living on borrowed time.

Time is like money, or at least like something valuable that
would act as money in a similar situation. Traditional approaches
to metaphor might regard these instances as isolated figures of
speech trying to convey messages more effectively. But the perva-
siveness of the metaphor and the casual way in which we use and
regard such usages suggest the degree to which they are part of the
fabric of our conceptions. Understanding that the metaphor "time
is money" is central to our conceptions of the world does not pre-
clude our using it; rather, it merely argues for an awareness of the
extent to which values and prior experiences are present in the
choices we make as users of language.

Lakoff and Johnson also point out how some metaphors are
orientational, the most prominent of which are up-and-down metaphors. Certainly based on physical, especially bodily, experience,
our conceptual orientation regarding up or down is often tied to
metaphorical usages in which up is good and down is bad. When
we talk about "feeling up," "something that boosted the crowd's
spirits," or "getting a lift from a phone call," we are equating up
with good. Similarly, "feeling depressed," "falling into a depres-
sion," and "feeling low" equate down with bad. Consciousness is
associated with up, and unconsciousness is down ("wake up,"
"sank into a coma"). Health and life are up; sickness and death are
down ("the peak of health," "down with the flu"). More is up; less
is down ("incomes rise and fall"). Virtue is up; depravity is down
("high-minded," "a low-down thing to do"). (Lakoff and Johnson,
1980, pp. 15–19.)

These metaphors suggest that not only are they pervasive in our speech and conversation but also systematic in our habits of explaining ourselves and our worlds. Metaphors are not detachable figures that we choose to use or not to use. Rather, they are part of the way we articulate ourselves and our understandings about the people and the things around us. If Arlo Guthrie is right about our being what we eat, then it is also true that we are what we say. The words we use often articulate much more than we may intend. Because our language is rooted in our values and experiences, our sayings spell out our assumptions and our aspirations, even assumptions and aspirations that might be better left unsaid in some contexts.

With this information in mind about the way metaphors undergird our utterances, it is possible, and I would argue advisable, to regard the metaphors we use as part of the message we are sending. Looking at texts we read and write and listening closely to our own utterances and those of others can tell us when the metaphors and the messages are working together or creating unproductive dissonances. Becoming more sensitive to how metaphors work in our language is a matter of practice and attention. Looking at the play of metaphors in a given text will alert all speakers and readers to the dynamics of metaphors, just as developing the habit of looking at how metaphors work will enable all speakers and readers to gain greater control over the impact of their utterances.

The point of this paper is to focus this kind of attention on the language that fund raisers use and especially the metaphors that often operate in the ways that fund raisers talk about their work. For instance, "Keep Those Names Coming," an article by Carol Enters in *Fund Raising Management* (Jan. 1990), discusses the need for fund raisers to continue to use direct mailing even as the costs have risen remarkably and as many have questioned its value. In the course of the discussion she talks about getting funds in the face of government budget cuts "to stay alive, much less grow," thereby introducing a metaphoric connection between the organization and an organic body and between the funds and blood or sustenance of some sort. So, without saying anything about the urgency or the harshness of the budget cuts, she has established the situation as desperate. The organic metaphor is a common one in the culture at large, and Enters elicits the reader's sympathy by aligning organizations such as hers with all living things, including the readers of her piece. The metaphor is consistent with her sense of the importance of the survival of her organization.

In other places she draws on theological contexts ("the sins of direct-mail fund raising") and mechanistic images ("what pushes their philanthropic buttons"). At first glance these metaphors seem casual, but they reveal her connection with other attitudes about fund raising. She has some reservations and strong feelings about some direct-mail practices, and the "sins" metaphor articulates those feelings as it simultaneously distances her from the suggestion with its "exaggerated" comparison. The mechanistic image reveals a practitioner's routinizing of the focus of his or her work, the kind of routinizing that occurs in most fields. But when donors are routinized into automatons having philanthropic "buttons," then the position taken toward the donor is at odds with many of the other assumptions about donors that fund raisers make. In other contexts, no doubt, Enters understands these conflicts and acts as a responsible professional. Her metaphor here raises some of those issues as she treats the many facets of direct-mail solicitation.

Perhaps the most prominent metaphors in the field of fund raising in general, however, are military. Examples are: "You are currently fighting attrition," "direct-mail acquisition campaign," "prospects bombarded by solicitations" (a figure that grows out of the previous metaphoric definition of the government cuts as the equivalent of an attack), "enlist volunteers," and "target prospects." Much of this language derives from the undergirding metaphor of a military campaign: "Capital campaigns" are among the chief activities in which fund raisers engage.

The image of a military campaign is a useful metaphor for the organization needing to raise money, to create a sense of urgency and to promise that the duration will be short. But the metaphor is perhaps not so useful for the sense of mission and for the position taken toward the people the campaign will address (the enemy?). In addition, although it is easier to get people to help raise funds if you promise a short duration for the effort, more and more nonprofits are recognizing that fund raising is a perpetual activity and that promises of short campaigns may disenchant people who otherwise might have signed on for the long term. Fund raisers might heed the example of all the generals who faced mutinies after unfulfilled promises to their troops of a quick fight and short-term rewards. Certainly such a pervasive metaphor might explain why some people have difficulty relaxing around fund raisers.

The military associations surrounding "campaign" are all the more surprising when considered in relation to the helping and caring motives and goals that characterize so much of philanthropic activity. Although philanthropists and fund raisers may be attracted to the sense of organization and clarity of purpose the metaphor offers, they could hardly have engaged a metaphor more disparate from the healing and nurturing they so often support. The ease with which the two contexts coexist suggests the degree to which the metaphors any group uses are embedded in cultural assumptions and attitudes. Recent discussions of the ways gender, race, and class determine linguistic choices suggest how thoroughly language embeds these attitudes. It is likely, for instance, that the increasing feminization of fund raising as a profession will influence the metaphors fund raisers use, pushing back the prominence of military metaphors and substituting metaphors that emphasize cooperation and mutual dependence. But it is unlikely that this process will move at a much faster pace than the change in language use in the culture at large.

Sometimes, however, using mixed metaphors creates confusion instead of clarity. For example, an article by J. Patrick Ryan in *The Journal* (Spring 1989, p. 8), urging American fund raisers to become more aware of and more respectful of fund raisers in other countries, repeatedly returns to organic metaphors ("growth," "flourish") to suggest a widespread, simultaneous increase in philanthropic efforts around the world. The article then undercuts that image by suggesting that philanthropic activities could be the "glue" that binds various nations in human understanding, a figure that changes the dominant organic image. The piece ends with a call for serious fund raisers "to lead the way," introducing a journey/search metaphor and so once again confusing the rootedness of the organic metaphor. The article creates problems for the reader because it keeps shifting the basis of its appeal and so loses the reader's focus and, ultimately, commitment.

The dissonances that competing metaphors create in a text are visible in the following passage in a promotional flyer for Michael O'Neill's *The Third America: The Emergence of the Nonprofit Sector in the United States* (1989): "In this new book, Michael O'Neill provides an up-to-date, comprehensive examination of the complex and diverse nonprofit sector in the United States, bringing the 'invisible sector' into the spotlight and revealing the enormous and dramatically increasing impact it has on American society, business, economics, and government. In a single volume he identifies and explores all the major subsectors of the nonprofit world—for example, religion, education and research, health care, and arts and culture, among others—describing how each developed and what it must do to achieve its mission and meet key challenges, problems, and policy questions."

The first sentence draws on the image of the laboratory analysis of physical specimens and on the practice of giving final exams over the whole field of study. Both types of examinations are undertaken by experts and have the authority usually accorded to objective and scientific inquiries. This pattern of claiming for O'Neill's book the power and importance of scientific treatises is extended to the promise of bringing new light to the subject, a common metaphor in Western civilization for new knowledge. But in this case, the light is a spotlight—most properly used in connection with stage productions. Theatrical spotlights are reserved for celebrities or for something that is to be applauded or enjoyed rather than objectively examined. In the next sentence O'Neill is said to "explore" the nonprofit world, thus shifting from an authoritative and sedentary scientific undertaking to an adventure involving treks into uncharted territories.

O'Neill cannot be both a plodding laboratory scientist and a swashbuckling explorer of new worlds. Although no one blames the writer for wanting to create excitement about O'Neill's work, the reader is asked to hold together simultaneously images of O'Neill as Jonas Salk and as Marco Polo or Indiana Jones. The dissonance between the two images causes the reader to lose sight of exactly what it is that O'Neill does. Once the connection between the activity and the context is lost, the reader has difficulty following the pattern of what is being presented or the claims that are being made for it. More than just a mixing of metaphors, the inclusion of mutually exclusive or competing metaphors asks the reader to sort through the dissonance and is apt to distract the reader from the point of the writing. Furthermore, there is a conflict between the values and motives at stake in each enterprise.

O'Neill's book itself keeps a tighter control over the metaphors it uses, much of the book being devoted to a description of what constitutes the nonprofit sector. An interesting pattern of values and their attendant metaphors emerges as O'Neill begins to speculate about future directions for study of the nonprofit sector. O'Neill regularly describes the connections between government and the nonprofit sector in terms of fluids ("revenue flowing," "funds channeled," "services funneled") whenever the direction is from government to the nonprofit sector, but in terms of solids ("supports," "provides mechanisms") when the connection heads from the nonprofit sector toward government. This difference in metaphor may reflect his point of view (as inside one sector and outside the other), and it may be a function of his spatial metaphor, which defines institutions in terms of "sectors."

O'Neill uses another spatial metaphor when he describes the providing of social services in America as a field and then specifies the metaphor as that of a game when he describes the government as the "biggest player on the field." Then he suggests a further extension of the game metaphor to apply to the context of military campaigns when he raises the possibility of nonprofits being the "vanguard" of social experimentation.

The last sentence of the quote about O'Neill's book introduces one of the most prominent metaphors used by fund raisers: the combat metaphor arising out of the chivalric tradition. For example, the writer paraphrases O'Neill on the nonprofit sector's achieving "its mission" and meeting "key challenges." "Challenge" originates in the practice of formalized one-on-one combat and brings with it all the suggestions of glamour and romance that surround the chivalric tradition. "Challenge grants" and other manifestations of the images in fund raising attract attention because they associate the fund-raising activity with the noble and courageous deeds that chivalric literature offers about knights in shining armor, whatever the record of actual knights might tell. The other relevant parts of the cluster are the journeys that knights undertake, their quests, and the valuable object of the quest, whether the Holy Grail or a damsel in distress. The fund raiser taking on a challenge wraps himself or herself in these romantic associations. The metaphoric cluster is especially useful for fund raisers because it blends the nobility and purity of motive usually expected of a person with a cause, the emphasis on bold and determined action required of fund-raising campaigns, and a valuable prize as the object of the quest. (It should be noted that too often the luster of such romantic associations is lost when the grail-object is represented by an oversized thermometer that gets redder and redder as the campaign succeeds.)

The grail-object is central to the repertoire of metaphors fund raisers live by in another way. In addition to being valuable, it is sitting passively waiting to be found, and its capture raises no questions about authority or dominion: The object of the quest wants to be found. This passive, controversy-free treasure makes the search worthwhile and avoids any questions of the appropriateness of the search. It is important to fund raisers that the object of their efforts be free of controversy. The funds to be raised are best if they are otherwise uncommitted, not discovered at the expense of other worthwhile projects, and without any taint in their origins. Money earmarked for another worthwhile use would complicate the role of the fund raiser, who would become the competitive and manipulative wheeler/dealer trying to capture the big account from other fund raisers.

Being cast in such a heroic image is helpful and flattering to fund raisers, but it has its own drawbacks. It puts pressure on fund raisers to perform at an extraordinarily high level, but it also complicates the image of fund raising by associating it with the world of high romance where heroes use magic and miracles to get their jobs done. Fund raisers would be better off with a realistic budget and some manageable time lines. Searching for treasure may sound exciting and is wonderful when it works, but there may be no sadder sight than an unsuccessful searcher.

The hero image also suggests that the fund raiser will do it alone. Indeed, the latest survey of philanthropy in the United States points out that many fund raisers work alone and fill a number of different roles in their jobs (American Association of Fund-Raising Counsel, 1989). Heroism can lead to burnout. The loneliness of fund raisers is apparent also in their use of the term "prospects" for the objects of their energy, which, of course, refers to the people who might give in the future. But the repeated use of the term often comes to suggest that fund raisers are, then, "prospectors," solitary searchers for treasures that sit out in the world waiting to be found.

The passive reward waiting for the searching fund raiser shows up also in the common phrase fund raisers use: "tapping new sources of support." Perhaps the first thing that comes to mind, and that is the way metaphors work, is the skillful and patient rural person tapping maple trees for their sap to make maple syrup. The image is pleasant and reassuring because the tradition surrounding the activity and the assurance that the trees will replenish the resource guarantee that the tapping is appropriate and of value to all concerned.

Perhaps the next most immediate image for "tapping" is the removal of natural gas and oil from the ground. Here the tapping is more controversial because the source is not replenishable and the harsh and exploitive procedures of so many developers have created questions about the ethics involved in tapping these new sources. Clearly, fund raisers want to be associated with the first image of tapping the trees, but the needs of their operations usually relate more to the kind of big strike commonly associated with the second image. The metaphor "tapping new sources" may tell more about a fund raiser than he or she wants known, its complexities undercutting his or her impact.

None of this analysis of the metaphors that characterize the language of fund raisers suggests that fund raisers should change their metaphors, but they may want to think about the assumptions they are making and the values they are inscribing into their practice. Fund raisers should take seriously the means by which they construct the world of their profession. One or another of the metaphors discussed above may embody a set of values or point to a set of practices that may require reflection, and reflection may lead to change.

References

American Association of Fund-Raising Counsel. *Giving USA: The Annual Report on Philanthropy for the Year 1988.* New York: American Association of Fund-Raising Counsel, 1989.

Enters, C. "Keep Those Names Coming." *Fund Raising Management,* Jan. 1990, pp. 38–44.

Hawkes, T. *Metaphor.* London: Methuen, 1982.

Lakoff, G. *Women, Fire, and Dangerous Things.* Chicago: University of Chicago Press, 1987.

Lakoff, G., and Johnson, M. *Metaphors We Live By.* Chicago: University of Chicago Press, 1980.

O'Neill, M. *The Third America: The Emergence of the Nonprofit Sector in the United States.* San Francisco: Jossey-Bass, 1989.

Packard, V. *Hidden Persuaders.* New York: McKay, 1957.

Random House Dictionary. (2nd ed.) New York: Random House, 1987.

Ryan, J. P. "We Have Much to Learn from Our International Friends." *The Journal* (NSFRE), Spring 1989, pp. 8–10.

PART TWO

THE MORAL DIMENSION
OF FUND RAISING

Chapter 4

A Historical and Moral Analysis of Religious Fund Raising

Thomas H. Jeavons

Jesus told his disciples: "No one can serve two masters; one cannot serve God and mammon" (Matt. 6:24).* Human history and experience confirm this judgment. The love of money, even if it is not "the root of all evil," seems to displace too readily the love of God—or if one prefers more secular terms, the love of "the good"—in human affairs and so unravels the moral fabric of life. However, human experience also tells us that while we may not be able to serve both God and mammon, neither can we easily separate the two.

As the history of the Judeo-Christian tradition demonstrates, there has always been a tension between the imperative to keep one's attention and obedience directed to the moral, to the spiritual, to God, at the center of religious life and the need to garner material resources necessary to support "the practice of faith," which involves giving witness to the world, in worship and in service, of the reli-

---

*All scriptural quotations in this essay come from the New International Version, Zondervan Press, 1979.

gious community's experience of God's love. So one finds that the
Scriptures, commentaries, and theological treatises of this tradition
are replete with instructions and admonitions about giving and getting worldly goods, with exhortations about the graciousness, and
warnings about the greed, that may accompany this process.

Of course, neither the Old nor the New Testament actually
has a chapter on fund raising. In a number of places, however, the
Scriptures do offer us examples of the circumstances in which and
purposes for which the Jewish and early Christian communities
sought contributions—for instance, for the maintenance of a place
of worship and for religious services (Exod. 30:11-16) or for the care
of less fortunate members of the community (Acts 6:1-6). And in a
number of places these biblical passages articulate or expound on
the manner and rationale that should characterize such giving.

A Proposal and a Problem

In this essay I propose to draw out a list of the motives the Judeo-
Christian tradition assumes might undergird the practice of giving
from a review of relevant passages in the Old Testament, or Hebrew
Bible, the New Testament, and other literature central to this tradition. Moreover, in considering the ways these different motives are
presented and treated, and by juxtaposing them with historical
practice (as far as we can know that), I propose to expose the relative
moral value this tradition assigns to different reasons for and approaches to giving. The point of this exercise is to work toward an
articulation of what constitutes "appropriate practice" in religious
fund raising based on religious values.

In these days, organized religion is confronted by the most
pressing needs for material resources to make its witness practical
in the face of worldly problems—for example, to make real the
Christian ideal of compassion in the face of homelessness and fam-
ine. But, at the same time, the world faces the most ludicrous examples of self-serving appeals for money from organized religion,
such as threats by one fund raiser that God will "call him home"
if he does not make his goal.

Many believe that making God's love visible and tangible by
serving and empowering those who are in need, hurting, vulner-

able, and often oppressed goes hand in hand with "preaching the good news" as the essence of the church's work in the world. Obviously, though, because of situations such as the one described above, those who want to do this work will have an increasingly difficult time raising the resources required in the face of increasing skepticism. Thus, we command our attention to questions of appropriate practice for the raising and giving of money in a religious context.

This chapter will argue that the key element in defining appropriate practice in religious fund raising (and perhaps, more broadly, all fund raising for philanthropic purposes) is the kinds of emotions to which requests for funds appeal. Beyond this, it will suggest that a key indicator of the nature of the appeal to which persons are responding is found in the manner of their giving. The latter point recognizes that while people will generally offer the most positive (socially acceptable) answer if queried about the reasons for their giving, their behaviors in giving may provide more trustworthy information about their real motives and intentions.

We must acknowledge before we begin that "real life" is always marked by ambiguity: Mixed motives are the rule, not the exception, of our experiences of philanthropy. Nevertheless, the arguments and cases explored will be presented with few if any qualifications in order to better highlight some central questions, issues, and principles, with the understanding that matters often (perhaps regularly) are less clear in "real life." The purpose of this historical examination of the rationales for and practices of giving and asking for money in the Judeo-Christian tradition, then, is to illuminate as best we can which motives, attitudes, and approaches to charity or philanthropy are seen as good and which are not.

I argue that, to the degree that this tradition still plays a key role in shaping our culture's moral assumptions, secular as well as religious approaches to fund raising need to be attentive to these norms. The history of this religious tradition shows us that the uses of inappropriate fund raising practices (for example, the selling of "indulgences") have often proved destructive to the very fiber of the body that employs them, whatever the short-term gain. Furthermore, there is evidence in recent years that public concern and uneasiness over fraud, greed, and questionable fund-raising practices

in the religious sphere is threatening to undermine the credibility
of the broader philanthropic tradition in American culture.

An Overview

A survey of the literature of the Judeo-Christian tradition of the Old
and New Testaments, the commentaries on these texts, and theological treatises related to them suggests that this tradition expects or
understands giving for what we might now call "charity" or "philanthropy" to be motivated primarily by one or more of five types
of emotions, ideals, beliefs, or commitments: (1) fear and/or guilt;
(2) a sense of belonging, or obligation, to a specific community; (3)
a sense of fairness or reciprocity, or obligation to justice; (4) a desire
for self-aggrandizement; and (5) love and/or gratitude. As we review
a wide variety of passages, we will see how these motives or ideals
are prominent.

It is interesting to note, by way of external confirmation, how
this analysis and set or schema of motivations drawn from biblical
literature seem to be supported by empirical data from a very different source. It was exciting to discover recently the striking cor-
respondence between this list of rationales or motives for giving that
emerges from a careful exegesis of biblical texts and an analysis and
list developed by psychologists working on the motivations for volunteering (Clary and Snyder, 1990).

Using a "functional analysis," which is "concerned with the
reason and purposes that serve as the foundation for psychological
phenomena," Clary and Snyder have looked at voluntary behavior
and derived a schema for examining the motivations of volunteers.
This highlights the way voluntary service fulfills one (or more) of
five functions for people: (1) a "value-expressive function," which
includes what we generally call "altruism;" (2) a "socially adjustive
function," "to help one fit in and get along with one's reference
group"; (3) an "ego-defensive function," "to reduce guilt, or make
one more deserving of desirable (future) outcomes"; (4) a "knowledge function," to gain greater understanding of something one
wants to know about; and (5) an "instrumental function," to help
persons gain useful skills or knowledge for a career purpose (Clary
and Snyder, 1990, p. 81).

Obviously, just giving money to some cause or person generally cannot fulfill either of the latter two functions these scholars speak about, as gaining greater understanding or developing a particular skill requires a different kind of involvement. But it is remarkable how the first three functions seem to embrace the rationales for giving that the Scriptures suggest we should expect. Fear, guilt, and self-aggrandizement all clearly fit the "ego-defensive function" as the psychologists describe it. The sense of belonging or obligation to community that is so prominent as motivation for giving in Old Testament texts quite obviously fits into the desire for "social adjustment." And giving out of a commitment to justice, or from a sense of love and gratitude, are both clearly "value expressive." In short, it would appear that the reflections on human nature we find in the Scriptures come to conclusions quite similar to the results of psychologists' empirical studies when they explore people's motivations for giving and volunteering.

The motivations described here are, of course, those that fund raisers, secular and religious, have thought of, built upon, and even exploited for some time. The interesting thing about considering these in the framework of religious tradition, however, is the way they are treated (as one would expect) in a normative context—that is, on their relative moral merit. Let us look then at that treatment, starting with the perspectives found in the Bible.

Biblical Perspectives

The Old Testament. In the Old Testament, or Hebrew Bible, three perspectives on giving are represented, two much more fully and affirmatively than the third. To understand what is being said about these perspectives, it is important to keep in mind one crucial characteristic of the Old Testament narrative: This is the story of a people, a story of a communal experience, where the frame of reference for practically every question and concept is that of "community." This must be stressed because it is so very different from our way of looking at things in modern Western cultures, where the individual is basic and virtually all issues are framed and considered in terms of their implications for individuals. Most of what the Old Testament teaches us cannot be understood in those terms.

The first reference in the Old Testament to raising funds for religious purposes is found in the book of Exodus (Exod. 30:11-16). In this passage God commands that each of the Israelites contribute to "the service of the Tent of the Meeting" (the edifice of worship and religious services), paying "the Lord a ransom for his life." The way this is presented is clearly an appeal to guilt: The payment is, to use some other biblical language, "atonement money." This commandment is put forward plainly, without moral commentary, although today we could hardly avoid judging negatively the notion of "paying ransom" as a form of contribution.

As we consider the implications of this, though, two things should be noted. First, the tone and substance of this passage is entirely congruous with the understandings of other, contemporaneous cultures and religions in the ancient Middle East (which surrounded and undoubtedly influenced Hebrew culture and religion); giving for religious purposes—often in the form of "sacrifices"—served primarily to appease or forestall the wrath of an angry God. Second, such an understanding of and rationale for religious giving virtually never appears again in the Bible, and is even ridiculed in later passages, especially in the Prophets (for example, Amos 4:4-5).

Indeed, the pervasive and dominant understanding of the reasons for giving in the Old Testament emphasizes (1) the obligation of each member of "the people of God" to contribute to the common welfare of the covenanted community and (2) the obligation of each member of "the people of God" to "act justly and love mercy" (Mic. 6:8). In this respect we need to see that in their self-understanding as "a chosen people," promising to obey and "delight in the law of the Lord" (Pss. 1:2), support of the priesthood and the temple (or Tent of the Meeting) through which their vital relationship with God and their identity was sustained was necessarily as important to the Israelites as care for "the sojourner, the orphan, and the widow."

Thus on the one hand we encounter a range of passages that emphasizes the obligations of every person to contribute to the support of the community's religious services and rituals (for example, Num. 18:21 and 25-29; Lev. 27:30-32); on the other hand, we find many passages that lift up the importance of the contribution of those of means to the support of other members of the community who are in need (for example, Exod. 23:10-11; Lev. 19:9-10; Prov. 14:31). Indeed, we also find passages that bring these two themes together, as in Deuteronomy 14:28-30.

It is probably important here to say a word about the practice of tithing, which has its roots in Old Testament times and has been central to many assumptions about giving through the long history of the Judeo-Christian tradition. The Hebrew word translated as "tithe" means literally "a tenth part." Tithing, as it was most simply interpreted in Old Testament times, was the practice of giving "a tenth of property or produce for the support of a religious institution." This was common to non-Hebraic cultures of the time. Biblical scholars have noted that the practice as presented in the Deuteronomic tradition in the Old Testament serves three spiritual and practical functions: (1) It acknowledges God's ultimate ownership of all "the earth . . . and the fullness thereof" (Pss. 24:1); (2) it provides support for religious institutions; and (3) it garners resources for charitable distribution.

Finally, the point of all these passages taken together is the apparent understanding that the quality of the common life of the community of God's people would be compromised by inadequate support for the community's worship and liturgy, as well as by any failure to show compassion and maintain the dignity and necessities of a decent life for all its members. Obviously, falling short in both respects would represent an even more serious breach of "the covenant" between God and God's people.

At the same time, whoever enhances the quality of the community's life in either respect brings blessings on him- or herself as well as the community. So, for example, the Israelites are told, "When you have finished setting aside a tenth of all your produce . . . you shall give it to the Levite [the priests], the alien, the fatherless, and the widow. Then say to the Lord your God, 'I have removed from my house the sacred portion and have given it to the Levite, the alien, the fatherless, and the widow, according to all you commanded. . . . Look down from your heaven . . . and bless your people Israel and the land you have given us'" (Deut. 26:12-15).

To frame this in more modern terms, the thrust of the Old Testament perspective is that what we call "charity" is, in this view, a matter of "righteousness" and "justice," maintaining right order in the community in accordance with God's law, simply the right thing to do. In the frame of the Old Testament's prevailing concern for community, "righteousness" is whatever contributes to the integrity and healthy ordering of the community's life; "justice" is a function of reciprocity, treating others as one would like (or has a right) to be treated oneself. This last element is especially crucial, though, for it dictates the need to extend compassion beyond the immediate (in this case ethnic and religious) community.

Thus God tells the Israelites, "When an alien lives with you in your land, do not mistreat him. The alien living with you must be treated as one of your native born. Love him as yourself, for you were aliens in Egypt" (Lev. 19:33–34). God assumes that, from the experience (or memory) of having been aliens or "sojourners" who were in need of kindness and charity, the Israelites should have the empathy to extend kindness and charity to those who come from outside their community. If this is taken seriously, for the Jewish community (or any other) that follows this tradition, charity may begin at home but it should extend out into the world.

At its origins, then, as motivations for giving, the Judeo-Christian tradition lifts up and affirms a sense of belonging; a feeling of obligation to one's own community; and a sense of moral obligation to uphold standards of justice, mercy, and decency (even for those not of one's own community). The texts of the Old Testament suggest that these were the emotions that should have been appealed to, as they are presented as good motivations, in whatever fund raising occurred in the ancient Israelite community.

It is, of course, hard to know what fund-raising practices were actually followed in that community, given the almost complete absence of any records regarding such activities. Still, a number of passages (especially from the Prophets) indicate that then, as today, many persons gave (and we can assume were asked to give) not for such ennobling reasons but rather primarily in self-serving terms.

Indeed, the Prophets had a few strong words for those who merely "followed the rules" for ritual observances—one assumes in matters of charity as well as worship—without their heart in it, or worse yet just to make themselves look good. Isaiah voiced God's condemnation of such behavior, telling them: "The Lord says: These people come near to me with their mouth and honor me with their lips, but their hearts are far from me. Their worship of me is made up only of rules taught by men" (Isa. 29:13). The Old Testament seems to tell us that what God hopes is that the people, when confronted by the need for charity, "will give freely . . . [with] a heart not grudging, because for this God will bless [them] in all [their] work and in all that [they] undertake" (Deut. 15:10).

The New Testament. As one might expect, the New Testament follows in this current, although it extends and modifies these teachings about giving in a variety of ways. As we move into looking at the issues in the New Testament perspective, the first thing we must do is note the shifting frame of reference. As the Old Testament is a narrative of a people, addressing a community's collective relationship with God, the New Testament is much more a story of one person, and of other persons whose lives he touched, and it is concerned with addressing individuals' relationships with God. In the Christian perspective, it is understood that people are called into relationship with other believers as well as with Christ, but the vertical dimension of this calling has traditionally been seen to come first, both in experience and in emphasis.

So we find very little is said about obligations to a particular religious community or tradition in Jesus' teachings about giving. In fact, such notions are frequently devalued, as in his comments about the Sabbath (Mark 2:27); or even condemned as the basis for hypocrisy, as in his attack on the Pharisaical practice of "Corban" (Mark 7:9-13). On what principles, then, are Jesus' teachings about giving based?

Jesus brings forward the expectation that people will give out of a commitment to justice and a sense of reciprocity ("Do unto others as you would have them do unto you") similar to the Old Testament's teachings. However, he also extends and subtly but radically alters that idea. "If you love those who love you, what credit is that to you? And if you do good to those who do good to you, what credit is that to you? . . . Love your enemies, and do good, and lend expecting nothing in return," Jesus tells his followers (Luke 6:32-36). Such exhortations go beyond reciprocity (see also

Matt. 5:40–42) and shift the tone of the rationale for giving and serving from obligation to opportunity. Combining these with passages that emphasize the importance of giving of oneself as well as one's resources, we can see this perspective assumes that one can induce people to giving and service by appealing to the love and gratitude they will feel and want to express for the grace and love of God they have experienced.

So Jesus sends out his disciples with the simple instruction, "Freely you have received, freely give" (Matt. 10:8). Moreover, Jesus indicates the clear expectation that one will be able to see if someone has come to know God's grace and power in her life, and is so chosen to be in relationship with God, by the evidence of her participation in acts of charity and compassion (Matt. 25:31–45). Other documents of the early church make similar assumptions when they ask questions like, "If anyone has the world's goods and sees his brother in need, yet closes his heart against him, how does God's love abide in him?" (1 John 3:17).

Some people would discount these teachings by observing that Jesus tended to devalue (or put in proper perspective, depending on your point of view) all material things, for instance in Matthew 6:25–33 or 19:16–21. But this misinterprets such passages, which are not intended primarily to demean the material world and its potential significance but rather to emphasize the safety and necessity of trusting in God in all concerns and circumstances.

(It is true that such readings and interpretations of Jesus' teachings emerged as a problem early in the life of the church, using a supposed deprecation of "the material" as an excuse for the neglect of worldly responsibilities. But, in fact, later Epistles [for example, 1 Tim. 5:3–8] seemed to make some attempt to correct those whose asceticism and neglect of material responsibilities went too far.)

So Jesus encouraged his disciples to lives of service and giving rooted in their experience of God's love, understanding of God's trustworthiness, and acceptance of God's grace. And looking at the larger vision encompassed in Jesus' teachings, one can immediately see that there is no place in this message of "good news" for manipulating people by playing on their guilt or fear.

Throughout the Gospels, Jesus encourages people to admit

and acknowledge their own guilt (whatever its sources), only so that they can come to terms with previous failures or sins, repent, and be enabled to accept the forgiveness and grace of God to move on into a new life of wholeness. His message to those struggling with fear is that they can trust in God. A central message of the whole Christian tradition (at its best) is that "perfect love"—the love we come to know in God's grace and share in acts of true charity— "casts out fear" (1 John 4:18). Therefore, appeals that engage people's guilt or fear in an effort to get them to support charity (or any other cause or institution) are clearly inconsistent with this tradition.

Another shift evidenced in the move from the Old Testament to the New Testament perspective is a new emphasis (or at least an emphasis previously less evident) on the importance of the reasons or motives behind a gift. Here we encounter passages that speak of one motivation for giving we should expect to see but reject self-aggrandizement. This point is made first in the Gospels, where Jesus teaches the people (in the "Sermon on the Mount") about the attitudes that should characterize true charity and warns them against seeking worldly rewards for their good works. "Thus when you give alms, sound no trumpet before you, as the hypocrites do in the synagogues and in the streets, that they may be praised by men. . . . But when you give alms, do not let your right hand know what your left hand is doing" (Matt. 6:2–3).

We then see the same kind of concern expressed in the ministry of the Apostle Paul. Paul may well be seen as the prototype of the "certified fund-raising executive"; he clearly worked hard and fairly systematically as he traveled in the ministry to raise funds to ensure the material support of the early church and its members. Yet, he is also the one who tells the church at Corinth, "If I give away all that I have . . . but have not love, I gain nothing" (1 Cor. 13:3). And he is the one who later congratulates them "that they were the first not only to give, but also to have the desire to do so" (2 Cor. 8:10). Motives are as important as results in this view.

In his travels and letters, Paul frequently appealed to the churches and individuals he visited for funds "for supplying the needs of God's people" (2 Cor. 9:12), that is, money to support poorer brethren and congregations and those facing persecution. In these efforts he sounded notes familiar to us from the Old Testament, striking the chords of the obligations of all believers to care for one another as members of the community of the faithful. But he also consistently emphasized the importance of giving as an opportunity to express gratitude. He also reminded his brothers and sisters that "God loves a cheerful giver" (2 Cor. 9:7).

In the Old Testament and the New Testament, we can thus find some very interesting and fairly clear indications of the principles that should underlie and circumscribe the approaches to giving and raising money in a religious context. As these are the source documents of the Judeo-Christian tradition, all those who claim affiliation with and see themselves as working on behalf of this tradition should take these indications very seriously.

The principles the Scriptures point to emphasize those potentially positive, affirmative, even celebratory motivations for giving. They strongly suggest that requests for support for the work of religious institutions and charities should be made in the context of appeals to members' sense of community, or to their commitments to justice and mercy, or in terms of the opportunity that giving (or serving) represents to express and share one's experience of God's love. They deemphasize, indeed warn against, the more self-serving motivations, and they clearly suggest that appeals to such self-serving motives and the manipulation of negative emotions such as fear and guilt in fund raising are inconsistent with the moral base and central principles of this tradition.

Admittedly, the application of general principles to specific, often ambiguous situations is always tricky, but consider one example of how we might do that in thinking about religious giving and fund raising. One question that should be asked of religious bodies that build on the concept of tithing as a tool for encouraging giving is whether they do so with all three of the spiritual and practical purposes suggested by the Scriptures. Do they encourage persons to participate in this practice in such a way that it is a reminder of God's ultimate ownership of all creation, provides support for religious institutions, and garners resources for charitable distribution? If they raise up the tradition of tithing only for the second purpose, only to garner institutional support, then there may be reason to doubt their commitment to the moral and spiritual ideals this tradition is meant to embody.

As is often the case, as the Jewish and Christian traditions evolved in history, some practices upheld the best principles of their original revelations and others represented unfortunate, even embarrassing, deviations from these principles. Let us look briefly at examples of both.

The Middle Ages, Enlightenment, and Reformation

The cultural context in which charity or philanthropy is practiced changed dramatically for both Jews and Christians after the conversion of the Emperor Constantine and the Christianization of the Roman empire at the beginning of the fourth century. The changes occurred in different ways at different times and had different effects on Christians and on Jews (respectively). There were essentially two kinds of changes to which we must pay attention.

First, the understandings of and rationales for philanthropy and charity in a religious context were inevitably altered by the emergence of new, previously nonexistent, or at least relatively insignificant, secular conceptions of these matters. The Greco-Roman cultural heritage, pervasive in the Western world and becoming more influential inside the church, carried forward its own ideas about giving and raising funds for public purposes, ideas not entirely consistent with the Judeo-Christian principles just discussed.

The Greco-Roman tradition does emphasize the rationale of responsibility for community needs, evoking giving for the purposes of improving the life of the community, city-state, or nation as a whole. However, it often conceives of such improvements in more political and cultural terms (for civic buildings and affairs and the arts) and less personal and pragmatic terms (for the care of the needy, the orphans, and the widows) than do the Jewish and Christian traditions. And it legitimizes, perhaps because it embraces a more political view, the motives of self-aggrandizement that the religious tradition rejects.

Second, as the Christian tradition has melded with the Greco-Roman heritage to become the dominant cultural influence in Western civilization, faith and politics have become inexorably intertwined. This has had different ramifications for Christians and Jews. For Christians, it began to make the distinction between giving for religious purposes and giving for secular purposes less and less meaningful, as the interests of the state and the church more and more closely identified. As a function of these same dynamics, though, the Jewish community became increasingly isolated from civic life and indeed was often persecuted, especially in the Middle Ages. Consequently, the focus of Jewish philanthropy, at least until after the Enlightenment, was that of a minority community increasingly concerned especially with caring for its own. These differences are reflected in the writings of the two traditions concerned with the practice of charity and philanthropy.

When we look at the writing of Maimonides (circa 1150 C.E.) in the *Sefer Mishneh Torah,* we find implicit in his codification of Jewish teachings on these matters the assumption that the basic purposes of giving are for the benefit of the immediate (Jewish) community. In this context the ennobling ideal of "righteousness" is again raised up, presenting the practice of philanthropy in terms of obligations to care for the common life of the community of faith and the requirements of justice and mercy. As the scholar Jacob Neusner put it, "Many people think charity is voluntary . . . while in Judaism, philanthropy in all its forms constitutes an act [simply] of what is right: righteousness, which is a matter of moral obligation" (Neusner, 1988, p. 16).

In the "Book of Agriculture" in the *Sefer Mishneh Torah,* Maimonides emphasizes that philanthropy at its best is directed toward equipping and empowering the poor to help themselves by "strengthening their hand" and is carried on anonymously, thus maintaining the dignity of the recipients. Slightly less desirable is "giving alms," giving just to relieve the immediate needs of the poor. But either way, Maimonides stresses that in the ideal practice of philanthropy the donors do not know to whom (in particular) the gifts are going, and the recipients do not know from whom (in particular) their help has come. This minimizes the potential for the humiliation of the recipient and reduces the possibilities of the donors becoming proud or condescending. Whether or not these teachings were strictly adhered to in the Jewish communities of those times we cannot know for certain, but the fact that they continued to be affirmed in principle and studied regularly suggests that they strongly influenced actual practice.

The teachings just cited address only giving for charitable purposes. It is true that the practice of tithing for the support of religious institutions, the rabbis, and synagogues, as well as for support of those in need, was common in one form or another in many Jewish communities in the Diaspora. Thus, it seems that much of the Old Testament teaching about giving and raising money was carried forward and followed fairly closely in Jewish communities of that time.

In contrast, in the Christian tradition of the Middle Ages, the disparity between ideal and practice was widespread and widely recognized. Indeed, this disparity may best be described, in the modern view, as "notorious."

Writing only a few years after Maimonides, Thomas Aquinas eloquently articulated the rationales and principles that should govern the Christian practice of philanthropy. In the *Summa Theologiae* he says plainly, "Now one aspect of neighborly love is that we must not merely will our neighbors' good, but actually work to bring it about" (Aquinas, 1964, 2a, 2ae 32, 5). Clearly such an assertion could undergird many forms of philanthropic practice: giving of one's time as well as one's money for the immediate needs of the poor as well as to alleviate the causes of poverty and for all aspects of the life of the church, for worship as well as for service.

Most important, Aquinas's writings on this subject appeal to love, *caritas*, as the best, perhaps the only "right" motive for philanthropic giving and service. In the section of the *Summa Theologiae* devoted to *caritas*, Aquinas also clearly delineates the different ways in which charity is made manifest in "corporal" and "spiritual" works of mercy. Aquinas's work still stands as a remarkable illumination of the elements and dynamics that should characterize Christian charity and philanthropy.

Unfortunately, this moving and elegant statement of principles stands in stark contrast to what we know of the actual practices of giving and fund raising of the medieval church. In the church of the Middle Ages we find giving and appeals for funds obviously based on motivations of self-aggrandizement, political control, and pure and simple greed. (Interesting examples of the last situation

include cases where persons "donated" money to the church to secure positions that would allow them to exact more money from
that position for themselves than they gave; for example, an ap-
pointment as abbot of a monastery that controlled particularly fer-
tile lands.) At least equally disturbing is evidence of the widespread
use of fund-raising techniques that played upon people's fears and
guilt and made a mockery of supposedly sacred aspects of the
church's life, as was the case with the sale of indulgences.

Thus we had patrons encouraged to contribute to the building of cathedrals that were actually as much monuments to their
egos and power (or the ego and power of some prince of the church)
as to the glory of God. Peasants who could hardly take care of the
simplest material needs of their own families were terrified into
giving what little cash they had to ransom their relatives out of
purgatory (and to fatten the coffers of Rome or the local bishop).
And a small but significant element of the clerical hierarchy used
such fund-raising techniques to support a life of self-indulgence or
political power brokering while the needy, the orphans, and the
widows starved outside their gates. Suffice it to say that malfeasance
and greed in religious philanthropy were not invented by modern
televangelists.

These disparities between the ideals of the gospel and the
practices of the church were so blatant and heinous that they undermined its legitimacy in both the temporal and the spiritual
realms. There is no question that such practices contributed pow-
erfully to the development of Protestantism and the collapse of
Catholic hegemony in Europe. On the bright side, at least the Reformation brought with it some recovery of the Gospel message and
some renewal of emphasis in Christianity on true charity, service,
and philanthropy.

More Recent Times

Since the Reformation, many of the patterns that developed in the
Middle Ages have continued, but also some further evolution occurred in both Christian and Jewish philanthropic practices.

For instance, much of the Jewish community's collective,
organized philanthropy is still directed primarily to the care of its

own. Yet, as persecution has lessened and genuine integration has become more the norm, individual members of this community have contributed enormously to the broader philanthropic tradition of American society in the arts, social services, and social reform. Jewish philanthropists, in keeping with the counsel of Maimonides, have created and helped sustain some of our most important institutions for empowering and serving those in need (from all faiths and backgrounds) and creating a more just society.

Similarly, in modern Christianity we see many churches and church organizations exemplifying the ideals of the Gospel about giving and serving out of gratitude and love, caring for those in need no matter who they are, and giving without thought for their own interests. Unfortunately, at the same time, appeals for funds that have played upon people's guilt and fear have continued to be all too common. When we have so-called ministers of the Gospel encouraging a dependency on their ministry in their followers, and then threatening that this ministry will be taken away without extraordinary support from those followers, the integrity and credibility of the whole Christian tradition and its message is undermined.

So some of the best and some of the worst elements in the practices of giving and getting money that have developed over the history of the Judeo-Christian tradition continue to be apparent in the present. Yet it may be that the most interesting facets of the changes we see in religious philanthropy and fund raising today result from a change in societal context that I describe as the "secularization" of charity and the "sacralization" of the larger culture—especially American culture.

As James Douglas noted, "The fields of activity we most readily associate with nonprofit organizations [and so with charity and philanthropy] include health care, education, religion, the arts, and a vast array of social services. In medieval times, these activities would have come primarily within the jurisdiction of the Church rather than the state" (1987, p. 43).

In other words, what was once seen as the responsibility of religious institutions has increasingly come to be seen, at least in Western societies, as the business of secular institutions. But, simultaneously, and perhaps in part because of this phenomenon, what were once ideals attributed particularly to religious people and traditions (for example, the sacredness of life, the dignity of the individual, and the responsibility of those of means for caring for those in need) are now assumed to be accepted by most (if not all) people, whether or not they have espoused a commitment to the Judeo-Christian tradition. Some persuasive evidence of this appears in the statement of the values that the organizing committee of IN- DEPENDENT SECTOR thought nonprofit, philanthropic organizations should foster (Payton, 1988, pp. 33-34). The similarity to a simple statement of central values of the Judeo-Christian tradition is striking.

Such a transformation of societal values has led to a situation in which the practices of fund raising and philanthropy should be more attentive to the ideals that derive from religious tradition, since that is the apparent basis for so much of this activity. On the other hand, it has also led to a situation where religious fund raising and philanthropy must be ever more cautious about unconsciously imitating secular approaches to fund raising and philanthropy that are inconsistent with their core principles.

One noteworthy example of this last situation comes immediately to mind: It has become common practice in religious fund raising to appeal directly, even primarily, to potential donors' self-interest in seeking a gift. Whether this takes the form of encouraging giving for its tax advantages or for its potential for self-promotion and "image enhancement," these practices need to be scrutinized carefully and critically. One is struck by the number of buildings and stadiums at religious colleges, as well as pews and windows in churches, that bear the names of donors. One wonders whatever happened to Jesus' teaching about "doing your giving in secret," or Maimonides's advice about making donations anonymously. When religious fund raisers seek a gift by appealing to people's self-interest, rather than to their commitment to embody the principles of the faith they espouse, what witness is the fund raiser making about his or her own commitment to those principles, or the commitment of the organizations they represent?

Summary and Lessons

What can we learn from this historical analysis? I believe we can learn about the principles that will best govern religious giving and fund raising and how they can be discerned in the source texts of the Judeo-Christian tradition: the Old and New Testaments. These principles center on issues of motivations and manner of giving and indicate what kinds of emotions, ideals, beliefs, or commitments should be engaged by appeals for contributions. They commend giving and appeals for contributions that derive from and build upon a sense of belonging, or moral obligation, to community; a sense of fairness or reciprocity, or commitment to justice; and feelings of love and/or gratitude that are the fruits of one's own experience of God's grace and love. They generally condemn appeals that exploit people's fear and/or guilt, and they explicitly condemn giving that is motivated by the desire for self-aggrandizement, making it clear that such giving does not represent true charity at all.

These original principles are sometimes usefully embellished or extended in later commentaries or theological treatises, so that insights about how to apply these principles in specific situations, in different times and places, may be derived from reading and reflecting on this literature. We learn that the manner of implementing these principles in action will vary in different contexts, but the principles themselves seem to remain constant and true.

Finally, I believe that these principles are generally applicable to secular philanthropy and fund raising as well. This broader philanthropic tradition depends on being perceived as good, as engaging the more noble elements of human nature, and as carrying forward the finer aspects of our common life, which are largely defined by our religious heritage. In order to remain vital, then, secular philanthropists and fund raisers need to honor these principles in their efforts as well.

On the other side of this coin, we can learn from the mistakes of this history. Fund raising and philanthropy that are motivated by the desire for personal gain or are in any other sense primarily self-serving, that seek to manipulate potential donors by playing on their fears or guilt, or that are in any sense finally false will ultimately destroy the cause they seek to support. We should learn this, if nothing else, from the history of the church. Noble ends cannot be long sustained by ignoble means; giving and getting need to be marked by grace, not greed.

To do "the work of God"—or if one prefers more secular

language, to do truly "good works"—in the world generally requires some social intercourse with mammon. It requires worldly resources to care for "the sojourner, the needy, the orphans, and the widows." It is also true that a community of faith undertaking such work is sustained by its experience of common worship; and so it is entirely appropriate for it to expect its own members to contribute materially to the physical elements required to support that worship.

Ultimately, the history of the Judeo-Christian tradition tells us, God and mammon cannot be easily separated. But if we wish to serve God, or "the common good," faithfully, we need to remember and be constantly mindful of which one is supposed to be our "master" in these efforts.

References

Aquinas, Thomas. *Summa Theologiae.* (O. P. Batten, trans.) New York: Blackfriars (with McGraw-Hill), 1964.

Clary, E. G., and Snyder, M. "A Functional Analysis of Volunteers' Motivations." *Spring Research Forum Working Papers.* Washington, D.C.: INDEPENDENT SECTOR, 1990.

Douglas, J. "Political Theories of Nonprofit Organization." In Walter W. Powell (ed.), *The Nonprofit Sector: A Research Handbook.* New Haven, Conn.: Yale University Press, 1987.

International Dictionary of the Bible. Nashville, Tenn.: Abingdon Press, 1962.

Maimonides, M. *Sefer Mishneh Torah.* New York: Maimon, 1927.

Neusner, J. "Righteousness, Not Charity: Judaism's View of Philanthropy." *Liberal Education,* 1988, *74* (4), 16–18.

Payton, R. L. *Philanthropy: Voluntary Action for the Public Good.* New York: American Council on Education/Macmillan, 1988.

Smith, T. L. "The Biblical Ideal in American Christian and Jewish Philanthropy, 1880–1920." *American Jewish History,* 1984–1985, *74,* 3–26.

Chapter 5

What Counts as Deception in Higher Education Development

Deni Elliott

Is development in higher education like a friendly poker game where development officers are allowed, by convention, to "bluff" foundations and potential donors? Or is it more like a business relationship where the development officers straightforwardly exchange goods, services, and goodwill on behalf of the institution in return for the donors' dollars? Maybe it is like the lawyer-client relationship, in which the development officer has a fiduciary responsibility to the donor.

Which of these metaphors we choose for the donor–development officer relationship tells us something about the conventions of the relationship. What counts as deception depends in part on what kinds of expectations participants have of one another and what professional duties are implicit within the relationship. Not many people would claim that it is justifiable to deceive a potential donor, but just what should count as deception is not clear. The problem with deception is not that development officers say, "Yes, I think in this case it's OK to lie, cheat, and steal." Rather, in questionable cases, they say that what they are doing is not really deceptive at all.

Here I provide a systematic analysis of what counts as deception in development with the goal of identifying those acts that require moral justification. If an act has the potential of causing an evil, then the actor has a duty to justify that action. Society could not continue if people were allowed to cause evils indiscriminately and without justification. We need to know what counts as deception because only then can we know which acts need justification and which do not.

Sometimes it is okay to withhold information. Failure to disclose is not the same as deception, even if the person from whom the information is withheld would very much like to know it. Therefore, in the interest of promoting ethical fund raising, it matters a great deal to know what counts as deception and what does not.

The Nature of Deception

To make the claim "I have been deceived" is to make a moral judgment, because to deceive is to violate a moral rule (Gert, 1988). When I use the word "deception" without attaching moral culpability—such as saying that a twisted street sign "deceived" me—I am not using the term in a literal context. When I say that a person deceived me, I imply that that person is blameworthy, although I may later find that her deception is justified.

A person can act deceptively even if no one ends up being deceived, or someone can feel deceived without the actor doing anything wrong. If I dress up like a doctor and am caught when I try to sneak past a hospital guard to get an exclusive interview with an ailing public official, I have acted deceptively. On the other hand, if I walk through a hospital corridor in white slacks and a jacket with no intention of being taken for a medical person and someone says "Oh, I thought for a minute that you were a doctor," I have not acted deceptively.

Some philosophers make a moral distinction between lying and more passive forms of deception, a distinction that is not helpful in the moral analysis. The problem with deception is that people want to avoid being led to have a false belief. They do not want to be misled, no matter what the method of misleading happens to be. There is a morally relevant difference between lying and failing to disclose information, but the important distinction is not the passiveness of the actor. Let us look at a variety of deceptive acts, actions for which the actors are blameworthy unless they have justification. Note that passivity or activity is irrelevant.

A lies when *A* asserts a proposition, *p*, that *A* believes to be false with the intention of having *B* believe that it is true. If I tell you that I am a good athlete and I am not, I have lied to you.

There are also nonverbal moral equivalents to lying. *A* acts deceptively through a nonverbal equivalent to lying when *A* presents herself in a way intended to lead *B* to a false belief, such as in the example above of dressing up like a doctor. Nonverbal equivalents to lying include gestures and physical appearance. If I am not a police officer, but I dress up like a police officer in order to initiate a belief in others that I am a police officer, I have deceived in a way that is morally equivalent to a straightforward false utterance.

However, withholding information that one knows is not always deceptive, even if the person from whom the information is withheld ends up having a false belief. *A* acts deceptively through withholding only when the following conditions are met: (1) *A* intentionally withholds a proposition that she believes to be true, and *A* believes that withholding that proposition will lead *B* to form or maintain a false belief; and (2) *A*'s withholding of the proposition involves breaking a promise, cheating, disobedience to law, or failing to do one's duty.

The moral rules to which I refer are from philosopher Bernard Gert's moral system. They are ten in number: (1) Do not kill, (2) do not cause pain, (3) do not disable, (4) do not deprive of freedom, (5) do not deprive of pleasure, (6) do not deceive, (7) keep your promises, (8) do not cheat, (9) obey the law, and (10) do your duty (Gert, 1988).

First, I will lay out the general conditions under which withholding of information includes these other morally questionable acts, and then I will turn my attention to the relationships development officers share with donors.

Deception by Withholding Involving Breaking a Promise. If *A* promises *B* that he will never let anyone use their jointly owned sailboat without getting *B*'s permission, and *A* subsequently lends the boat to some third person without telling *B*, then *A* has deceived *B*. He has acted deceptively by withholding information that he has promised to tell, and he continues to deceive *B* for as long as *B* erroneously believes that *A* has not lent the boat to anyone.

However, *A* is not acting deceptively in failing to tell his next-door neighbor that he lent the boat because there is no promise that he would tell.

Deception by Disobedience to Law. This is just as straightforward as breaking a promise. If I fail to disclose income to the IRS, I have acted deceptively; if I fail to disclose income to my neighbor, there is no deception.

Deception by Withholding Involving Cheating. Sometimes the withholding of information is cheating. Cheating refers to violations of rules (explicit or assumed) that govern people who function together within a system. Our societal conventions are rules of this nature. We all know what is expected when a stranger asks us for the time or for directions; we all understand the minimal expectations that govern letters of recommendation and the completion of credit or employment application forms. The withholding of information counts as cheating when someone conventionally expects that the information will be given.

For example, suppose that *A* stops to ask directions from stranger *B*. *B* listens with seeming attention while *A* says, "I'm trying to get from Hanover, New Hampshire to Woodstock, Vermont, so I'll just drive north on Route 5." *B*, by presenting herself as listening to *A*'s planned route, voluntarily enters into a social relationship that includes the convention of not intentionally misleading. If *B* withholds what she knows to be true, that is that Woodstock is nowhere near Route 5, she will have acted deceptively.

Other people on the street who have not entered into this special relationship with *A* have no similar obligation even though they may have heard the conversation and know that *A* is mistaken. It would be laudatory for *C*, standing nearby, to say to *A*, "Wait a minute, that's not how to get to Woodstock," but there is no special obligation for *C* to do so. *C* would not have acted deceptively in keeping silent about *A*'s faulty sense of direction.

Deception by Withholding as a Failure to Do One's Duty. Duties to tell certain kinds of information are often required by professional relationships. For example, if your internist finds, during a routine medical examination, that you have a growth on the back of your hand that looks like a melanoma, she would be acting deceptively through a failure to do her duty if she withheld this information from you. If, on the other hand, a different physician were to notice the growth as he passed you on the street, he would have no duty to tell you his belief. The doctor on the street has no professional relationship with you and therefore no duty toward you.

A Few Words on Justification. These are all examples of deception, but it is not the case that all deceptive acts are necessarily immoral. Sometimes violations of the rule "Do not deceive" are justified.

Consent is one kind of justification: Sometimes we like to be deceived. When I go to a magic show, I give implicit consent to limited deception. I have not given consent for someone to lie to me about what time the show starts or how much the ticket costs, but, within the limits, it is justified for the magician to act deceptively.

Consent is a justification because an impartial, rational person could permit deception in cases of consent to be publicly allowed. For example, although it is a duty for doctors to tell patients their condition, a doctor would be justified in withholding details if a terminal patient said, "Doc, don't tell me when I'm getting near the end. I'll enjoy my life better if I'm not thinking about dying."

Deception in the World of Development

Let us take a look at some examples of situations where development officers might be tempted to withhold information from potential donors.

1. A development officer does not tell an alumnae donor that the college has made the decision to begin to matriculate men. The donor is in the process of handing over a check and reflecting with

pride that the college has managed to resist solving its financial problem by caving in to pressures to go coed.

2. A donor who is giving money for student activities with the express intent that "the young people not turn to homosexuality" is not told that the college is considering the establishment of a gay and lesbian student support group.

3. A donor is particularly supportive of a scholarship and assistance program for inner-city women admitted to the college. The development officer, who is hoping to increase the size of the gift, stresses the expenses of the program in such a way that the donor ends up believing, falsely, that the program's future is in danger.

4. A donor specifies that his gift should be used for educational purposes. Reasoning that everything the college does has an educational purpose, the development officer puts the gift in unrestricted funds, without so informing the donor.

Whether the development officers in these situations are acting deceptively depends on the nature of the relationship that exists between potential donors and development officers. The operative questions are (1) Is the development officer cheating if she fails to disclose the relevant information? and (2) Is disclosure of the information required through professional duty? (I have not included cases of promise-breaking or law violation because these cases seem reasonably straightforward.)

The essential professional duty for a development officer is to secure funds for the institution. Development officers also want to engage donors in continuing relationships with themselves as agents of the institution, but this is a secondary duty. Without the first it is alumni relations, not development.

No particular obligations toward donors follow from that professional duty of raising funds. What keeps that duty from being interpreted as "any means to an end" is that doing one's professional duty cannot cause others to suffer evils. That is, "I'm just doing my job" does not provide moral justification for causing people pain, depriving them of pleasure or opportunity, deceiving them, cheating them, or breaking promises made to them. Any special moral obligation to give information to the donor will follow from the conventions governing development officer-donor relationships from what is reasonable for people within that relationship to expect from one another.

It is clear, then, how the questions with which I began this discussion are relevant: Is the relationship like a poker game, like business, or like a trust? Different conventions govern these relationships, and the withholding of information that would not be deceptive in one relationship (for example, the poker game) would certainly be deceptive in another (for example, the fiduciary relationship).

Let us take a look at how two professional organizations, the Council for the Advancement and Support of Education (CASE) and the National Society of Fund Raising Executives (NSFRE), describe the development officer-donor relationship within their codes of ethics.

Among other things, CASE suggests that "institutional advancement professionals" should use "words and actions [that] embody respect for truth, fairness, free inquiry, and the opinions of others; should safeguard privacy rights and confidential information" (CASE, 1982). Although the CASE code does not mention donors in particular, it is reasonable to assume that they are included in how development officers ought to act in relation to others.

The NSFRE code is more explicit. Professional fund raisers, we are told in the preamble, recognize a trusteeship that includes assuring "donors that their purposes in giving are honestly fulfilled." Specifically, the code tells us that "members should encourage institutions they serve . . . to use donations only for the donors' intended purposes." In addition, "Members shall make full disclosure to employers, clients, or, if requested, potential donors all relationships which might pose, or appear to pose, possible conflicts of interest." It seems that while full disclosure of potential conflicts is required on its face to employers and clients, disclosure to donors is not required, absent a direct question. (See any issue of the NSFRE *Journal*.)

The NSFRE code suggests, in its reference to trusteeship, that there may be a professional duty to the donor. However, since members are required to encourage the institutions that they serve to use donations only for the donors' intended purposes, it may be too strong to stipulate that assuring the donors that their purposes are fulfilled is a professional duty. Development officers cannot assure donors of anything without the power to carry out the promise.

It certainly seems to be a convention of the relationship, however, that donors designate use of their gifts and that development officers be responsible for seeing that donors' wishes are fulfilled. Development officers can attempt to influence the designation, but when the donor hands over the gift, there is an understanding that the donor's wishes will prevail. And, in the interest of truth (in the CASE code) or in assuring the donor that their purposes are being fulfilled (in the NSFRE code), the development officer can legitimately be expected to disclose any information relevant to the donor's intention.

That is why cases 1 and 4 are examples of development deception. The development officer can be sure, in case 1, that the donor would not make the donation if she knew that the college had decided to admit men. The development officer is therefore acting deceptively in accepting the donation without disclosing the pertinent fact. To the extent that the decision has not been made public, the development officer has an obligation at least to suggest that the donor wait a week (or however long it will be before the public announcement is made) before writing the check.

In case 4, the development officer is acting deceptively in following the letter rather than the spirit of the donor's intentions. The development officer has an obligation to uncover what the donor has in mind and to restrict the gift accordingly.

When trying to decide when he or she has a duty to disclose information, the development officer should consider (1) whether the withheld item of information relates directly to the potential gift and (2) whether the information might make the donor reconsider his or her gift. All information relating directly to the gift should be disclosed. (But information that might make the donor reconsider must be disclosed only if it also relates directly to the gift.)

It is that last stipulation that makes case 2 borderline. First, the college is considering starting a gay and lesbian support group; no decision has been made. And even if the decision had been made, whether that information relates directly to the potential gift depends on whether the gift would be used to fund the group. If, for example, the donor had said, "I want my gift to go to athletics; that's a great deterrent to homosexuality," there would be no need to disclose the support group to the donor. While it might be laudatory for a development officer to do some careful consciousness raising with such a donor, it is not a case of cheating if she does not.

Case 3 involves deception of a different sort. This is also a case of withholding, but rather than withholding negative information, this development officer is withholding positive information, so that the overall picture painted for the donor is not reflective of reality. The unjustified withholding of positive information can be just as deceptive as the unjustified withholding of negative information.

The development officer-donor relationship, at least as alluded to within two professional codes, is more like a trust than a business or bluffing relationship. The convention is that donors have a right to expect that development officers will provide an honest assessment of the context for their philanthropy.

It is hard to imagine a situation when it would be justifiable to deceive a donor. Paternalism provides justification for deception some of the time for some professions, and the prevention of large societal evils justifies deception at times for others. For example, it might be justified for an emergency room doctor to withhold some information from an accident victim in shock who is demanding to know the medical conditions of other family members. Or it might be justified for a black reporter to pretend to be seeking housing to investigate a report that a white-owned real estate agency was discriminating against minority buyers.

Donor-development officer relationships rest on a gift exchange, an action that is ideal rather than required behavior. Philanthropists are praised for their beneficence, but they are not compelled to be gift givers. To justify deception, one must balance the evil caused by deceiving against that caused by refraining from deceiving. The evil caused by the deceptive withholding of information to donors includes loss of credibility to the profession of fund raising and the cheating of individual donors. Since the donor's act is not morally required, no evil is caused if the development officer refrains from deceiving. The nature of gift giving implies a special obligation for the fund raiser to be honest with potential donors even if the fund raiser's primary professional duty is to the institution rather than to the donor.

References

Council for the Advancement and Support of Education. *Statement of Ethics*. Washington, D.C.: Council for the Advancement and Support of Education, 1982.

Culver, C., and Elliott, D. "An Analysis of Journalistic Deception," unpublished paper.

Gert, B. *Morality: A New Justification for the Moral Rules*. New York: Oxford University Press, 1988.

Chapter 6

Conflicts of Interest Between Nonprofits and Corporate Donors

Barbara J. Lombardo

Fund raisers sometimes face the difficult decision of whether to seek or accept much-needed funds from corporate grant makers whose objectives or activities represent a conflict of interest with their own organization's mission. Examples include the funding of women's groups by the Playboy Foundation (Goss, 1989); grants made by alcoholic beverage companies, such as Anheuser-Busch, to organizations dealing with alcohol abuse (Montague, 1989b); and contributions made to environmental groups by companies widely perceived as environmentally irresponsible, such as Exxon.

This chapter is intended to assist fund raisers in making decisions about corporate grants that represent potential conflicts of interest. It first draws on the managerial ethics literature to establish the ethical basis for alternative positions taken in such circumstances. It then uses interviews with a small sample of fund raisers regarding such situations to develop criteria for making decisions about such grants. The chapter does not attempt to make prescriptions for behavior in such situations but rather to serve as a starting

point for thought and discussion about the ethics of receiving
grants from corporations where conflicts of interest are likely.

Conflicts of Interest in Perspective

The conflicts of interest addressed in this chapter are by no means
new, nor are they unique to corporate grant seeking. In fact, the
concept of tainted money and the suspect motives of benefactors,
which underlie many such conflicts, are probably as old as philanthropy itself. For example, early Roman emperors distributed grain
and gave lavish public banquets; historians interpret such "false
charity" as an attempt to avoid the revolutions and political instability that could result from mass hunger (Marts, 1966). The possibility that the largesse of early philanthropists like Rockefeller
and Mellon was motivated by a desire to burnish tarnished reputations (Bremner, 1960) raised questions for their beneficiaries. More
recently, the controversial past of the Japanese philanthropist Ryoi-
chi Sasakawa has been problematic for some of his beneficiaries,
which include many major American universities. Sasakawa's jaded
past, including his association with a private fascist army during
World War II, his arrest for war crimes during the Allied occupation
of Japan, and his alleged involvement with Japanese organized
crime, has led some to interpret his considerable philanthropy as
part of a campaign to improve his image and to buy respectability
(Goode, 1990).

A related situation also occurs when researchers receive funding from organizations with a vested interest in their results, leading
to questions about the objectivity of the research. For example,
certain medical researchers investigating the effects of alcohol on
health were criticized because their research was partially funded by
alcoholic beverage companies (Montague, 1989b). The objectivity of
policy research on Japan has also been questioned, given estimates
that three-quarters of all university research conducted in the United States about Japan is funded by Japanese interests (Judis, 1990).

Although the issues discussed may be relevant to many of these
situations, this chapter focuses specifically on instances where the
objectives or activities of a potential corporate benefactor represent a
conflict of interest with the nonprofit beneficiary's own mission.

The media regularly bring to our attention conflicts of interest in the public sector and the private sector. For example, we are all familiar with situations in which public officials accept gifts from corporations whose contracts they must renegotiate, or in which corporate executives recommend contracts with firms in which they own substantial stock (Macklin, 1983). Conflicts of interest involving the nonprofit sector, however, have received less attention, either from the media or from scholars of managerial ethics. Nevertheless, managers in the nonprofit sector often face such situations and need to be prepared to handle them. Conflicts of interest have been defined as existing when "a subsystem attempts to enhance its own interests or those of an alien system to the detriment of the larger system of which it is a part" (McGuire, 1983, pp. 231–232). The nature of the conflict addressed here is more specifically between the short-term goal of the nonprofit organization to acquire funding and its long-term goals to achieve its mission. But since the short-term goal is necessary for the continued existence of the organization, it must be met in order for the long-term goal to be realized. At the extreme, the organization is forced to choose between survival and adherence to its mission. Such a conflict may be especially problematic for nonprofit organizations, which by their nature are commonly assumed to be oriented toward purpose.

Appeals to Ethical Theory

The motives behind potentially conflictual corporate grants can be interpreted in various ways. At one extreme, the grants can appear as attempts to defuse hostility, appease critics, or buy favor. Alternatively, such grants can be seen as genuine efforts to compensate for the potential damage caused by the corporation's activities. In the former case, the grant recipient is a pawn in the corporation's attempts to manipulate its critics and the public; in the latter case, the grant recipient is merely a beneficiary of the corporation's efforts to provide recompense for past damages. Fund raisers' positions on whether to accept such grants are likely affected by how they interpret the corporation's motives.

Positions taken by fund raisers in such situations can range along a spectrum from idealism to pragmatism. Some may take an idealist position and refuse funding from any source whose objectives or activities are inconsistent with their own goals; others may take the pragmatic position that all money is to some degree tainted, and it is the use to which the money is put, not the source of it, that matters.

There are, of course, other positions along the spectrum of response. An organization could refuse such a grant, not on the principle that the benefactor's objectives are in conflict with its own but on the pragmatic basis that it wishes to avoid adverse publicity or criticism from accepting the grant. Nevertheless, the idealist and pragmatist positions will be used here to represent the two ends along the spectrum of alternative responses to the situation. The idealist position is likely to be viewed as the more virtuous of the two, possibly because it involves sacrificing immediate gain in the interest of long-term goals. Also, the pragmatist position exposes the organization to the potential perception or accusation that it is being compromised or controlled by the benefactor in question.

However, it is crucial to acknowledge that both positions can be justified on ethical grounds. The explication of these grounds requires a brief discussion of moral theory and terminology. Two basic approaches to moral reasoning have prevailed in philosophical thought: the teleological and the deontological. The term "teleological" derives from the Greek word *telos,* which means end or purpose. The teleological approach determines the rightness of an act based on its consequences; utilitarianism is its most common form. Basically defined, utilitarianism holds that an action is right if it produces the greatest amount of good for the greatest number of people. Defenders of utilitarianism hold that it systematizes and makes explicit what most of us actually do in our moral thinking (DeGeorge, 1982, p. 40).

The term "deontological" derives from the Greek word for duty. It maintains that "actions are morally right or wrong independent of their consequences . . . one's duty is to do what is morally right and to avoid what is morally wrong, irrespective of the consequences of so doing" (DeGeorge, 1982, p. 55). Whereas teleologists look to the consequences of an act in order to evaluate it, deontologists look to the motives and character of the agent (Beauchamp and Bowie, 1983, p. 33). Deontological theories include Kant's formalistic theory as well as more contemporary ones, such as Rawls's, which present moral arguments in terms of justice and rights.

The pragmatist and idealist positions on potential conflicts of interest are analogous to the teleological and deontological approaches to moral reasoning. The pragmatist position evaluates the acceptance of the potential grant based on its consequences, or the use to which the money is put. It essentially employs a teleological approach to evaluate the rightness of the act, and can be justified on teleological grounds. The idealist position evaluates the potential grant based on the duty of the actor to uphold the mission of the nonprofit organization, despite the consequent loss of funding. It is consistent with a deontological approach and can be justified on those grounds. In sum, both positions appeal to prevailing ethical theory for their justification.

Methods

In order to provide some preliminary insight into how fund raisers handle potential conflicts of interests, and to develop criteria to be used when faced with potential conflicts, interviews were conducted with twelve fund raisers or executive directors of organizations that have been or could conceivably be faced with such a decision. The individuals interviewed represent organizations in three nonprofit subsectors, including the environment, women's issues, and alcohol abuse. These subsectors were selected because they are involved in causes where such conflicts are particularly likely. An attempt was made to contact organizations that vary in size, location, and age. The identities of the interviewees and their organizations are not disclosed; the interviewees were assured confidentiality in order to increase the likelihood of an unbiased response, as well as to protect their privacy.

The interviews addressed whether the organization had in the last few years been presented with a grant that represented a conflict of interest, how such a grant was handled, and what criteria were used in evaluating whether to accept a conflictual grant. They also covered whether the organization has formal guidelines or policies regarding conflictual grants or the perceived need for such guidelines. Information about the percentage of total funding received from corporate donations was also collected.

Based on the interviews, the organizations were categorized along the spectrum of positions with respect to potential conflicts of interest. Such categorization is admittedly subjective but is nevertheless necessary to summarize results in a meaningful way.

In many cases, a hypothetical grant from a specific corporation whose objectives or activities represent a conflict of interest with the organization's mission was used as a basis for discussion. In evaluating the responses of these organizations, the hypothetical nature of the situation discussed must be emphasized, for it does not necessarily indicate how they would respond in an actual situation. Nevertheless, hypothetical grants provide a reasonable alternative basis for discussion.

The preliminary nature of this study should be emphasized. Given the very small number of organizations contacted, the results discussed below cannot be considered representative of all nonprofit organizations, nor of organizations in their particular subsectors. Survey research on a much larger scale will be necessary to ascertain the prevailing views of the sector on these issues. Nevertheless, this small sample provides us with some preliminary insight.

Following is a brief synopsis of the responses of each of the twelve organizations. The order in which they appear follows the pragmatist/idealist spectrum developed earlier in the chapter.

Summary of Interviews

Organization A

> Approach to potential conflicts: Pragmatist
> Purpose: To preserve endangered species and habitat
> Percent funding from corporations: 10 percent
> Members: 450,000   Formal guidelines: No

This organization accepts funding from corporations that many consider to be environmentally irresponsible. The development director explained their position that "not to take their money doesn't do any good." However, in the last year it rejected a potential grant that they felt was just a public relations effort by a company with a very poor reputation.

Organization B

> Approach to potential conflicts: Pragmatist
> Purpose: To promote responsible decisions regarding the use
>   or non-use of alcohol among college students
> Percent funding from corporations: 55 percent
> Budget: $500,000   Formal guidelines: Yes

This organization receives about 30 percent of its total funding from the alcoholic beverage industry. Its guidelines regarding contributions are expressed in a policy statement that explains that since alcohol is a legally manufactured product, it "does not fall outside of the realm" of desirable corporate contributions.

Organization C

> Approach to potential conflicts: Moderate/Pragmatist
> Purpose: To improve the economic status of women through
>   their integration into all occupations
> Percent funding from corporations: Less than 40 percent
> Members: 120,000   Formal guidelines: No

Although this organization has not been presented with a potentially conflictual grant in the last several years, there has been some discussion among board members about accepting funding from the tobacco industry. Some perceive this as a conflict because the organization is active in women's health issues. The development director expressed the belief that the use to which the funding is put may take precedence over its source. The need for guidelines is currently under consideration.

Organization D

> Approach to potential conflicts: Moderate
> Purpose: To help corporations foster career and leadership
>   development of women
> Percent funding from corporations: 98 percent

Budget: $1.9 million   Formal guidelines: No

Although this organization has not been presented with a potentially conflictual grant in the last several years, the development director states that the organization would reject grants from corporations that are "clearly outrageous to women." They decided not to pursue funding from a particular corporation that they learned supported views offensive to women. Since they seek to influence companies that do not have a good working environment for women, they would not necessarily reject grants from them.

Organization E

Approach to potential conflicts: Moderate/Idealist
Purpose: To provide legal assistance to women and to educate the public on equal rights issues
Percent funding from corporations: 10 percent
Staff: 25   Formal guidelines: No

This organization has not been presented with a potentially conflictual grant in the last several years. It is particularly aware of its role as a litigator when considering potentially conflictual grants. The development director is certain that they would not accept funding from corporations that are "blatantly obnoxious to women." She expressed concerns about the degree of recognition that corporations request in return for funding, particularly in cases of event sponsorship. In potentially conflictual situations, "principles would prevail over finances."

Organization F

Approach to potential conflicts: Moderate/Idealist
Purpose: To reduce exposure to toxic substances in air, on land, and in water
Percent funding from corporations: Less than 5 percent
Members: 25,000   Formal guidelines: No

Although in the last two years this organization has not been presented with a potentially conflictual corporate grant, it will not accept funding from one particular corporation because of the corporation's poor environmental record, its alleged ties to organized crime, and its practice of requesting seats on the boards of organizations it funds as a stipulation of its grants. The development officer expressed a "pretty strong feeling among the staff" that accepting potentially conflictual grants would compromise their programs.

Organization G

> Approach to potential conflicts: Moderate/Idealist
> Purpose: To provide support, networking, and skill development services for women
> Percent funding from corporations: 70 percent
> Members: 1,500   Formal guidelines: No

This organization has not been presented with a potentially conflictual grant in the last several years. However, the organization was approached by a cigarette manufacturer with an offer to sponsor their annual convention. Because the cigarette manufacturer asked to display samples of its product at the convention, the organization denied the grant. While the tobacco industry does not represent a conflict with their mission as a women's organization, they did not want to be perceived as endorsing the product or being compromised by the company.

Organization H

> Approach to potential conflicts: Idealist
> Purpose: To educate the public about the environment
> Percent funding from corporations: Minority
> Members: NA   Formal guidelines: Yes

This organization has rejected numerous grants from corporations it does not consider environmentally responsible. It accepts no funding from the pulp and paper industry or the waste management industry.

Organization I

> Approach to potential conflicts: Idealist
> Purpose: To preserve and restore the global environment

Percent funding from corporations: Minority
Members: 20,000   Formal guidelines: No
This organization has not been presented with a potentially conflictual grant in the last several years, but it is strict about not accepting
funding from corporations it considers environmentally irresponsible.

Organization J

Approach to potential conflicts: Idealist
Purpose: To prevent death and economic loss caused by
    drunk drivers and chronic offenders
Percent funding from corporations: Less than 10 percent
Members: 11,000   Formal guidelines: No
This organization refuses grants from the alcoholic beverage indus-
try. It will accept no funding from companies "which could even
be perceived as a conflict."

Organization K

Approach to potential conflicts: Idealist
Purpose: To increase public awareness of and urge students
    to take action against drunk driving
Percent funding from corporations: See below.
Local groups: 20,1000   Formal guidelines: Yes
This organization used to receive over half of its funding from
corporations, with about 30 percent from the alcoholic beverage
industry. Concerned about the degree to which the alcoholic beverage industry was targeting underage drinkers in its advertising,
the organization polled its members about its funding from this
industry. When the members responded that they felt the messages
conveyed in the alcoholic beverage companies' advertisements were
in conflict with the organization's programs, the organization's
board issued an indefinite moratorium on funding from the alcoholic beverage industry.

Organization L

Approach to potential conflicts: Idealist
Purpose: To support victims of drunk drivers and to lobby
    for the passage of more effective drunk driving laws

Percent funding from corporations: 1 percent
Budget: $130,000   Formal guidelines: Yes
This organization accepts no funding from the alcoholic beverage industry. The founder believes that they should not take money from an industry that would lose income if their goals are met. The founder also believes that as a watchdog organization, it should be especially careful to avoid any behavior that could damage its credibility.

Discussion

Of the twelve organizations interviewed, five can be characterized as idealists in that they take a strict position regarding potential conflicts of interest. Three of these are anti–alcohol-abuse organizations that have a firm policy of accepting no funding from the alcoholic beverage industry, and two are environmental groups that will not accept funding from any company they find to be environmentally irresponsible. There is considerable variation among them, but five other organizations could be characterized as moderate to some degree in their positions regarding conflicts of interest. These organizations have no firm policies regarding conflicts, yet they have rejected or would reject grants from particular companies that represent a conflict. Notably, all of the women's organizations fall in this category, perhaps because there is no particular industry that presents a conflict for them as a group. Only two of the organizations interviewed could be characterized as pragmatists, in that they consistently accept funding from companies or industries whose activities are considered to be in conflict with their mission.

Three criteria for making decisions about potentially conflictual corporate grants emerge from these interviews, including the degree of control requested by the corporation as a stipulation of the grant, the organization's particular goals, and the reaction of the organization's members. Each of these three considerations is discussed briefly below.

Degree of Control. Regardless of any potential conflict between the objectives and activities of the benefactor and the mission of the beneficiary, conflicts can arise due to the degree of control that the corporation requests as a stipulation of the grant. Board seats, excessive recognition, and product promotional tie-ins are examples of the kinds of stipulations that can accompany corporate grants.

In such situations, the nonprofit needs to evaluate the degree to which these stipulations may compromise its own objectives, convey a message inconsistent with its purpose, or give excessive control to the corporate grant maker. For example, one environmental organization rejected a grant, not because of the environmental record of the company, but rather because the company requested what the organization believed to be excessive recognition for the grant. The organization believed the grant to be an overt attempt to improve the company's public relations and chose not to be affiliated with such an effort. Another organization was approached by a cigarette manufacturer to sponsor their annual convention. Because the cigarette manufacturer asked to display samples of its product at the convention, the organization refused the grant. While the tobacco industry did not represent a conflict with their mission as a women's organization, they did not want to be perceived as endorsing the product or being compromised by the company.

Goals. Nonprofits faced with potentially conflictual grants need to consider the degree to which meeting their own goals would harm the corporate grant maker. To what extent would the company suffer if the nonprofit succeeds? These considerations are especially important to organizations active in lobbying for changes in legislation or litigation. For example, one women's organization active in litigation is especially sensitive to the possibility that their corporate benefactors may be at some future time defendants in legal suits that they instigate. This consideration may cause some nonprofit organizations that are especially political or confrontational to reject funds that a less politically inclined organization working for the same general cause would accept. If a nonprofit considers its role to be a watchdog of the industry, perceptions of excessive ties to the industry could damage its credibility and ability to fulfill this role, as, for example, in the case of the founder and executive director of one alcohol-abuse organization to whom we spoke.

Reaction of Members. In assessing whether to accept a potentially conflictual grant, nonprofits need to consider the reaction of and impact upon their members or constituents. This is important not only to avoid alienating those the nonprofit serves but also to indicate the nonprofit's adherence to its mission.

Acceptance of a potentially conflictual grant is more likely to offend members who have been directly harmed by the corporation or industry in question than members whom the nonprofit seeks to prevent from being harmed. For example, one alcohol-abuse organization that serves the victims of drunk drivers does not accept any funding from the alcoholic beverage industry, while another that educates students about responsible alcohol consumption does accept such funding.

In another case, an alcohol-abuse organization polled its members about its funding from the alcoholic beverage industry. When the members responded that they felt the messages conveyed in these companies' advertisements were in conflict with the organization's programs, the board issued an indefinite moratorium on funding from the alcoholic beverage industry.

Another alcohol-abuse organization not interviewed for this chapter is losing members who believe that its funding sources have compromised its goals. According to one former member, the organization "is reluctant to support tough legislative insurance reforms against drunk drivers or initiatives to raise the sales tax on alcohol, and the reason is that they are afraid to step on the toes of some of their biggest contributors" (Snyder, 1990, p. A7).

An Additional Criterion. In light of the ethical theory introduced earlier in this chapter, one additional criterion may help nonprofits make decisions about potentially conflictual grants. It may be useful for the nonprofit to consider whether its mode of operation is more results-oriented or more principles-oriented.

Though many associate accountability and results more with the private sector than with the nonprofit sector, the nonprofit sector includes a wide spectrum of organizations that vary markedly in their modes of operation. Some nonprofits operate much like private corporations. Also, the differentiation between the private and nonprofit sectors is becoming increasingly less clear. Observers have noted that the nonprofit sector is undergoing "a shift from empha-

sis on the 'good cause' to emphasis on accountability and results"
(Drucker, 1988, p. 26).

Those nonprofits that emphasize accountability and results
may find that a results-oriented or pragmatist approach to potentially conflictual grants is better suited to their organization than
a principles-oriented or idealist approach. This consideration,
made together with the three described above, could facilitate decisions about potentially conflictual grants by making explicit the
ethical approach implicit in the organization's mode of operation.

Guidelines. Of the twelve organizations interviewed, only four had
formal guidelines or policies addressing potential conflicts of interest with benefactors. The attention alcohol-abuse groups have received in recent years regarding these issues could explain why three
of the four are in that subsector. However, there was general agreement that developing guidelines would be a useful exercise, especially for larger organizations. Many fund raisers felt that the process of
developing guidelines would serve as a useful exercise for both staff
and board members, because it would stimulate discussion and bring
issues to the forefront.

External sources may be useful in establishing objective
guidelines. For example, one environmental organization interviewed in this study will not accept funds from organizations that
violate the Valdez Principles. These principles are a code of conduct
developed by a coalition of environmental groups and investors to
be used in determining which corporations are environmentally
responsible. If guidelines are in place, an organization is less likely
to be unduly swayed by an unusually large grant at a time of great
financial uncertainty.

Dependence on Corporate Support. One concern raised by the conflicts of interest addressed in this chapter is that the financial status
of a nonprofit may influence its decision regarding a potentially
conflictual grant. A nonprofit's degree of dependence on corporate
support may play the same role.

In light of these concerns, it is notable that none of the organizations interviewed for this study that receive more than half of
their total funding from corporations are characterized as idealists.

Furthermore, all of the organizations characterized as idealists receive considerably less than half of their total funding from corporations. This suggests a relationship between a nonprofit's degree of dependency on corporate funding and its position regarding potentially conflictual corporate grants.

The causal direction of this relationship is unclear. It could be that organizations taking an idealist position are less successful in obtaining corporate support. It could also be that organizations heavily dependent on corporate support tend to take a pragmatist position in order to sustain corporate funding. This apparent relationship has important implications for nonprofits and fund raisers and merits further study.

Conclusions

As the brief discussion of ethical theory above reveals, both the pragmatist and idealist positions regarding potential conflicts with corporate grant makers can be justified on ethical grounds. Nevertheless, both positions also present a degree of risk.

The idealist position takes the obvious financial risk of forgoing potential funding, and, furthermore, it may encourage premature assumptions about the motives of corporate grant makers. Fervent idealism may foreclose any meaningful dialogue with corporations, thereby preventing a resolution from taking place.

The pragmatist position takes the risk that peer organizations, members, or the public will accuse the organization of being controlled or compromised by potentially conflictual corporate funders. More significantly, it risks the possibility that its programs and capacity for action will be weakened to avoid harming or alienating the corporations on which it relies for funding.

Two measures can mitigate some of these risks. First, to the greatest extent possible a nonprofit should seek a wide range of funding sources. This protects them from being excessively dependent on or controlled by any one funding source, and it further protects against the perception of such dependence or control, which can be damaging in itself. Second, open disclosure of funding sources is a proactive way of avoiding the adverse publicity that can result when the media or another watchdog group discovers what can be perceived as excessive control or a conflictual relationship. The appropriate position with respect to potentially conflictual corporate grants is contingent upon many factors, including the degree of control stipulated by the corporation, the nonprofit's own goals, the reaction of members, and the nonprofit's mode of operation as results-oriented or principles-oriented. Careful assessment of these criteria can help an organization make decisions about corporate grants that represent possible conflicts of interest.

References

Beauchamp, T., and Bowie, N. *Ethical Theory and Business*. Englewood Cliffs, N.J.: Prentice-Hall, 1983.

Bremner, R. *American Philanthropy*. Chicago: University of Chicago Press, 1960.

DeGeorge, R. *Business Ethics*. New York: Macmillan, 1982.

Drucker, P. "The Non-Profits' Quiet Revolution." *Wall Street Journal*, Sept. 8, 1988, p. 26.

Goode, J. "Fascist Endows Fellowship." *Daily Californian*, Feb. 8, 1990. p. 1.

Goss, K. "Reparations or Tainted Money? Women's Groups Face Dilemma over Playboy's Grants." *Chronicle of Philanthropy*, Jan. 24, 1989, p. 4.

Judis, J. "The Japanese Megaphone." *The New Republic*, Jan. 22, 1990, pp. 20–25.

McGuire, J. "Conflict of Interest." In T. Beauchamp and N. Bowie (eds.), *Ethical Theory and Business*. Englewood Cliffs, N.J.: Prentice-Hall, 1983.

Macklin, R. "Conflicts of Interest." In T. Beauchamp and N. Bowie (eds.), *Ethical Theory and Business*. Englewood Cliffs, N.J.: Prentice-Hall, 1983.

Marts, A. *The Generosity of Americans: Its Source, Its Achievements*. Englewood Cliffs, N.J.: Prentice-Hall, 1966.

Montague, W. "Drunk-Driving Foes Accept Big Gifts from Alcoholic Beverage Producers." *Chronicle of Philanthropy*, July 25, 1989a, p. 1.

Montague, W. "Brewers' Grants for Research on Alcohol Issues Prompt Questions About Objectivity of Studies." *Chronicle of Philanthropy*, Aug. 8, 1989b, p. 1.

Snyder, G. "Reports of Revolt and Defections Among MADD Volunteers." *San Francisco Chronicle*, Mar. 12, 1990, p. A7.

PART THREE

THE PROFESSIONALIZATION
OF FUND RAISING

Chapter 7

Fund Raising in Transition: Strategies for Professionalization

Harland G. Bloland
Rita Bornstein

Development, the primary occupation of fund raisers, plays an increasingly central role in institutional decision making. Indications of its centrality include the high level of involvement in fund raising by presidents and trustees of institutions, the increasing resources devoted to fund raising, and the impressive levels of salary, status, and involvement accorded to development officers. Despite its current important place in institutions, however, the occupation is viewed as vulnerable by development leaders and practitioners. Changes in tax laws, government regulations, and negative public perceptions of fund raisers could severely reduce the significant position that development currently holds.

To improve and preserve the status of development so that it has a more secure institutional role, fund raisers aspire to what professions and occupations generally seek: effectiveness and efficiency in the work, control over work and work jurisdiction, and recognition of the legitimacy of the work and those who perform

Note: This study was conducted under a grant from Lilly Endowment, Inc.

it. The most attractive path to that end appears to many to be professionalization. James L. Fisher states that advancement (including fund raising) is "accepted at the academic conference table largely out of a pressing need. . . . rather than out of appreciation" for its activities. The key to remaining at that table, he wrote, is for advancement people to define themselves "more surely as professionals" (Fisher, 1985, p. 12).

In the 1980s, development-related associations, such as the Council for Advancement and Support of Education (CASE), the National Society of Fund Raising Executives (NSFRE), the National Association of Hospital Development (NAHD), and the American Association of Fund-Raising Counsel (AAFRC), led the movement toward professionalization. These associations generated large-scale programs to improve recruitment, training, knowledge, and ethical behavior. During the same period, a number of development-related academic courses and programs were instituted in colleges and universities around the country.

The purpose of this study is to evaluate the potential of professionalization strategies to strengthen the occupation of development. The questions are fundamental. How can the occupation maintain its current important role in institutions? What costs and benefits are associated with the quest for professionalization? Can an administrative area be a profession? Can an occupation in which amateurs do much of the technical work be a profession?

The research is largely qualitative, involving both an extensive review of the literature from the sociology of occupations, organizational analysis, development, and philanthropy and interviews with forty development officers. Three theoretical frameworks are employed: functionalism, pluralist power, and institutionalization.

The focus of this study is on the general occupation of fund raising, set in the context of the philanthropic tradition. Since the authors and most of the interviewees are based in higher education, the study is particularly oriented to academic fund raising. However, because the occupational issues and professionalization questions are much the same throughout the fund-raising world, statements and assertions are deemed to be applicable to the general field of fund raising.

The Work of Development

The everyday work of development consists of planning, researching on donors, cultivation, solicitation, organizing staff and volunteers to solicit, providing information on tax laws and methods of giving, recognition of donors, administering the office of development, processing and acknowledging gifts, and other related tasks. These activities are organized around the core task, fund raising, but the concerns of development officers extend beyond this framework. They participate in institutional long-range and strategic planning, in relations with external individuals and organizations, and in furthering the mission of the institution.

In their work, however, development practitioners are faced with a series of skill, jurisdiction, and legitimation circumstances that both restrict the occupation and provide it with opportunity. Although fund raising is the core task of development, the skills involved are not held exclusively by development officers but shared with volunteers who are enlisted to do much of the work. Sharing expertise with amateurs considerably weakens the occupation's power to define its work and establish jurisdictional control and legitimacy.

Other development activities are purely administrative and the result of a division of labor within institutions. Except for the technical aspects of the work related to tax laws and planned giving, much of it could be conducted by another administrative unit. Although development officers cannot claim exclusive jurisdiction if other administrators have similar skills, they have the legitimacy attendant to all administrative areas as well as a bottom-line, measurable standard of achievement that others often do not have.

Development Culture. The sets of deep, sustained values and cultures in which development practitioners participate are often incompatible, and conflicts of loyalty and identification may result. Fund raisers identify with their own careers, the missions of their institutions, and the general ideal of philanthropy in a broad sense. These positions are not always compatible, and fund raisers may experience considerable internal conflict in reconciling their disparate commitments. Because the development occupation is so inextricably bound to the institutions that house it, commitment to a particular institution and to its goals and mission looms very large. Each institution has its own culture, and successful careers are bound up in the ability to understand, accept, and be a part of an organization's values and beliefs.

At the same time, fund raisers need association beyond the confines of a particular institution. Although identification with a career in a cosmopolitan community may attenuate commitment of development officers to a particular institution, it does strengthen the professionalization aspirations of the occupation.

Figure 1 illustrates combinations of high (+) and low (-) commitments to two variables: the occupation (cosmopolitanism) and the institution (localism). Four recognizable development types emerge from a consideration of an individual's commitments to an institution and/or an occupation.

Orientation to Occupation
(Cosmopolitanism)

+   -

Orientation to	+	Professional	Booster	+
Institution				
(Localism)	-	Careerist (Migrant Worker)	Placebound Worker	-

+   -

The four development types are defined as the professional, the booster, the careerist, and the placebound worker.

For the professional, high loyalty to both the local institution and the occupation is most desirable but is difficult to achieve in practice, for loyalty to one tends to attenuate commitment to the other. The booster has a high level of commitment to an institution, often the one from which the booster has graduated. Identification with the occupation is minimal. The route to development is frequently through the alumni office. The careerist, sometimes called a "migrant worker," is committed to the occupation but not to a particular institution and often moves from institution to institution. The placebound worker has little loyalty to either the occupation or the institution. The development office is viewed as a convenient site for employment and for tuition and other benefits. Any other office in the university would do as well.

Each of the four quadrants in the figure represents a different concept of the jurisdictional boundaries of the occupation. Each also reaches for recognition of legitimacy within its commitment boundary.

Identification with the institution and not with the occupational collectivity, as in the booster quadrant, narrows the jurisdiction of an occupation considerably, giving it an idiosyncratic character. It greatly reduces the autonomy of the occupation and makes it dependent upon the particular institution in which the booster operates. This is a legitimate commitment for those stakeholders heavily invested in an institution, but it lacks legitimacy for those who are interested in transforming the occupation of development into a profession. Those who are committed to the institution are not interested in the cosmopolitan aspects of the occupation. They do not participate in national association affairs, write for journals, or interact with their counterparts in other institutions.

The careerist might be viewed as a professional if employed with a consulting firm but a "migrant worker" when employed by a series of institutions. The careerist sees the boundaries of a career as much broader than a particular institution or job. Legitimacy in the field of development requires a cosmopolitan orientation but also a large measure of commitment over an extended period of time to a particular organization.

Placebound workers include those who have very low commitment to either the occupation or the institution. They cannot move and are working in the field because they are not mobile and need a local position. They tend to acquire little autonomy, do not rise in the field, and have difficulty increasing their legitimacy.

Development Careers. Most development officers came into the field accidentally, after having done a number of other things. The vice presidents interviewed in this study had undergraduate majors primarily in the liberal arts. Their graduate majors were in such areas as journalism, engineering, law, chemistry, economics, education, physics, and business. Early work experiences included teaching, business law, research, and sales. A number of vice presidents for development began their careers in advancement-alumni relations, public relations, or admissions. Career lines in fund raising are problematic so that it is difficult to trace a smooth upward career path.

Development, at present, is a wide open field, with many positions available and remuneration at an all-time high. There is little regulation governing entry to the field—persons come from a variety of backgrounds and with little prior applicable experience. This provides opportunity for individuals coming into the field, but it also presents them with a sense of precariousness, for it is not clear what experience, talents, training, and expertise they must have to be successful. Our respondents believe that a recruit to the field should have a liberal arts education, some business administration skills, experience in some other administrative position, talent in writing and speaking, and a pleasant personality.

For an occupation in which time spent in one location is viewed as adding considerably to the worth of the practitioner, development currently operates with a high rate of turnover. Thomas found that "17.3 percent of the positions in the average advancement office changed hands during the year. . . . The highest rate (19.5 percent) occurred among development offices" (1987, pp. 7–8).

A central concern in development is the socialization and training of new and inexperienced development officers to ensure the maximum efficiency and effectiveness of performance; to gain control over the access, composition, and organization of the field; and to gain legitimacy for an occupation lacking definition and enforceable standards of practice. Professionalization is viewed as the overarching mechanism for achieving these goals.

Professionalization

Definitions and Usages of the Term "Profession"

Profession is an emotionally loaded word. It can connote strong praise, as in "That person is a real pro," or it can convey powerful condemnation, as in "That person's conduct is unprofessional."

When an occupation is not described as a profession, it is often defined as low status and unattractive. At the same time, those who receive money in exchange for sexual favors or who steal on a regular basis are negatively termed "professionals." Many activities divide certain tasks between those who work full time and for money (professionals) and those who participate without pay or on a part-time basis (amateurs). But, in most contexts, the term "profession" refers to a high-status occupation that commands respect, admiration, and trust; is associated with contributing to society's needs; and affords its practitioners comfortable and often high incomes.

Although sociologists have sought to rid the term "profession" of its powerful normative implications by seeking its "true" characteristics through objective, scientific studies of occupations, they have been singularly unsuccessful in draining the term of its highly emotional, value-laden connotations. Individuals continue to care very much how the word "profession" is used in relation to their occupations. People wish to have others see their work as significant, attractive, prestigious, and well paid—that is, as professional.

However, the long-standing disagreement that plagues discussion of the core characteristics of a profession strongly suggests that no single definition is presently acceptable to those occupations that would claim ownership of the term or deny others the right to use it. The preoccupation with definitions stems from a recognition that the "status professions" (Elliot, 1972, p. 14)—medicine and law (including professors)—have enjoyed prestige and remuneration well above most other occupations. Medicine in particular has been so successful that all definitions of what a profession is have been influenced by its form and characteristics. Much of the study of occupations has been directed toward determining the set of traits that medicine encompasses and differentiating that privileged profession from other occupations.

Theoretical Perspectives

Attitudes toward professions are ambivalent, reflecting the belief that professions are quite powerful and that their power can be used for good or evil. So society rewards professions handsomely, while searching for ways to restrict their power. The great rewards that accrue to recognized professions lead many occupations to seek professional status, but it is not easy to achieve. Most occupational aspirants to this status are either ignored or come to be seen as self-serving, noncontributors to society's needs. Beginning in the 1950s, a variety of overlapping, often contradictory perspectives on professions were generated.

The Functional Approach. This sociological paradigm provided the rationale for asserting that professions contribute crucial services to society and to individuals, based on high levels of expertise and exemplary ethical standards. High-status professions, such as medicine, are said to embody ideal traits. The standard functional approach begins with an analysis of successful professions, deciding what their basic characteristics are, and then applying these traits to determine which occupations, in addition to the high-status professions, qualify as professions.

Ideally, low-status occupations can become professions by acquiring the traits associated with high-status professions. This "trait" approach to professions has spawned many lists that purport to authoritatively inform any occupation what characteristics it has to have to be considered professional. Ernest Greenwood (1957) produced a widely cited list. For him, undisputed professions possessed (1) a theoretical base that produces and supports the skills of the profession and stimulates "theory construction via systematic research"; (2) a monopoly of control over the profession's clients; (3) sanction from the community to control training, entry to the profession, and admission to practice; (4) a code of ethics that regulates colleague relationships and professional/client interaction; and (5) a culture consisting of professional values, norms, and symbols.

A variant of the trait approach is to determine the stages through which an occupation must go to be recognized as a profession (Wilensky, 1964; Ritzer and Walzcek, 1986; Abbott, 1988). Although the stages vary, the assumption is that the destination, professionalization, is the same for any occupation, and arrival at the destination is confirmed by identifying the set of professional characteristics possessed by the occupation.

Functional analysis assumes that effectiveness is a primary goal and that it is achieved as a consequence of acquiring the appropriate traits and/or progressing through the appropriate stages.

Power Approaches: Monopolist and Pluralist. In the 1960s there was a backlash against the functional assumption that professions were universally positive contributors to the well-being of society. Books and articles were published that portrayed professions as monopolistic conspiracies against weakly organized clientele and a defenseless public. Professions were accused of using their ethical codes to reduce competition but not to police themselves or improve services. They were seen as occupations with privileged positions in society that they did not earn and that they used to their advantage. Their claims to expertise were said to rest on arcane language and tacit knowledge that simply excluded nonprofessionals without benefiting them. Professions were portrayed as aiming more for control over work and work jurisdiction than for service as an end (Johnson, 1967; Roth, 1974; Larson, 1977).

During the same period, another power approach developed. Pluralists were also concerned with control over work and jurisdiction. However, they viewed professions as less capable of asserting and enforcing monopoly, more vulnerable to internal conflict, and deeply involved in competition with other occupations and professions over control over work and work jurisdiction. Occupations and professions in this approach are not viewed as monolithic structures but as divided into segments, each with its own identities, orientations, and definitions of what should be emphasized and rewarded in the work of the occupation (Abbott, 1988; Freidson, 1970, 1988).

Occupations seeking professionalization and professions attempting to maintain or expand their areas of exclusivity do so within a network of similar occupations and professions attempting to do the same. This means that no occupation striving for professional status can do so in isolation: Other occupations and professions are always major factors in the process, so that jurisdictional questions and disputes are of constant concern. From the pluralist perspective, at no point can an aspiring profession be assured that it has become a profession and that its place in an occupational status hierarchy is permanent. Occupations are not headed for the same necessary destination, nor is the place they occupy at any one time secure. Even the older professions, medicine and law, are viewed as having no permanent, fixed position high in the hierarchy of occupations. Rather, they are viewed as constantly subject to incursions from other occupations upon their control over work; as fighting for favored position in organizations; and as threatened by new technology, by the rationalizing imperatives of organizations, and by external forces that upset their claims to safe and stable niches in the panoply of occupations in the United States.

Attempts to professionalize an occupation are characterized by the pluralist techniques of negotiation or bargaining, compromise, coalition building, temporary settlement, trial balloons, and retreats. There is a sense of the fragility of power and of the potential temporariness of control and status in this pluralist orientation. The pluralist perspectives in the study of professions are similar to pluralist approaches to the study of politics. They differ from monopolist perspectives in ways much like the differences between pluralist and elite perspectives in community power structure studies (Hunter, 1953; Dahl, 1961).

The Institutional Approach. The institutional approach emphasizes the concept of legitimacy and the processes by which it is sought, obtained, and used to move an occupation to a higher-status level (Zucker, 1987; Scott, 1989). In this study, the institutional perspective is applied to occupations and focuses on the processes by which work is organized for legitimacy and comes to be taken for granted (institutionalized). The institutional view suggests that nonprofessional occupations borrow methods and processes from established professions to gain in status and legitimacy.

One branch of institutional studies looks to the environment to provide "rational myths" that may be imposed or emulated by an organization or occupation (Meyer and Rowan, 1977; DiMaggio and Powell, 1983). From this perspective, institutionalization focuses upon isomorphism, the taking on of characteristics approved by strong external forces, as a way of acquiring greater legitimacy—

for example, strategic planning for organizations or professionalization processes for occupations.

The special attraction of an institutional approach is that it provides an alternative to conventional analyses of professionalization. It deemphasizes the rational, technical perspective, which assumes that the sole rationale for seeking to professionalize is to acquire more efficiency or effectiveness. Institutional (and power) approaches emphasize that the most powerful incentives for change may stem from the desire for legitimation and control without any necessary increase in technical effectiveness or efficiency.

The institutional and pluralist power approaches allow us to view the professionalization process as other than a series of traits or stages that, once attained, will result in professional status. Instead, the approach here is that the so-called "traits" of professionalization may be depicted as a series of strategies and tactics that an occupation might use to obtain authority (power and legitimacy) in relation to its work, its clientele, the public, and the state (Klegon, 1978).

This chapter draws upon all three theoretical perspectives on professionalization: functional, pluralist power, and institutional. Each approach provides a concept that can be translated into a goal that every occupation and profession seeks to accomplish. Thus, from functionalism, we derive the concept of traits (redefined here as strategies) and the goals of effectiveness and efficiency. The pluralist power perspective provides concepts of autonomy and occupational segmentation with goals of control over work and jurisdictional control. Institutionalization gives us values and prestige and the goal of legitimacy.

Goals, Strategies, and Tactics

Strategies and tactics promote the goals of increasing effectiveness, augmenting control over work and work jurisdiction, and increasing legitimacy. Although there is no accepted test of how much of an increase is enough, occupations that are successful in moving toward the goals are called and believe themselves to be professions. The ultimate test of successful professionalization is that the appropriate stakeholders and publics of an occupation recognize that occupation to be a profession.

Among the strategies that aspiring professions use are (1) development of a knowledge base; (2) instillation of a service orientation among members; (3) organization of national and regional associations; (4) construction of codes of ethics; and (5) introduction of certification, licensing, and accreditation.

The strategies have different positive and negative effects on the goals. That is, some strategies and tactics may be more successful in moving the occupation toward the goals, and some strategies may be better than others for achieving a particular goal. This chapter will analyze the first of these strategies.

Building a Knowledge Base: Benefits and Costs of Three Tactics. The most important strategy for gaining professional status is the development of a substantial, legitimate knowledge base that aids the occupation in progressing toward the three goals: effectiveness, control over work, and legitimacy. Generating a knowledge base involves the following tactics: (1) developing a set of skills appropriate for improving development's fund-raising capabilities, (2) creating a theory base related to the skills, and (3) initiating research that modifies the theory base and improves the skills.

Skill development and improvement speaks primarily to two goals: (1) effectiveness, that is, the ability of fund raisers to increase their capacities to garner more resources and (2) control over work and work jurisdiction. There is hope as well that skill enhancement will aid in promoting the legitimacy and status of the occupation. Fund raising is rooted in practice, and developing skills is viewed as the major means of improving effective practice.

Competence is highly prized in fund raising, and much effort is devoted to determining appropriate skills and improving them. CASE members, for example, at the 1985 Greenbrier II Colloquium on Professionalism, made a series of professional and training recommendations (Shoemaker, 1985). More recently, a report was issued that assessed the association's 1985 workshops and other programs designed to "educate advancement officers about their profession" and identified "core and professional area knowledge, skills, and attitudes needed of advancement officers at the entry, middle manager, and senior levels" (Edwards, Chewning, and Raley, 1989, p. 1).

In development there is a strong tradition of learning skills on the job. In mentoring, a senior officer takes a neophyte in tow and is both a teacher of skills and an inspiration. Professional consultants are also primary leaders in the development of practical skills. The appropriate sites for teaching skills have been the home institution and the national and regional association meetings. In both development offices and association meetings, the teachers are successful senior development practitioners and consultants, and the development officers who benefit the most from skill-enhancing sessions are junior development officers.

The control aspect of skill acquisition involves claiming a monopoly of expertise and demonstrating persuasively that only bona fide practitioners can have that expertise. Developing special skills that others do not possess enhances development's ability to control access to and organization of the field of fund raising. Significantly, the methods to improve skills and the locations where skill development is likely to take place emphasize strongly a desire by occupational members to have control firmly in the hands of practitioners.

Development skills are highly prized by the field and training programs and workshops are intended to improve the legitimacy of fund raising through the improvement of skills.

What are the costs of skill development? Skill development can come at the cost of professional legitimacy if it is too insular and narrowly focused. Claims based on exclusive competence and skill are precarious. The potentiality for needed change through restructuring or innovation is restricted if knowledge of skills and control over instruction are the exclusive property of current practitioners. Unless an occupation has a continuous flow of new ideas and modified techniques from sources that go beyond practitioners, it may lose its connection to changes taking place in the larger institution or the society and become obsolete. National and regional meetings for the exchange of ideas and technical skills are very helpful in providing innovations and fresh ideas, but some means for including abstract, theoretical knowledge is necessary also for the occupation to retain its drive toward ever-greater effectiveness.

If skills are performed in relation to a technology, changes in the technology can lead to skill obsolescence. A skill base that remains unchanged over time will be open to rationalization, a process whereby large and complicated tasks requiring judgment and a variety of skills are divided into small, easily learned operations and taught to novices. Such deskilling renders an occupation accessible to anyone seeking a position.

Organizations such as universities are prone to what Abbott (1988, p. 65) calls "workplace assimilation," whereby those untrained, when called upon to perform tasks, learn quickly some usable version of the skills a profession claims sole jurisdiction over. These nonprofessionals can then be called upon to perform that skill when no recognized professional is present and the organization needs someone to do the task.

Jurisdictional claims based on expertise are significant, and the CASE curriculum study, which designates skills, knowledge, and attitudes appropriate for entry, middle, and senior levels in the bureaucratic hierarchy, is important because it signals an attempt by those in the field to gain some control over the work, and it begins the process of determining bases for training people in the development field. However, many of the skills and attitudes identified as needed for fund raising by the CASE curriculum study are already shared by anyone who does administrative work in any kind of organization. Examples include these characteristics: "portrays personal integrity, honesty, and fairness . . . is competent in budget preparation, support, and control . . . possesses the ability to delegate and prioritize issues" (Edwards, Chewning, and Raley, 1989).

Shared jurisdiction is much weaker than exclusive jurisdiction. Skills that all administrators might be expected to have do little to add to the strength of jurisdictional control by development. In addition, professional skills in fund raising are amenable to teaching and learning, but, like law and medicine, they are challenging and time consuming to learn. The skills to be learned must also include a place for tacit knowledge, knowledge the practitioner possesses, that is understood from experience rather than explicitly taught.

A preoccupation with skill development, important as it may be, combined with a neglect of theory construction and research, will be costly to the occupation. As Robert Carbone accurately points out, "If . . . an occupation aspires to be recognized as a 'true profession,' competence cannot be its predominant concern. . . . Competence is not enough" (Carbone, 1989, p. 7).

Creating a theory base that is changed by research and a research base that is informed by theory are considered by many students of the professions to be the most important tactic in the professionalization process. Abbott (1988), particularly, stresses the significance of scholarly, abstract knowledge as the most important means of obtaining and maintaining a competitive position among professionals. Theory and research are so important that one of the major bases for distinguishing established professions from non-professions is the characterization of the former as theory- and research-based and the latter as theoryless.

An occupation with sufficient abstract knowledge and a research agenda related to the theory has a flexibility that allows it to respond to both its environment and its ambitions. According to Abbott: "Any occupation can obtain licensure (for example, beautician) or develop a code of ethics (for example, real estate). But only a knowledge system governed by abstractions can redefine its problems and tasks, defend them from interlopers, and seize new problems" (Abbott, 1988, p. 9). For example, fund raising might claim jurisdiction that could include all external affairs as well as administrative arenas.

The generation of basic theory adds greatly to occupational control. Although the work of fund raising by full-time people is shared with amateurs, if a theory and research base is in the hands of professionals, the distinctions between professional and amateur can be more sharply drawn, and fund raising can have a greater ability to define and defend its work boundaries. If the theory base changes through research and is tied to practice, the attenuation of control through rationalization is discouraged.

Jurisdictional battles are serious. They can be won and lost. For example, alcoholism as a problem has been variously defined as legitimately within the jurisdiction of lawyers, clergy, and medical doctors. It has thus been defined as a legal, a moral, or a medical problem. The battle for jurisdiction through defining the problem has been fought with theory and research, and medicine clearly, when it decides to focus on the problem, has an edge in claiming jurisdictional control.

Theory and research can enhance prestige and legitimacy. Engineers who apply their abstract engineering formulas to the concrete activity of building bridges are identified as professionals. The construction workers who actually build the bridges are in an occupation not driven by theory and research. Without a dynamic changing theory and research base, an occupation is considered a static enterprise, trapped in its own rigidities, and not a profession.

The development of theory and research find their most natural homes in the academy. Teaching and learning theory seem to be best accomplished by formal courses in universities and colleges taught by professors who make the field their scholarly interest. Professors who teach a subject matter area are usually the most committed to doing research and theory building in that area. Placing teaching and learning, and theory and research generation in the academy adds considerably to the legitimacy of an occupation. Programs in universities attract scholars and students and provide the possibility for controlling entry into the field. They may also increase the legitimacy of the occupation to the outside world.

Building a theory and research base may also have costs. The distance between theory and practice is often large, and every professional field tends to be impatient with the apparent lack of direct payoff in terms of increasing effectiveness through research and theoretical efforts. Our respondents generally view research on donors, research that increases statistical knowledge, and research on practical matters positively. Practitioners are interested in and encourage research that provides information that appears useful to increasing the flow of funds to the institution.

However, if the research is of such a practical nature, it may have little salience in the academy. Problems may result even when programs are housed in the academy. Theory construction is a basis for academic reward giving and is therefore highly competitive. Theories of fund raising, if constructed and disseminated in the academic milieu, will be judged by the tough competitive standards of university scholarship and efforts to emulate other successful academic fields.

Housing knowledge generation in institutions of higher education requires that a different kind of fund-raising professional be added to the field: the professor who specializes in research and theory building whose home is an academic department and not the development division. Professors not only have their own reward structures and values, however, but tend to follow their own research agendas, which may be perceived as providing little to serve the needs of practitioners. A central characteristic of the world of professions is the structural conflict between scholars and practitioners that threatens the solidarity of whole fields of endeavor. For example, the split between academics and practitioners is so severe in psychology that it has divided the national association in two.

Efforts to gain legitimacy in the academy are problematic. Student affairs has all the formal attributes of a thriving field of administration housed in the university structure. There are courses, majors, degrees, theory-generation, and research agendas with professors working full time on the subject matter, and it has had these attributes for more than forty years. Yet it is a field that has not yet gained the status and legitimacy it desires (Bloland, 1988; Penney, 1969; Stamatakos, 1981).

Application of just one strategy—development of a knowledge base—to enhance effectiveness, control, and legitimacy demonstrates the extraordinary complexities involved in moving toward professionalization. Each of the three tactics associated with the strategy of developing a knowledge base raises questions of who is responsible and where it should be done. A complete analysis of the potential for professional status requires a similar review of the implications of the strategies of a service orientation, a code of ethics, and licensure for their impact on the goals of effectiveness, control, and legitimacy. Each strategy raises questions about the locus and nature of the responsibility for its implementation.

Summary and Conclusions

This study is concerned with fund raising as an occupation and with professionalization as a series of strategies by which it can reach its goals of effectiveness and efficiency, control, and legitimacy. A review of the three current major perspectives on professionalization—functional, pluralist power, and institutional—

indicates that each of the three orientations can be employed to achieve the primary goals in the professionalization process. Traits derived from functionalism are viewed as strategies used to professionalize, and the most important professionalizing strategy, generating a knowledge base, is analyzed in terms of its three significant components: skill development, theory generation, and research. Each strategy has benefits and costs that must be considered in terms of implications for furthering the basic goals of the occupation.

Most fundamentally, fund-raising officers are concerned with their effectiveness and legitimacy in their institutions and among their publics. They believe their present position is precarious. They see their present relatively high status as dependent upon current demands for income in a time when many other sources of income have leveled off or been reduced. They fear that unrealistic demands will be made upon them concerning the size of capital campaigns in the future.

There is also considerable anxiety about the image that fund raising presents to the world, but there is consensus that the image is far better than it was twenty years ago. Development vice presidents see their position as enhanced or protected primarily in terms of whether they are able to secure continually increasing resources. Therefore, they are quite eager to increase their organizational and fund-raising skills but are far less interested in augmenting their theory and research bases. Skill enhancement through workshops and courses conducted by senior practitioners and consultants is viewed by practitioners as the most useful means for training new entrants to the field. At the same time, there is concern that there are few opportunities for senior practitioners to enhance their skills.

Although there is considerable interest in professional status in the fund-raising occupation, it is primarily the association of professionalization with legitimacy that interests fund raisers. Even as they see themselves as professionals, fund raisers do not see development as a mature profession. Fund raisers do not focus upon the relationships between professionalization and the occupation's control over work and work jurisdiction, nor do they see a connection between bottom-line effectiveness in fund raising and the generation of theory and research. There is little interest among practitioners in the creation and support of university graduate programs and graduate degrees in fund raising, philanthropy, or related areas, but there is strong support for on-the-job and association training programs.

Recognition by the appropriate stakeholders that an occupation has become a mature profession is difficult to acquire. It involves aiming for high levels of effectiveness, control over work, and legitimacy. All three of these goals are worthy of pursuit even if the desired level of professional recognition is far in the distance. This chapter has presented and analyzed what is involved in the professionalization process for development and what might be gained and lost in undertaking the strategies and tactics necessary to pursue professional status.

Only the members of the occupation of fund raising will decide how far and in which ways the pursuit of professionalization will take place. The intention of this study is to help clarify the pathways to a more fully informed and rationally articulated plan for enhancing the status of fund raising.

References

Abbott, A. *The System of Professions.* Chicago: University of Chicago Press, 1988.

Bloland, H. G. *Associations in Action: The Washington Higher Education Community.* ASHE-ERIC Higher Education Report no. 2. Washington, D.C.: Association for the Study of Higher Education, 1985.

Bloland, P. A. "The Art of Becoming Professional." Paper presented at the annual meeting of the American Counseling Psychology Association, Miami, Fla., Mar. 22, 1988.

Bornstein, R. "Career Development for the Foundations Relations Professional." In M. K. Murphy (ed.), *Cultivating Foundation Support for Education.* Washington, D.C.: Council for Advancement and Support of Education, 1989.

Carbone, R. F. *Fund Raising as a Profession.* College Park, Md.: Clearinghouse for Research on Fund Raising, 1989.

Dahl, R. *Who Governs?* New Haven, Conn.: Yale University Press, 1961.

DiMaggio, P. J., and Powell, W. W. "The Iron Cage Revisited:

Institutional Isomorphism and Collective Rationality in Organizational Fields." *American Sociological Review*, 1983, *48*, 147–160.

Edwards, R. A., Chewning, P. B., and Raley, N. "Executive Summary of the Delphi Study and Case Curriculum Study." Washington, D.C.: Council for Advancement and Support of Education, 1989.

Elliot, P. *The Sociology of the Professions*. London: Macmillan, 1972.

Fisher, J. L. "Keeping Our Place at the Academic Table." *Currents*, 1985, *11*, 10–13.

Freidson, E. *Profession of Medicine*. New York: Dodd, Mead, 1970.

Freidson, E. *Professional Powers*. Chicago: University of Chicago Press, 1988.

Greenwood, E. "Attributes of a Profession." *Social Work*, 1957, *2*, 45–55.

Hunter, F. *Community Power Structures*. Chapel Hill: University of North Carolina Press, 1953.

Johnson, T. J. *Professions and Power*. London: Macmillan, 1967.

Klegon, D. "The Sociology of Professions: An Emerging Perspective." *Sociology of Work and Occupations*, 1978, *5*, 259–283.

Larson, M. S. *The Rise of Professionalism*. Berkeley: University of California Press, 1977.

Meyer, J. W., and Rowan, B. "Institutional Organizations as Myth and Ceremony." *American Journal of Sociology*, 1977, *83*, 340–363.

Murphy, M. K. (ed.). *Cultivating Foundation Support for Education*. Washington, D.C.: Council for Advancement and Support of Education, 1989.

Penney, J. F. "College Student Personnel: A Profession Stillborn." *Personnel and Guidance Journal*, 1969, *47*, 958–962.

Ritzer, G., and Walzcek, D. "Rationalization and Deprofessionalization of Physicians." *Social Forces*, 1986, *67*, 1–22.

Roth, J. A. "Professionalism: The Sociologist's Decoy." *Sociology of Work and Occupations*, 1974, *1*, 6023.

Scott, W. R. "The Adolescence of Institutional Theory." *Administrative Science Quarterly*, 1989, *32*, 493–511.

Shoemaker, D. *Greenbrier II: A Look at the Future.* Washington, D.C.: Council for the Advancement of Education, 1985.

Stamatakos, L. C. "Student Affairs Progress Toward Professionalism: Recommendations for Action." *Journal of College Student Personnel,* 1981, *22,* (Part I) 105–113; (Part II) 197–207.

Thomas, E. G. "Flight Records." *Currents,* 1987, *13,* 6–11.

Wilensky, H. "The Professionalization of Everyone?" *American Journal of Sociology,* 1964, *70,* 137–158.

Zucker, L. "Institutional Theories of Organization." *American Sociological Review,* 1987, 443–464.

Chapter 8

Effective Business Practices in Fund Raising

Margaret A. Duronio
Bruce A. Loessin

Well, I think the most important thing of all is to do the right thing, all the way through.

Senior Development Officer
Higher Education Institution

Fund raisers are currently discussing whether fund raising is a profession. One reason for this discussion is the rapid growth of the fund-raising enterprise in dollars raised, in numbers of organizations and staff involved, and in importance to the survival and prosperity of many nonprofits. Another reason is the concern for the improvement of fund-raising practice, both to assure continuing success and to prevent abuse. Still another reason, separate from the "increased effectiveness" motive, is practitioners' desires for more credibility and increased prestige. The purpose of this chapter is to examine the "business" of fund raising—not as an alternative to the idea of fund raising as a profession but as another perspective on the field.

In this chapter, using examples from our recent case studies on effective fund-raising programs in higher education institutions, we examine the ways in which effective fund raising utilizes good business practices but is more than just a business enterprise. For our research, we selected ten institutions (one private and one public each from the categories of research university, doctoral university, comprehensive university, baccalaureate college, and two-year college). Using multiple regression analysis of institutional characteristics to predict fund-raising outcomes resulted in a pool of 100 institutions with actual outcomes that exceeded predicted amounts. From this pool the ten were selected. We made site visits to these institutions and interviewed over 100 people, including presidents, vice presidents, deans, and fund-raising managers and practitioners. Full details of the study appear in *Effective Fund Raising in Higher Education* (Duronio and Loessin, 1991).

One of the things that made conducting this study both interesting and enjoyable was the high degree of candor and openness in the discussions of fund-raising programs. In addition to all that was going well, we heard about programs and efforts that had failed, and we saw people struggling, sometimes as we talked, to understand the causes for the failure. We heard a lot of willingness to share credit for fund-raising success and also willingness to take responsibility for efforts that had not been successful. And, in most institutions, fund raisers had a clear sense of their responsibility to be educators in the fund-raising process with all constituencies. Many development officers recognized that serving faculty was one of their most important functions and that, in order to serve them well, faculty had to be better informed. Development officers, many of whom were engaged in uphill struggles with deans and faculty who "think they have a better handle on fund raising than they really do," were taking responsibility for this.

The Connection of Fund Raising with Philanthropy

It should go without saying, but it does not, that giving and fund raising are elements of the same enterprise, as Payton (1988) has observed. There is a general view that philanthropy is one of America's most exemplary social characteristics. Philanthropy is good, as are donors (usually even if they do not have "pure" philanthropic motives). Fund raisers, on the other hand—unless they are volunteers or people with "real" jobs, such as college presidents or agency directors—are often ignored or considered to be the necessary evil in an otherwise highly meritorious exchange. What is wrong with this picture? [For a dissenting view of philanthropy, see Odendahl's view (1990) that American philanthropy is primarily a system by which the wealthy help finance their own interests, rather than a system by which the fortunate distribute resources to the less fortunate.]

In the nonprofit world, fund raising attracts the same kind of disparagement with which business is often regarded, and especially that associated with sales. Salespeople, however, may be the most disparaged of business practitioners in the eyes of the general public, but they do not generally experience the same lack of esteem within their own industries or organizations as fund raisers often do in theirs. The scholarly literature and the general press on nonprofit organizations are full of references that imply that these organizations are passive recipients of income from private support, for example, "nonprofit organizations receive a substantial portion of their revenues from voluntary support." An article in INDEPENDENT SECTOR's 1989 *Compendium of Resources for Teaching about the Nonprofit Sector, Voluntarism, and Philanthropy,* for instance, includes information about donors' motivations for giving but says nothing about the fact that they are often stimulated *only* through a deliberate and skilled fund-raising process. A basic fact in fund raising is that most gifts result because someone asks someone else to make the donation. Unsolicited gifts represent only a very small portion of money given to philanthropy each year. The *Compendium* also includes a section on teaching fund raisers about philanthropy. Although we are in full agreement about the need for this endeavor, the treatment seems one-sided and implies that there is no corresponding need for other participants in philanthropy to be better informed about fund raising.

There is a need for a change in the perception of the field. For instance, a fund-raising executive (Lawson, 1987) wrote that a wealthy donor once said that paid fund raisers were parasites in the philanthropic process, using quite an unflattering metaphor to express his opinion that all fund raisers should be volunteers. As another example, in a critical and rather bitter book about the $350 million campaign at Harvard University, Vigeland (1986) described a time when fund raising was "an innocent marriage of artful appeal and traditional school spirit" (p. 27), in contrast to the "big business" orientation of the Harvard campaign.

If these examples represent general expectations of the way fund raising ought to be, nonprofits are in desperate need of another vehicle for acquiring resources, because fund-raising programs based on those expectations are not going to get the job done today. Many factors, including increased competition for funds, more knowledgeable and discerning donors, and higher stakes and higher levels of accountability, require that fund raisers be highly skilled and rigorously professional in their approach. Images of fund raising as a totally voluntary activity or as one lacking in commercial sophistication are completely out of date.

All parties in the philanthropic exchange—the donor, the fund raiser, and most constituents of the fund-seeking organization—are motivated by an unequal combination of economic self-interest, competitiveness, pride, and ego, as well as a concern for good (Freeman, 1987), but society is the most leery of the fund raiser in the middle. What is the basis for this disdain?

In our case studies, we were consistently impressed with the caliber of the people we interviewed: their respect and appreciation for their institutions and the donors who support them, their commitment to being successful in carrying out their charges, their high levels of competency and technical skill, and, in many cases, the degree of statesmanship and concern for higher values explicit in their work. We did not directly "test" their ethics and integrity, and we assume that all of them are operating from a combination of self-interest and altruistic motive. Yet there was not one of them who, in our opinion, seemed to warrant the low esteem in which the field is held.

One president we interviewed, four years into his first presidency, told us about the orientation to fund raising he received from colleagues, most of them college or university presidents. He said, "When I started to look for a new chief development officer, I was told that it would be difficult because there are not that many good people out there. Several presidents said, 'You're not going to

find loyal people because they're a highly upwardly mobile group
and they're already thinking about their next job when you hire
them.' They also told me that I'd find people with showy resumes
making exaggerated claims about what they'd done. Since I had
never hired a development officer, I was concerned after I heard
these things, but, as it turned out, that was not my experience in
recruiting development staff. It was no more difficult finding the
right development person than it was finding the right provost."
(Nevertheless, this president noted that he had not been "warned"
about provosts.) Now he said he discounts many negative allega-
tions about fund raisers and considers those who make them, asking
himself what role these presidents might have played in their negative experiences with fund raisers.

In a dissenting view on the subject, J. P. Smith suggested that
fund raisers are treated with disdain because the field is populated
by too many unprofessional people who "rely on the 'old boy network,' war stories, and old worn-out jokes," and "traffic in football
tickets and parking privileges" (1981, pp. 10–13). These reflections
do not contradict our judgments of the caliber of the group we
interviewed. After all, we were studying programs in institutions
with demonstrably effective fund-raising programs.

One possible answer to the question "What's wrong with
this picture?" is that ambivalence about money is deeply ingrained
in this society's Judeo-Christian values. Contemporary society
values having money, earning money, spending money, and, certainly, giving it away but is basically and deeply ambivalent about
money itself and about people who make their living as brokers of
money. Literally, brokers negotiate sales or contracts in return for
a fee or commission, which does not describe the situation of most
in-house fund raisers, but we use the term to connote the fund
raiser's *role as agent* and *position in the middle* of the transaction.

In light of the extreme dependence in most nonprofits on
skillful fund raising, this fundamental discomfort is in need of reex-
amination. How fund raisers are perceived and valued in their own
organizations can have a great deal to do with how effectively and
honorably they perform. Similarly, how fund raisers function will
affect how they are perceived.

The Essential Difference Between Fund Raising and Business

A business is an organization with the primary and unambiguous mission of generating money. Bottom-line performance is of utmost importance: Business is results-oriented, focusing on outcomes achieved. Although there may also be secondary concerns, such as meeting customers' needs, these are always subordinate in the long run to making a profit.

A nonprofit organization conducts business in pursuit of a social mission. Nonprofits are generally considered to be process-oriented, focusing more on how the mission is carried out and less on outcomes. Overall outcomes in nonprofits are often very difficult to measure, which is one reason for the focus on processes.

Fund-raising units generate money in order to provide the host organization with the means to achieve its social mission, and many fund-raising outcomes are measurable. Fund raising is results-oriented. Nevertheless, people, including most fund raisers, believe that doing things right in fund raising is as important as doing the right things and that fund raising does not have two missions but a single mission with two parts that cannot be separated. Fund-raising units doing good without raising money, or raising money without doing good, are neither successful nor acceptable. Therein lies a fundamental difficulty in fund raising: balancing concern for results with concern for how results are achieved. Society and the fund-raising field alike abhor fund-raising mercenaries and expect fund raisers to be value-driven as well as proficient.

Thus, the essential difference between fund raising and business is based on mission. In business, all concerns are secondary to making a profit. Even though there may be organizational ethical values about the way in which business is conducted, these are subordinate to the primary mission. In fund raising, generating revenues is inseparable from the value to do so in a manner consistent with the mission to do good.

Business at Work in Fund Raising

Our case study research was a follow-up to our earlier research to analyze relationships of institutional characteristics to fund-raising

outcomes in different types of institutions and among different donor groups. Our results (we are oversimplifying them for brevity's
sake) indicated that while these relationships differed, it was clear
that studying institutional characteristics alone shed no light on why
some institutions raised more money than others of the same type
with similar resources. We concluded that the differences might be
attributable to fortunate circumstances not reflected in the quanti-
tative data (geographical location, for instance) but probably more
likely the result of effectiveness in the fund-raising program and in
the performance of fund-raising staff. In short, there were programs
and staff in place that were effectively mobilizing institutional resources, whatever they were, to generate high levels of private support. Several of the aspects we explored in our site visits reflect
business practices and methods. The remainder of this chapter focuses on a description and discussion of these practices in actual
fund-raising programs.

Products and Advertising. The cardinal principles for business success are that you must have something consumers want and you
must make consumers aware that your product exists. There was a
high degree of understanding of these principles in every institution
we visited. Most fund-raising staff did not use the term "marketing"
to describe what they did, but all the programs were built on these
principles. (In a recent "how-to" book on fund raising, Lord [1987]
wrote that the most profound change in philanthropy has been the
transition from begging to marketing). The current substitute for
the word "marketing" in fund raising is "telling our story," or
"getting our story out to our constituents."

In all these institutions, "telling the story" was preceded by,
and proceeded contemporaneously with, a commitment in the institution to ensure that there was real substance to the story. We
found a high degree of understanding of what we call the push-pull
relationship of fund raising and institutional qualitative growth. In
order for fund raising to be successful, the institution has to merit
external support. Fund raising must provide the resources for the
institution to continue to make qualitative improvements. As fund
raising is more successful, the institution is pushed to grow, and
then it pulls fund raising along. Similarly, as the institution is more

successful, fund raising is pushed to grow and then pulls the institution along.

History indicates that association with higher education through philanthropic donations is a product many Americans want to "buy." The vice president for institutional advancement at a major university said that he continues "to find amazing the kinds and numbers of people who want to be associated with colleges and universities. The damndest people return my phone calls, not because of me, but because I'm from _____ University. People gain status by being associated with this institution and [our task in development is to] manage that to the benefit of the institution."*

Fund raising occurs in these institutions to support the educational mission. In many institutions we were told that although at one time they raised money first and then decided what to do with it, that is no longer the case. One vice president said, "Fund raising doesn't drive academic planning but is the logical extension of the academic planning process. If we don't have academic plans that are as interesting, exciting, and important to the outside as they are inside, there isn't any reason to raise funds." At another institution, a senior development officer said, "We're not raising money to put in a bank account. We're raising money to make something happen. And where does that happen? At the hands of the faculty." Institution-wide priorities for fund raising have been set in nine of the ten institutions studied. Staff at the tenth institution anticipated that this process would occur as soon as the new president, scheduled to arrive a few months after the site visit, took office.

We were struck by the clear image that all ten institutions' fund-raising staffs had about what their institutions stood for, what was unique or outstanding, and who their constituencies were. In many cases, this institutional knowledge had been developed not for fund-raising purposes but in response to the institution's tradition of providing service in its city, region, or state. Eight of the ten had a strong history of service, and, in these institutions, fund raisers had turned these traditions into fund-raising resources.

*Because of the authors' promises of anonymity, the individuals quoted in this chapter are not identified.

Role of the Chief Development Officer. In most business operations, the vice president for sales is a major participant in setting
company direction, because the sales staff are most closely in touch
with the market and what customers want. Similarly, in most of
these effective institutions, vice presidents and other senior development staff played an important role in helping to set institutional
long-range goals and directions. This has not always been the case,
however. Until recent years, most institutions did not have development officers in executive positions. Directors of development
reported to vice presidents who were sometimes far removed from
fund-raising practice.

There are numerous examples of college administrators setting a course dependent upon private resources that were simply not
to be found. In many such cases, if their advice had been sought,
experienced development officers could have advised that funding
for particular programs would be difficult or impossible to secure.
Because of the increased importance of effective fund raising, the
expertise and specific knowledge of the chief development officer is
more valued. In many institutions, the position has been elevated
to the vice president's level, and the chief development officer now
serves as one of the president's key advisers.

Goals and Results Orientation. One private institution among the
ten, which we describe as a "maverick," had a strong, openly acknowledged sales orientation. A senior development manager at
this institution said, "Fund raising is a professional activity. This
is a corporation with a $6 million annual budget and 120 employees
that will turn a 600 percent profit this year." An intricate planning
and goal-setting process involving dollar and activity goals for each
fund raiser is in place. The development staff (which, incidentally,
has a very low turnover in contrast to national averages where the
present length of stay in a given institution is only about two to
three years) told us they were considered "pariahs" in the development community and compared to used-car salesmen. We found
that unfortunate, however, because we not only respected the considerable fund-raising success this institution experienced over the
past ten years, but we were quite impressed with the seriousness of
purpose and professional stature of this group.

One of the reasons the staff stays on in this institution, continuing to meet very demanding goals, is that development officers "own their own programs." Within the structure of very clear expectations (clearer here than anywhere else we visited), practitioners had a great deal of autonomy and thought the rewards of working in such an environment were greater than they would be elsewhere, even if they might earn more money. Operating almost entirely without a volunteer network, these development officers "are used to getting on the phone with chief executive officers and going to see them." One such fund raiser said, "A big difference here is that we are expected to deal directly with [major] donors, which affects our image of ourselves as professionals. I came from an institution where there was always a volunteer between me and the donor. Here, I feel like a builder. These are my bricks that get stacked together, my new building. This is my new professorship, too—something I help in a very direct way to bring about."

To ensure that concern for results is balanced with concern for how things are done at this institution, development officers participate in the planning and goal-setting process for their areas, and central development provides extensive direction and backup support. Staff and management widely agree that monitoring only what can be counted does not fully capture what is going on; there is also a management commitment to the principle that fund raisers are not held accountable for what they cannot control. Moreover, team effort and open sharing of information and resources receive a strong emphasis. The senior development manager emphasized that the most important thing he communicates to staff is that the success of the entire program and of each individual fund raiser is dependent upon their cooperation and communication with each other.

This description is not intended to imply that this is a model for fund-raising management that all institutions should adopt (although this particular institution has been among pacesetters in higher education for many years.) Although space does not permit full explanation here, the evolution of this university and its fund-raising history helps to explain why this particular approach has been so successful for this school. It did not have the "classic," traditional development of fund-raising programs and donors that has occurred over decades in many other institutions—reason enough for a nontraditional, highly entrepreneurial approach.

In contrast, at another institution in the study, a major public university, the fund-raising program is also results-oriented, but in a very different way. The chief development officer, who eleven years ago was the only development officer, built this institution's fund-raising program to include comprehensive programs involving twenty-eight professional staff. He was unusual among the chief development officers we interviewed because of his firm stand against setting dollar goals for any unit or individual fund raiser. He said, "I'm really interested in long-term development . . . I want relationships between prospects and disciplines to develop so that gifts are brought in at the right time. The bottom line is only one way to see how people are doing. Another way is to look at how successful the development officer is in attracting and involving the private sector. Have advisory boards been established and are they active and effective? In this outfit, involving the right volunteers is a strong measure of effective performance." Volunteers solicit almost 80 percent of the gifts this university secures.

Another measure of performance this executive uses is the confidence development officers gain among deans and faculty. Clearly, development officers in this institution function in a very different kind of environment, with different kinds of expectations, than in the university described earlier. The important implication of this finding is that it is critical for managers hiring development staff to pay close attention to the "goodness of fit" between candidates and institutional programs. (Incidentally, all persons interviewed at this institution, when asked why they were successful in fund raising, unanimously cited the leadership and management style of this chief development officer. Of all the comments made about him, one struck us as particularly insightful: "I think he is a man of vision, a very big person. He has the overall picture and therefore little things never become big issues with him. There's a team happening here because of his leadership. . . . He fosters camaraderie and team play.")

Professional Management. In 1987, Young commented on the lack of a strong management tradition in nonprofits and described the practice of promoting practitioners into administration, where they learn (or fail to learn) by trial and error. Young also noted that improvement of management in nonprofits requires "more explicit recognition of management as a critical area of activity . . . and the development of an appropriate mix of skills . . . [that] are more commonly associated with other sectors" (p. 177). We define "professional management" as management that is taken seriously as a valid process that contributes to achieving goals, not as something that gets in the way of achieving goals, as it is perceived (and practiced) in many nonprofits. At every institution we visited, whenever high-level managers also had fund-raising responsibilities, there was conflict about whether they should remain on campus "to mind the store" or be "out there raising money." If fund raising is still thought of as a necessary evil in higher education, management is still generally considered to be a necessary evil in fund raising. This is one way in which fund raising differs from sales: Sales staffs are not ambivalent about strong visible management and fund raisers are. Some of the institutions we studied have important management staff who do not have direct fund-raising responsibilities. That seems to be part of a good solution to the problem, because it seems clear that a good way to ensure that fund raising is both competent and honorable is through a professional management process that provides structure, guidance, and support for both high outcomes and ethical behavior.

Managing Staff. In one university, we met an experienced fund raiser who was now in a senior management position. Of all the managers we met, she most clearly articulated a balanced philosophy of concern for results, methods, and people. She said, "Most of my time has been spent recruiting and hiring, which is a very demanding task. It needs to be, because people are everything in this field. I also have put a lot of effort into building a team. We are all new to the kind of programs we're doing and new to each other."

Indicating that success as a fund raiser is no guarantee for success as a manager, she observed, "Being an effective manager of human resources, keeping the staff well-integrated and supported, takes real skill which I am working to develop and improve." She discussed the steps she is taking, which include requiring attendance at seminars and educational programs for executive managers and also involving the university's director of human resources as a facilitator for team building and problem solving at development staff retreats. It is important to her to create conditions that help staff enjoy their work, as well as perform well. "The whole staff, including secretaries, is going out to dinner tonight," she said. "We all think that activities such as this support our commitment to the university."

Managing Costs. A question about fund-raising management that plagues us and others who conduct research in this area is how the field can be so businesslike in some respects and so far removed from business practice in the understanding and use of cost/benefit ratios. The efforts of several researchers (ourselves, as well as staff from the Council for the Advancement and Support of Education and the National Association of College and University Business Officers) to collect valid, reliable data on fund-raising expenditures have been only minimally successful. Paton (1986) wrote that "no other single accomplishment will improve research about development so much as identification of *practical* methods for monitoring development expenditures routinely" (p. 37), and that this process cannot proceed until efforts to gather performance data *within* institutions improve.

There are enormous problems in comparing fund-raising costs and these are only some of the reasons: There are almost as many accounting and record-keeping systems as there are institutions; the way in which fund-raising costs differ in relation to life stage of program (new programs have higher costs), gift level (major gifts cost less per dollar to raise than smaller gifts), and donor groups (alumni dollars cost more to raise than, say, gifts from corporations); and the immeasurable cost and influence of the president's time and that of high-level volunteers.

Nevertheless, we cannot choose not to struggle with this problem. The expectation of accountability from within our institutions and from without is not going to diminish. Even televangelists, who have been saying for decades that they are accountable only to God ("Swaggart Criticizes Oral Roberts' Life-Extension Plea as 'Spiritual Extortion,'" 1987, p. 12), now are being forced to disclose information about expenditures and how much of the money raised actually goes to philanthropic purposes.

Since we have been conducting research in fund raising and disseminating our results, the most frequent requests we receive for further information are for comparative data on fund-raising expenditures. Chief development officers need accurate comparative information on costs and expenditures for designing programs, for defending budget requests, and to ensure that scarce resources are applied to the most profitable areas.

There is some evidence that not all fund-raising executives want more clarity about fund-raising expenditures, and one reason is that there is little understanding outside the field about these costs. Yet, there may also be cases where fund raisers are spending insupportable amounts of money. This reasoning is based on a fact that we do know for certain: Most fund-raising programs in higher education typically do not have sophisticated, systematic evaluation programs to measure results and costs. Fund-raising executives need to spend more time educating others about fund-raising costs and the factors that affect them and to become more skilled in cost/ benefit analysis and overall evaluation. Correspondingly, it is critical that other participants in the philanthropic process have a better understanding of costs. A lack of complete understanding and knowledge on the part of fund raisers and those outside the field contributes to the lack of clarity about fund-raising costs, and, until there is more learning on both sides, circumstances are not likely to improve.

Entrepreneurship. The term "entrepreneur" often indicates a person who is especially talented at seizing or creating an opportunity to do something that others would consider too risky, either because there is too slight a likelihood of success or because failure would cause considerable loss or harm. "Entrepreneurial" is also used to connote a situation in which decisions made or actions taken are outside of and/or contradict conventional practice. Five of the ten institutions we studied were characterized by an entrepreneurial approach, as defined above. Entrepreneurial activity is most often associated with business, but, as Young (1987) observed, after his analysis of risk taking in the private sector, government, and nonprofits, "comparing cases across sectors yields few clear-cut distinctions, and perhaps that is the most surprising conclusion in view of the conventional wisdom that business/entrepreneurs are the quintessential risk-takers in our economy" (p. 171). He concluded that managers in nonprofits faced the same areas of risk—financial outcomes, personal reputations, and credibility—as those in business.

It is important for fund raisers to be entrepreneurial because of the need to enlarge the base of traditional donors and reach new, nontraditional donors as well. It is also an aspect of fund raising that others need to understand, in order to more fully appreciate the creativity, substance, and ingenuity that fund raisers bring to their institutions. The entrepreneurial activities we learned about were both profit- and value-driven, and, in fact, some represented notable instances of statesmanship in higher education fund raising.

Entrepreneurial efforts almost always involved building creatively on existing institutional strengths. These fund raisers found that people already bound to the institution put their money where their hearts are, *if they are asked.* One public university, noted for its warmth and caring about students, has a long tradition of involving parents in institutional affairs. Major events on the campus each year are the two weekends designated either for "moms" or "dads" when parents stay on campus and participate in activities designed for parent and student to attend together. Enterprising fund raisers several years ago decided to begin a program of parent solicitation, in spite of reservations on campus that parents would be offended. This was an institution that parents already supported through their taxes, and most families with students at this university were not well-to-do. The program has had resounding success, with none of the feared negative consequences. The evidence seems to be that what works best in fund raising—directly asking for money—is what makes others most uncomfortable about the work fund raisers do.

Entrepreneurial Statesmanship. A veteran fund raiser in a large public university provided several examples of entrepreneurial statesmanship. For more than a decade, he has had the primary responsibility in his institution for raising scholarship funds. More than any other person we interviewed, he identified students as the most important constituency he serves.

In this time of increasingly depersonalized connections between massive organizations and individuals, this development officer continues to find time to solicit scholarships for individual students in financial crisis who fall outside the federal or institutional guidelines for financial aid. Although he acknowledged that this type of donor is less easily come by than once was true, he can still find donors who will help individual students, demonstrating that you do not get the gifts that you do not ask for, but you can get gifts when you ask. No one in any other institution talked about this particular kind of fund raising. At this large public university, there is still a member of the administration (in the development office, no less) to whom students can appeal for personal attention and help with serious problems.

This development officer's concern for students extends beyond his own institution but continues to benefit his own institution as well. He described a situation of several years ago, when he was approached by officials of a foundation in the state who wanted to create an ongoing program to provide twenty four-year scholarships to students attending any of the state's three public universities. The foundation officials wanted his advice about how the scholarships should be divided among the three institutions. The development officer said, "I suggested that they award the scholarships and let the winners make their own selections about where to attend, because I thought that would be best for students." The generosity of this suggestion impressed the foundation officials and resulted in considerable goodwill for the university. The program has been in operation for three years. Each year so far, seventeen out of the twenty winners have chosen to attend the development officer's institution. He noted, "We might get all twenty this year. I thought we'd get some of the winners, but I never dreamed we'd get as many as we do."

Long-Term Institutional Benefit. One area in which fund raisers are working to improve effectiveness and increase credibility is in their commitment to build permanent structures for the continued development of fund-raising efforts: a pervasive theme in the institutions studied. Although it is now better understood that fund-raising progress is essentially a developmental activity, in many institutions we heard of earlier efforts that were successful in reaching goals but did not create the foundation necessary for permanent and steady growth. In some cases, this might have been evidence of what one vice president called the "quick fix" phenomenon in fund raising, which he described as "finding some key people to give large gifts after which both the donor and the fund raiser walk away. The fund raiser looks like a hero, but there's nothing underpinning that" to promote the donor's continuing involvement in the institution.

The practice of all but eliminating the development function after a successful major campaign was once more common than it is now. The quick fix phenomenon may have been the result of shortsightedness in both fund raisers and institutional administration, rather than fund raisers' disregard for the institution's long-term welfare. However, this vice president noted that the fund-raising field needs to be more purposeful in its commitment to work for long-range benefits to the institution, saying "We do a disservice if we come in, apply the 'quick fix,' and move on." He also observed that institutions need to be more enlightened about market conditions underlying turnover in fund raising. He said, "It's a lot cheaper to pay extra to keep good staff than it is to hire new people every three years. It seems to me that is not well understood at many schools."

Ethics in Fund Raising

For our institutions to survive, fund raisers must be competent, and that is where management comes in; fund raising must be honorable, and that is where ethics comes in. Fund raising, like but *not more than* most other professional transactions, is fraught with potential conflicts of interests: between the donor and the organization; the donor and the fund raiser; the fund raiser and the organization; and among the fund raiser, the donor, and the organization.

As a field, we have only begun to address ethical issues in any systematic way. Carbone's (1989) recent research suggested that although fund raisers indicate a desire to be ethical in their work, there is confusion about ethical standards. The research also suggested that fund raisers are not particularly skilled or experienced in considering the more subtle aspects of their work. These results indicate the need for more widespread discussion and more serious attention to these matters by fund-raising leadership.

Yet this, too, is a two-sided problem. It is also important for those outside the field not to conclude that what they are personally uncomfortable about constitutes unethical behavior. For instance, many people in nonprofits are uncomfortable with activities that emphasize results, believing that this may lead to lying and cheating, and that pressure to achieve goals will cause people to distort the data or use methods that are ethically questionable. Of course, the potential is there, but there is no reason to believe that people will automatically be both more ethical and more productive if the focus is on how things are done rather than on the results achieved. There is no scarcity of unethical or incompetent behavior in the rest of the nonprofit sector, which operates primarily with a process orientation.

Furthermore, fund raisers without specific goals have another kind of burden, one that can also result in unethical and unproductive behavior. Being judged by what you accomplish, without an understanding of the standards or expectations, causes a very different kind of pressure and may result in the fund raiser's being judged for many things other than actual performance. The potential for things to go wrong, things that can greatly impair integrity and performance, is at least as great in this situation and perhaps even more dangerous because it is more subtle.

To improve fund-raising practice and increase understanding of ethical dilemmas, it is important to get more things out on the table, among fund raisers themselves and among fund raisers and others concerned with philanthropy. What fund raisers must bring to the discussion is an acknowledgment of whatever truth there is in criticisms leveled against them, along with the admission that sometimes the ethical ice they walk on is very thin. University head football coaches, surveyed for a recent study (Cullen, Latessa, and Byrne, 1990), said they knew there was widespread corruption in college athletics—but not at their schools. Most important, the study suggested that circumstances often beyond the coaches' control contributed considerably to the ethical conflicts they face, and that ethical problems in collegiate activities cannot be solved or controlled by holding only the coaches responsible. The institutions and all other parties concerned must also be held responsible.

The fact is that although ethical problems are inherent in the work of fund raising, development officers alone cannot solve or control these problems, and all of the ethical problems in fund raising are not created by fund raisers. Fund-seeking organizations, funding organizations, and donors all contribute to the ethical complexity of philanthropy.

We like the new attention being given to fund-raising ethics, but we do not like emphasizing only that good ethics are good for fund-raising outcomes, or that fund raisers had better police themselves or Congress will do it for them. Since fund raisers are more than salespeople, they must be forthright in saying that they practice good ethics not because it is pragmatic—which it is—but because it is moral. Salespeople in business cannot get away with that kind of talk, even if they mean it, because of their profit motive. Because of their mission, fund raisers cannot get away with anything less; they must stand for the proposition that fund raising is an honorable endeavor.

Conclusion

Fund raising has been phenomenally successful in this country because Americans believe in philanthropy and also because fund raisers work hard and use methods that work. It is naive to think that fund raisers should not use business methods, and those truly concerned with philanthropy will welcome the professional skill and honorable commitment most fund raisers bring to their work. Fund raising has become big business because that is what nonprofit organizations now require, which does not mean fund raising is not honorable. But it does mean fund raisers are more responsible than ever for balancing their concerns for results, methods, and people. Fund raisers and other participants in philanthropy need to work together to bring fund raising out of the hidden side of philanthropy into the place of respect it deserves.

References

Carbone, R. F. *Fund Raising as a Profession.* College Park, Md.: Clearinghouse for Research on Fund Raising, 1989.

Cullen, F. T., Latessa, E. J., and Byrne, J. P. "Scandal and Reform in College Athletics: Implications from a National Survey of Head Football Coaches." *Journal of Higher Education,* 1990, *61,* 50–64.

Duronio, M. A., and Loessin, B. A. *Effective Fund Raising in Higher Education: Ten Success Stories.* San Francisco: Jossey-Bass, 1991.

Freeman, D. K. "Ethical Considerations in Fund Raising." *Fund Raising Management,* June 1987, *72,* 74–77.

INDEPENDENT SECTOR. *Compendium of Resources for Teaching about the Nonprofit Sector, Voluntarism, and Philanthropy.* Washington, D.C.: INDEPENDENT SECTOR, 1989.

Lawson, C. E. "Leading by Example." *Currents,* 1987, *13,* 72.

Lord, J. G. *The Raising of Money.* New York: Third Sector Press, 1987.

Odendahl, T. *Charity Begins at Home: Generosity and Self-Interest Among the Philanthropic Elite.* New York: Basic Books, 1990.

Paton, G. J. "Microeconomic Perspectives Applied to Development Planning and Management." In J. A. Dunn, Jr. (ed.), *New Directions in Institutional Research,* no. 51. San Francisco: Jossey-Bass, 1986.

Payton, R. L. *Philanthropy: Voluntary Action for the Public Good.* New York: American Council on Education/Macmillan, 1988.

Smith, J. P. "Professionals in Development: Dignity or Disdain?" *Currents,* 1981, *7,* 10–13.

"Swaggart Criticizes Oral Roberts' Life-Extension Plea as 'Spiritual Extortion.'" *Fund Raising Management,* Mar. 1987, pp. 11–12.

Vigeland, C. A. *Great Good Fortune: How Harvard Makes Its Money.* Boston: Houghton Mifflin, 1986.

Young, D. R. "Executive Leadership in Nonprofit Organizations." In W. W. Powell (ed.), *The Nonprofit Sector: A Research Handbook.* New Haven, Conn.: Yale University Press, 1987.

Chapter 9

The Feminization
of Fund Raising

Julie C. Conry

In the closing months of 1989, a storm of discussion and debate followed the release of new statistical evidence that points to a growing dominance of woman entering and succeeding in the fund-raising field. A 1988 membership survey by the National Society of Fund Raising Executives (NSFRE) revealed that just within the prior three years, the percentage of males in the field dropped from 51 percent to 48 percent and that women are now entering the field at twice the rate of men ("Profile 1988: NSFRE Career Survey," 1988, p. 2). In higher education, women have assumed a new majority in the membership of the Council for the Advancement and Support of Education (CASE): 54.7 percent, up from 48.5 percent in 1986.

Note: Several personal interviews with fund-raising practitioners and executives were conducted during the spring of 1990 to provide perspective and background for this chapter. The subjects requested anonymity, and their comments are interspersed as such throughout the text.

A number of individuals provided critical review and assistance during the development of this chapter. They include Pam Creedon, Carol Ebbinghouse, Pranab Chatterjeo, Pat Pasqual, and David Ganzfried.

Although sheer numbers do not necessarily establish a revolution, concern has nevertheless mounted that the gender transition taking place in fund raising has negative implications. Many long-time fund raisers are voicing fears that should this trend continue, the salaries, prestige, and status of a previously male-dominated occupation will decline significantly (Goss, 1989). They argue that by becoming "feminized," the field will suffer the fate of other occupations that have switched from being predominantly male to female, such as teaching and library science.

Attendant issues surrounding this gender switch focus on the future of women choosing to pursue careers in fund raising. Will these women duplicate the patterns now being documented in parallel professions, such as public relations and grant making? Will they be clustered in technical "skills" positions, with few opportunities for advancement, making less money than male counterparts at all levels? Will they fall victim to what sociologist Barbara Reskin calls female "ghettos," lower-paid enclaves occupied almost exclusively by women within otherwise integrated organizations and institutions (Cowan, 1989, p. A14)?

Further, will their demonstrated effectiveness for successfully managing the details and personal relationships inherent in top-level fund raising be rewarded in a conservative system? Or will women be penalized in the "capital campaign" environment now so pervasive in fund raising, one that demands mobility and short-term performance to attain career advancement, while the values of loyalty and long-term cultivation diminish?

These questions and issues are the primary focus of this chapter, which examines the emerging gender-based transition of the fund-raising field and discusses the present status of women fund raisers. It addresses some assumptions about the field's possible destiny as another "velvet ghetto" as a result of the increasing numbers of women choosing fund raising as a career. The striking parallels with other professions are highlighted, as well as the troubling paradoxes that follow women's seeming progress in this demanding and very visible occupation.

An emerging and visible presence for generations, women have been the backbone of American philanthropy: organizing committees, staffing campaigns, soliciting gifts, and, in most cases, offering their expertise and skills for little or no compensation. Titles, money, and professional status were accorded to male counterparts, who as paid fund raisers officially represented institutions and organizations to donors and prospects. Just fifteen years ago, 79 percent of the fund raisers in higher education were men (Desruisseaux, 1987). The American Association of Fund-Raising Counsel (AAFRC), which represents the largest consulting firms in the field, was commonly referred to as a "male club" during most of its fifty-five-year history (Goss, 1989a).

Today, women direct and manage multimillion-dollar campaigns on college and university campuses, serve as vice presidents for development, and dispense significant funds as foundation executives. A female executive director heads the AAFRC. The portrait of women in fund raising is changing rapidly and dramatically, as the numbers reveal:

> As of 1988, female members of the National Society of Fund Raising Executives outnumbered their male colleagues by a ratio of 52 to 48 percent. In 1981, only 38 percent of the annual NSFRE survey respondents were women, compared to 52 percent in 1988. In the last three years women have entered the field at twice the rate of men ("Profile 1988: NSFRE Career Survey," 1988, p. 22).

> As of 1987, 42 percent of the active members of the National Association of Hospital Development were women, compared to 15 percent in 1977 (Bumgarner, 1987, p. 18).

> As of 1987 in higher education, women held 28 percent of Director of Development positions, 19 percent of Planned Giving Director positions, 36 percent of Director of Major Gifts positions, 60 percent of Director of Annual Giving positions, 42 percent of Director of Corporate and Foundation Giving positions, and 77.9 percent of Director of Prospect Research positions (Brakeley Recruiting, 1988, p. 7).

As of 1989/1990, CASE membership statistics showed that women held a 54.7 percent majority, compared to 48.5 percent in 1986 and 38.7 percent in 1982.

Women, the news reports are heralding, are becoming the dominant force in the field, and this gender transition has serious implications for the future of the profession, its status, compensation, and growth. Goss noted in a recent article on the trend: "Those observers, male and female alike, say that the 'feminization of fund raising' may be simultaneously helping and harming the profession. They note that women are enjoying tremendous success in a vocation for which they appear especially well suited. But at the same time, those observers say that if women come to dominate the field, their presence could depress the salary levels and prestige of this traditionally male career" (Goss, 1989, p. 1).

The question no longer appears to be a matter of *if* women come to dominate the field, but *when*, and how long it will take before the scales become irrevocably tipped to occupationally segregate fund raising as "women's work." Many commentators and practitioners share the view that the current intensive market demand for competent fund raisers of any gender will continue into the immediate future, creating widespread entry-level opportunities for women (Carbone, 1989; McIlquham, 1978). But if previous occupational feminization patterns are repeated in fund raising, the lower salaries paid to women may become the norm, and institutions will cultivate this new-found work force that supplies cheaper labor with no loss of the effectiveness or productivity that existed with higher-paid male staffs.

The Phenomenon of Feminization

Current economic theory states that an occupation can be defined as female-dominated if 60 percent or more of the workers in that occupation were female in 1980, or neutral if 21 to 59 percent were female (Rytina and Bianchi, 1984). A wide body of research exists that addresses the roles women have in the work force; the dynamics of how they have been occupationally typed into low-status, low-paying jobs; and the economic, social, and cultural forces that have contributed to the wage gap. There is a great deal of agreement about the status of women workers but far less consensus about how that status is perpetuated in capitalist systems and what remedies should be pursued to correct the problems.

Economists Strober and Arnold (1987) present an institutional theory of occupational segregation in explaining the forces that shape a gender transition. Their theory assumes that (1) social rules and customs as well as profit maximizing govern employers' personnel decisions; (2) male workers as a group decide, within race and class constraints, which jobs will be theirs; and (3) male workers maximize their economic gain in making this decision. Their study of the feminization of bank telling after World War II confirmed these assumptions, as men declined to return to banking jobs and sought out other, more lucrative and skilled occupations. The women who had temporarily gained access to the field, younger, less educated, and less experienced than the men they replaced, thereby inherited the jobs left behind. They also inherited a compensation and status system that had been altered by the banking industry to respond to a female-dominated work force. The result was a significant decline in the status and compensation of bank telling, conditions that still hold true today.

Hartmann (1976) theorizes that women's work was sex-typed from patriarchy. She argues that male workers have material motives for maintaining job segregation by sex because it ensures lower wages for women and keeps them dependent on and subordinate to men in the home and workplace. Marxist-feminist analysts believe women's work outside the home was ideologically determined, with women's work in the labor market equated with work in the home: Hence women were not viewed as workers but as women working (Grieco and Whipp, 1986).

Historically, gender transitions in the work place have several common denominators. Males in the occupation undergoing a transformation continue to dominate the highest-status, highest-paying positions, usually management (Reskin, 1988), such as those of superintendents and principals in education. As women gain access to previously male fields, the jobs become deskilled or redefined by management with consequent losses in compensation, prestige, autonomy, and responsibility (Reskin, 1988; Creedon, 1990).

As one female development executive explains it: "Women start at lower salaries and are not given the same raises and promotions as men. There is a set of built in social attitudes that undervalues women's work and worth" (Desruisseaux, 1987, p. 22).

Phillips and Taylor argue that skill definitions are stilted by sexual bias: "The work of women is often deemed inferior because it is women who do it. Women workers carry into the work place their status as subordinate individuals, and this status comes to define the value of the work they do" (1980, p. 94). Reskin (1988) concludes that whether or not women choose to be in the jobs they dominate, the outcome is the same—the more proportionately female an occupation, the lower its average wages. A 1987 census bureau study concurs in its summation that "the earnings of a person, regardless of sex, will be lowered as the ratio of women in his or her occupation increases" (Toth and Cline, 1989, p. 15).

Economists have observed in many studies of job segregation that within institutions women start at the bottom and move to the middle, while men start at the middle and move to the top. Numerous pressures exerted on women, both personally and professionally, keep the vast majority clustered in middle management, while few actually break through the "glass ceiling" or invisible barrier to top executive positions (Hymowitz and Schellhardt, 1986). The resulting wage stagnation, lack of career growth, and absence of women in policymaking roles all contribute to minimal progress for women in achieving management and leadership roles.

A more recent phenomenon has been the creation of what Reskin calls female "ghettos" within integrated work places that follows the shift of male workers to higher-paying, more rewarding positions (Cowan, 1989, p. A14). Reskin points to the real estate business, where male flight from the residential side of sales to the more financially advantageous commercial side created a lower-paid enclave of women who had gained entry to the field through lower commission sales. Reskin (1988) also points to the bakery and pharmacy industries as examples of occupations where women are now most prevalent in a clerk role behind pharmacy and supermarket counters, while males run the commercial bakeries and retail drugstore chains.

Even in tightly controlled professions, such as medicine and law, that have only recently exhibited any statistically significant increase of female practitioners, women have little visibility in high-status areas. Gross (1967) found women in medicine prevalent in pediatrics, psychiatry, and dermatology and almost absent in neurology, internal medicine, and the surgical specialties. In law, a similar pattern emerged with women appearing in low-status divorce, juvenile, and welfare law practices and absent from tax law and corporate litigation. Gross (1967) concluded from studying changing sex structures of occupations that whenever large numbers of women enter an occupation, men begin to seek employment elsewhere.

Social psychologist Touhey (1974) confirmed in studies of college students that perception (shaped by socialization and cultural norms and role expectations) plays an important role in the outcome of increasing proportions of women in certain occupations. He found that the mere presence of women in an occupation has a severe impact on the ratings of that occupation's prestige and desirability. Both male and female students reacted negatively when they were led to believe that a high-status occupation (such as medicine) was expected to increase its proportion of female practitioners.

Popular feminist theory, particularly that embraced by Reskin (1988), maintains that social control systems, including gender ideology, customs, socialization, institutional structures, and the cultural devaluation of "traditional" women's work, all conspire to keep female majority occupations from achieving the status and compensation levels accorded to male-dominated occupations. These are the same forces that relabel fields as less attractive, valued, and prestigious as women enter and men leave, hence the term "feminization" to describe the phenomenon.

Are women in fund raising inheriting a field that is becoming deskilled, an occupation being abandoned by men? Or, by contrast, are they exploiting an opportunity and contributing to fund raising's professionalization by bringing in more credentials and education than their male predecessors? In spite of their qualifications and talents, are women experiencing discrimination in fund raising? Will their sudden majority complete the feminization cycle? It is perhaps too early to make substantive conclusions, particularly in the absence of comprehensive comparative data, but a brief examination of women's current status in the field may offer some clues to their future in fund raising.

Limited Progress in Two Decades of Change. Women's increasing participation as professional fund raisers in some ways mirrors the greater presence of women in the U.S. work force. This is true also of their status—how they are compensated and where in the hierarchy they are located. There are 56.2 million American women in the civilian work force today, and they make up 45 percent of all workers, compared to 38 percent in 1970. By the year 2000, women are expected to represent almost 50 percent of the labor force. Almost half of all accountants and bus drivers are now women, and one of five of the nation's doctors and lawyers is a woman (Cowan, 1989, p. A14).

In the last decade, women have become the majority in six major job categories, as insurance adjusters; examiners and investigators; bill collectors; real estate workers; production line assemblers; and checkers, examiners, and inspectors (Prial, 1982, p. 1). However, 46 percent of all working women are still clustered in low-paying, "pink-collar" ghetto jobs as clerical workers, saleswomen, waitresses, and hairdressers. Since 1960, the number of female professional and technical workers has increased, but the majority are still nurses and teachers ("Women's Group Blames . . .," 1988, p. A1).

The statistical picture of women fund raisers is much less precise. Of the three professional associations that represent fund raisers, NSFRE, AHP, and CASE, only NSFRE has attempted to track through regular surveys the actual numbers of women in the field, which it estimates at just over half. CASE does not break out membership by gender, but in periodic surveys gender is analyzed along with other worker characteristics. Some estimates place the number of active fund raisers at nearly 40,000, many of whom are not members of professional organizations and do not have status and backgrounds represented in any formal surveys. The last in-depth survey that specifically addressed women in fund raising was in 1978—twelve years prior to the most dramatic changes the occupation has ever experienced. (The estimate of actual practitioners in fund raising was determined by polling several knowledgeable individuals. No authoritative source exists for exact figures because many fund raisers engage in the practice as a portion of their total job duties, particularly in the nonprofit sector.)

Positions, salaries, and other compensation are the most telling points of how women are faring in fund raising and the larger work force. The ratio between what the average woman earns and what the average man earns has risen to 70 cents on the dollar (roughly 30 percent less), up from 62 cents in the late 1960s, which is largely attributed to women's gains in securing high-paying professional and managerial jobs (Cowan, 1989).

In 1975, such positions accounted for only 27 percent of women's full-time jobs, and by 1986 the percentage rose to 32 percent. Simultaneously, the male share of these positions dropped from 34.6 percent to 29.4 percent. The ratio of women to men managers in industry and government was 54 to 100 by 1986, but men's professional and managerial earnings still averaged about 69 percent higher than women's in this category (Koretz, 1988). Only a small group of women has benefited at all financially from these gains—in 1986 less than 1 percent of women made salaries of $50,000 or more while 76.8 percent made less than $20,000. Further, economists Wagman and Folbre attribute women's progress in gaining professional and managerial posts to affirmative action programs "during a time when competitive pressures unleashed by demographic shifts and industrial change were putting tremendous downward pressures on wages in general" ("Mixed Results on Women in the Workforce," 1988, p. 8).

Such recurring themes are evident in the existing data on women's and men's fund-raising salaries. The 1988 NSFRE survey revealed that almost half (49.5 percent) of the female salaries were below $33,000, compared to one-fifth (19.9 percent) of the men. This shows some progress since 1985, when 65 percent of women earned less than $33,000. In 1988, however, almost half of all males (46.6 percent) earned $50,000 annually, while almost half of the women (50.4 percent) earned $33,000 or more. In 1988, men were more than twice as likely as women to earn more than $40,000 a year, and 5.2 percent earned more than $90,000. Only 7.4 percent of women in 1988 earned more than $60,000.

Some observers have attributed the discrepancy in overall

salary levels to the fact that women fund raisers are in organizations with smaller budgets, have less experience than their male counterparts, and are more likely to work part time (Carbone, 1989; Greene, 1990). Both CASE and NAHD survey data contradict this explanation and indeed offer statistics that point to gender being a significant factor in salary determinations when all other characteristics, such as age, experience, and education, are equal.

In the 1982 CASE survey of professionals in the field of institutional advancement, women earned 20 percent less than men, regardless of their experience, education, and other qualifications (Turk, 1986). Men also had a higher annual salary than their female counterparts in almost every job category. By 1986, the survey noted: "Gender—a factor that has nothing to do with preparation or experience in an advancement career—significantly influences salary. Other personal and professional characteristics being equal, a man earns 12 percent more than a woman . . . however, the gender gap has narrowed by nearly one-half from four years ago" (Turk, p. 8).

The 1986 CASE survey also showed that men's titles indicated a higher level of responsibility than women's, with men's mean salary at $38,817 and women's at $27,235. Men in every title category were paid more than women with the same title, with the difference greatest at the lower levels of responsibility. When a multiple regression analysis was applied to determine how much of the salary difference could be attributed to gender alone, it was determined that being male adds $3,686 to an annual salary—all by itself (Turk, 1986). Turk noted that "experience, educational background, and age do not fully explain salary differences between male and female advancement professionals. While all these factors do influence salary, gender is the greatest influence" (Turk, 1986, p. 20).

By 1989–1990, the CASE survey indicated that women's new majority had not carried into increased status or salary. Women were still clustered on the lower rungs of the ladder and still paid less. In 1989–1990, women respondents reported an average salary of $36,123, versus the men reporting $49,066—a 35.8 percent difference ("1990 CASE-Ketchum Survey . . .," p. 13).

The difference in salary that is gender based—the part of the gap that cannot be explained by different levels of education, experience, and age—worsened between 1986 and 1990. In 1990, men in advancement in higher education were paid 14.2 percent more than women, even with all other factors held equal. That gap was 12 percent in 1986. In 1990, being male added an average of $5,136 to a fund raiser's salary, even if both male and female subjects held the same title, worked at the same type of institution, were in the same area of advancement, were the same age, held the same degree, had the same experience and job tenure, and were the same race ("1990 CASE-Ketchum Survey . . .," p. 14).

NAHD survey figures reveal similar trends in medical development. A 1987 NAHD study of salary and benefits indicated large gaps in pay between men and women. Men with two years experience in administrative and executive positions had a yearly median salary of $61,000, compared to $48,500 for women. With years of experience, the pay gap widened for men and women: Female fund raisers with two years experience earned 85 percent as much as men; women with eight or more years earned only 73 percent as much as men (Melillo, 1989, p. 1).

NAHD survey data from 1990 showed little status improvement; findings concluded that women fund raisers at hospitals continued to make much less than their male counterparts (Greene, 1990). The survey noted that female executives with up to two years of development experience are paid 76 percent of what their male equivalents earn; women who have worked in development for more than eight years earn 70 percent of what males earn. Salaries between men and women become more equitable at the lowest job ranks, such as assistant or associate director, according to the survey, but after both groups obtain seven years of experience, men show huge gains over women (Greene, 1990, p. 1).

At the highest CEO levels in educational fund raising, women share somewhat more parity, but many are more educated and still make less than their male colleagues. The 1987 *Brakeley Compensation Report* of chief development officers in higher education noted: "The women CDOs in our sample earn 87.6 cents for each dollar earned by men. This is up 6.4 cents over last year's findings. . . . Twenty-one percent of the women CDOs hold Ph.D. degrees and earn an average base salary of $66,596 compared to 19 percent of men with Ph.D. degrees who earn an average of $67,636.

Forty-nine percent of the women CDOs have Master's degrees and earn $54,056, compared to 41 percent of the men who have Master's degrees and earn an average of $64,127" (Brakeley Recruiting, 1988, p. 5).

Women are also behind in every category of fringe benefits. The NSFRE survey shows women trailing men by four or more percentage points in each category. In higher education (Brakeley Recruiting, 1987, p. 16), only 21 percent of women CDOs are awarded use of a car, while 56 percent of the males receive the benefit; one-half of the males receive club privileges, compared to 33 percent of the women; 10 percent of the males receive housing assistance and only 2 percent of the women. It appears that women fund raisers, much like their female colleagues in the larger work force, pay a penalty for their gender in many cases as they struggle to establish a presence in a tradition-bound, male-dominated occupation. If unequal compensation levels are sustained as women become the majority in fund raising, it is likely salary levels for the field will diminish as organizations and institutions adjust their pay scales to accommodate female job candidates who will work for less and offer a standard of performance that is a bargain from the employer's point of view.

Implications for the Future. This scenario fulfills the primary assumptions about the feminization trend. As lower compensation levels become the norm, men will seek to preserve their advantages by continuing to dominate the highest-paying, highest-status positions. Or they will abandon entry-level opportunities altogether, leaving women to fill the technical roles of fund raising while they continue to manage the operations (Creedon, 1990).

There is already some evidence that female ghettos are developing in certain areas of fund raising with the most technical orientation, even at the directorial level. Almost 80 percent of prospect research director positions are now held by women, who earn an average of $24,759—the lowest salary level of all mid-level development director staff positions tracked in the *Brakeley Compensation Report.*

Just under 60 percent of annual fund and annual giving directors are now women, who earn an average of $32,126, the second-lowest salary level among director positions (Brakeley Recruiting, 1988, p. 5). Both research and annual fund positions are regarded as typical entry-level training jobs in fund raising because the work is routine and structured and offers few opportunities for donor interaction. The existence of negligible numbers of men in these departments suggests that they are bypassing this entry route to more direct line and management roles, or not entering the pipeline at all.

In addition to the discrepancies that appear in the salaries paid to men and women, current market forces in fund raising are exacerbating the problems of entry- and middle-level staff, causing additional salary deflation in some cases, and producing a double bind for women. The 1988 NSFRE survey revealed that in two years time, twice as many top fund raisers made more than $75,000 a year (8.4 percent), and more than 4.2 percent made more than $90,000. Those institutions most likely to pay salaries in excess of $90,000 are educational institutions, consulting firms, and medical centers. In a climate of increasing competition for the private dollar, these institutions are trying to buy expertise and acquire fund raisers who can turn on money machines.

One consultant observed that "colleges and universities still seem to be looking for the fund raising star who can champion their efforts to attract large-scale support, and they are financing the high salaries they must offer such officials by holding down the compensation of their other fund raisers. I think that approach is going to end up costing them dearly" ("Pay Gap Widens Among Fund Raisers . . .," 1987, p. 22).

With this kind of pressure and with fewer dollars to divide among middle- and lower-level staff members, it would appear financially advantageous for institutions to accept and cultivate a female labor force in fund raising. Salary demands would be appreciably lower for a female-dominated staff than a male-dominated one, freeing up more dollars to place high-priced star performers and managers—usually male—in the top tiers of fund-raising staffs. Turnover would also be less of a problem for institutions because many women do not exercise their option to move or transfer out of a community; hence they are a stabilizing force at lower staff levels.

At the same time, even the lower salaries women are paid in fund raising are often superior to what they could command in similar occupations, particularly in fields where women are the dominant work force. This is additional incentive for women to accept less in all aspects of fund raising—less money, less prestigious titles, less responsibility—as a trade-off for the opportunity to gain experience and a track record. As women prove themselves to be effective and successful paid fund raisers, as they still expect fewer rewards than men, and as they continue to provide a solid supply for the high market demand in the field at present, it is highly likely salary levels and prestige will fall. There is a strong possibility that fund raising will begin to resemble a two-tiered hierarchy similar to that in other professions where the value system rewards those who take the greatest risks: highly compensated superstars who move to the highest bidder at the top, and female-dominated mid- and lower-level staffs with short career ladders whose lesser rewards will become the standard.

The Status Question: A Gender or Occupational Issue. With the feminization process, declines in salary in the professions are generally accompanied by equal declines in status and prestige. As an occupation becomes predominantly female, it is consequently thought to be less desirable, less attractive to individuals with high ambitions, and less challenging. Reskin (1988) asserts that women begin to dominate an occupation or make significant gains when work content and functions shift to functions already socially labeled as "women's work," such as communications, clerical, or emotional and interpersonal work.

Fund raising has historically been intensively interpersonal, persuasive, highly dependent on skillful communicators and those comfortable with managing emotions and motivations. The conspicuous absence of women as paid fund raisers until fairly recently is all the more noteworthy in that it is a field that has personified these "traditional" female characteristics and traits. One could argue, even, that fund raising's status might already suffer because its associated job functions are more innately female than male, an issue that may be exaggerated as women assume more visible roles in the field.

In the barrage of commentary that followed the 1988 NSFRE findings that women were the new majority of fund raisers, several schools of thought emerged regarding the status question. One held that the increasing presence of women would enhance fund raising's status because women entering the field brought significant academic credentials, work experience, and technical skills and thus more credibility to their institutions and the public (Goss, 1989). A second view theorized that women would advance fund raising's professionalism, raise its standards of performance, and increase its acceptance as a legitimate occupation in an economy that offered organizations two choices: become sufficient at fund raising or become extinct (Goss, 1989b). A third view predicted that a status change would follow the inevitable match between the occupation and its rightful gender—women. And as women demonstrate their success in the field, the success is attributed not to professional preparation and strengths but to women's "natural" attributes as nurturers, intuitors, listeners, sympathizers, and motivators.

These traits in men or women are certainly necessary for successful fund raising, but this kind of devaluation of women's success repeats the feminization refrain: "women not viewed as workers, but as women working" (Grieco and Whipp, 1986, p. 117). This perception also poses a serious risk to occupational status and to women trying to achieve professional parity with men. It presents an even greater paradox for women who choose to exploit their own strengths to achieve advancement and recognition in fund raising. With success now defined by stereotyped gender traits, the line becomes very thin between women's attributes and "women's work."

The contribution of women in fund raising to the continuing struggle to establish it as a recognized profession is also a critical factor in the status debate. The increasing presence of women in the field has hit at a time when the occupation itself is undergoing rapid technological changes, as well as internal status changes. Until the severe economic realities of the 1970s and 1980s dropped full force at the doorsteps of educational institutions, hospitals, and health and social agencies, fund raisers often occupied roles of secondary importance. Fund raising's status was far from ranking at the highest levels of occupations and professions. As one veteran fund raiser summed it up: "At one time many felt that a fund raiser was someone who had failed at something else. Today, men and women enter development by choice rather than by default" (Bumgarner, Georges, and Luna, 1987, p. 16).

Many aspects of fund raising, however, still work against the efforts to define it as an occupation with professional standing, whether its practitioners are women or men. Carbone (1988) noted that fund raising is hampered by the numbers of people in part-time jobs, an overreliance on volunteers, the lack of a substantial knowledge base versus a focus on people management and technical know-how, no formal preparation program for practitioners, no standard credentials based on formal education, and no single, uniform professional association. Because of these factors, the success or failure of individuals pursuing a career in fund raising is often dependent on their access to training opportunities, the chance to work with and be mentored by an experienced fund raiser, and a willingness to be mobile to pursue career advancement.

Within these constraints, women will find personal and professional progress difficult—fulfilling the expectations of some that their ultimate success will be limited to technical roles rather than management. If this is the fate of women in fund raising, and if women continue to make up the majority in the occupation, status will be altered by issues of gender.

Statistics now indicate that many women are choosing fund raising as their entry-level field. Carbone notes (1989) that many women with extensive volunteer experience who are reentering the work force choose fund raising because their volunteer skills are transferable and moving from no pay to low pay is not viewed as a negative consideration. This phenomenon is also cited as a primary contributor to women's lagging salaries because women "are unprepared to fight for comparable pay" (Greene, 1990, p. 1).

For these reasons, many women in fund-raising jobs are clustered in one- or two-person shops with small budgets; many have little or no access to experienced mentors; and many have few resources to spend to participate in conferences, seminars, or training sessions. Even women in larger organizations in entry- and mid-level positions have their access to training opportunities controlled by a manager, who may or may not value spending resources to train staff in aspects of fund raising outside their immediate job responsibilities.

A majority of fund raisers in one survey indicated that mentoring, hands-on experience, apprenticeships, and working with a true professional, together with seminars and conferences, is the most effective training scheme possible to succeed and advance (Carbone, 1989). In this scheme, educational credentials, exceptional interpersonal skills, and previous job experience in a related field (all of which women are credited with bringing to fund raising) will not necessarily contribute to their professional advancement or the external perception of fund raising as a profession. The choice then becomes one of accepting the status quo and perpetuating the existing system, which may or may not serve their needs, or changing the accepted practices and creating new paths to success.

Perilous Parallels. Of the many occupations in the United States that are currently experiencing dramatic shifts in gender representation, two bear striking and prophetic parallels with fund raising in becoming feminized: public relations and private foundation grant making. The status of women in these two fields, unlike that in fund raising, however, has been exhaustively monitored, charted, and investigated at length. Because so many of the same dynamics are occurring in fund raising, it is appropriate to briefly examine the conclusions being drawn and the methods used to formulate them.

In 1986, the International Association of Business Communicators (IABC) published a research report entitled "The Velvet Ghetto: A Report of the Increasing Percentage of Women in Public Relations and Business Communication," which described the impact of women in the field and their success levels. Public relations, at that point, was almost 60 percent female, up from 27 percent in 1970. Student enrollment in public relations programs was approaching 80 percent female. In 1989, a follow-up study, "Beyond the Velvet Ghetto," was issued, which also evaluated the feminization trends established earlier.

Both studies (Toth and Cline, 1989) documented three main assumptions: (1) Women in public relations were paid substantially less than men; (2) women were more likely to perceive themselves as filling the technician role rather than the managerial role in public relations and business communication; and (3) practitioners were concerned that when other professions had gone from male dominated to female dominated, they had diminished in salary and status.

Much like Turk's (1986) finding of a $3,686 salary differential between men and women in fund raising, men in public relations, when all factors were controlled, made a $6,000 bonus for being male. One study (Cline, 1989, p. 265) indicated that the difference was as high as $30,000, and at the fifty to fifty-nine-year-old age level it was $25,000 a year. In light of this discrepancy, Cline (1989, p. 265) observed: "Over a lifetime of earnings at the high end, women could possibly pay a $1 million penalty for being female." In the late 1980s, annual salary decreases in public relations were attributed to two factors: an increase in younger, lower-paid professionals and the feminization of the profession (Cline, 1989).

In addition to salary deflation, indications of status changes were also becoming obvious as women became more dominant in public relations. Broom and Dozier (1985) surveyed 206 public relations practitioners and found that the number of women classified as technicians increased from 38 to 52 percent between 1979 and 1985, while women classified as managers moved only one percentage point, from 18 to 19 percent, during the same time period. The same subjects who responded to the survey indicated that, as experience increased, job status decreased.

The research (Creedon, 1990) also revealed concerns about institutionalized salary bias due to management's diminishing assessment of the value of communications and public relations, and a subtle socialization process working upon women in communications that resulted in their pursuit of the technical role versus the managerial role. Other fears voiced about the feminization trend revealed in the "Velvet Ghetto" study focused on the growing misunderstanding of the place of public relations in the corporate world, a bias against communications that would make it a dead-end job, and the tendency by too many women to accept lower salaries and lower positions than men just to get experience (Cline, 1989).

Further, participants in the study fulfilled expectations that gender stereotypes, rather than overt sexism, were believed by men and women, which caused women to be passed over for promotions, to lose jobs, and to accept the technician role more readily, resulting in job segregation and lower salaries (Cline, 1989).

Along parallel lines, the internal credibility of fund raisers within the organizations that employ them continues to be a source of struggle, controversy, and professional concern. Should the trends now apparent in public relations be repeated in fund raising, the increasing dominance of women may make that struggle more difficult because women in both fields report that not being taken seriously is their most compelling problem.

Carbone's (1989) data on the self-perceptions of fund raisers indicate that more than half of the respondents disagreed with the assertion that their employers regularly accepted their decisions. Their most common complaint was unrealistic expectations and a lack of understanding of the appropriate role of the development officer. Only 20 percent of the fund raisers polled agreed that the leaders of their institutions accepted "without exception" their judgments and decisions about fund-raising matters (Carbone, 1989, p. 28). It appears that women as fund raisers, much like women in public relations, have a double burden: to establish personal credibility and to defy gender stereotypes within an occupation that does not enjoy high esteem in the eyes of management.

In the grant-making field, as in public relations and fund raising, women are now the majority. Boris's (1988) research indicates that women now make up 74 percent of foundation staffs overall and 57 percent of professional staffs. Community and public foundation professional staffs are 62 percent female; independent, corporate, and private operating foundations are 54 percent female. Women have made major gains at the CEO level—41 percent of foundation CEOs are women, compared to 26 percent in 1982. Most, however, are still clustered in foundations with the smallest assets (below $100 million). Fewer than 13 percent of the largest foundations have female chief executive officers.

Within the foundation world, "the question that is being asked is whether feminization of the field is imminent" (Boris, 1988, p. 1). A male-female salary gap continues to be present in grant making, and rapid turnover is becoming as prevalent as it is in fund raising. In foundations in all asset groups, women CEOs make approximately $25,000 less than their male counterparts, with the largest discrepancies ($35,000) in foundations with $100 million or more in assets. Male program staffers average $12,000 more than women, and male executive staffers average $24,000 more (Boris, 1988).

Boris, Daniels, and Odendahl (1985), in their study of the status of men and women working in foundations, noted that there was ample evidence to predict that the increasing numbers of women in grant-making positions would generate significant changes in philanthropy. "The fact that some women are entering the field and are rising in it without referrals but at lower salaries suggests that there may be an incipient trend toward the feminization of foundation work, with women making progress in numbers. A great many, however, are still relegated to small organizations, with small budgets, where there are few opportunities to establish a high-profile track record. This type of job segregation and lesser reward system contributes heavily to the feminization process as certain categories and hierarchies begin to be associated only with women workers. Pressures to hire staff in order to professionalize giving in foundations with modest incomes lead to hiring individuals, usually women, willing to accept low salaries, who may gain experience and then go on to higher-paying positions in other foundations. However, our study suggests that both horizontal and vertical mobility at present require participation in a special kind of network, in which a background from elite schools and the possession of advanced degrees are important for entry.

"In fund raising and grant making, women must learn to navigate political networks to advance, and since both occupations attract and accept generalists, aggressively obtaining useful on-the-job training is essential to mastering one's position. With such similar ports of entry, the next decade will be crucial in tracking how women fund raisers and grantmakers achieve and maintain career success" (Boris, Daniels, and Odendahl, 1985, p. 73).

Troubling Paradoxes. In ten years time, what women fund raisers have observed about their unique roles in raising money for institutions has changed little. Much of their professional progress is offset by personal compromises, and the sacrifices inherent in these choices continue to be problematic. In a 1978 article, women fund raisers noted that the field offered women numerous chances to gain entry-level jobs, but advancement hurdles were often encountered in the route to upper management. Men, they said, felt women were not capable of handling major gift solicitations or planned giving drives. Being a woman was an additional disadvantage because most fund sources—foundations, corporations, and the government—were still headed by men and the old-boy rule still prevailed (McIlquham, 1978, p. 19). Not being taken seriously, being barred from corporate meetings, not being allowed to travel, not instilling confidence in male donors, and not being given the opportunity to speak for their institutions were all cited as significant handicaps to being a woman fund raiser (McIlquham, 1978, p. 21).

In 1987, female fund raisers polled about hospital development still echoed similar concerns. They agreed that enthusiasm and professionalism were the keys to alleviating the patronizing attitudes still held by some male colleagues and board members. They also sensed a need to prove themselves so they could get on with the business of raising money. Many felt they would be treated differently and paid more if they were men.

The characteristics attributed to women as making them more effective fund raisers—being more verbal, more sensitive, less afraid of emotion, more detail-oriented, more nurturing, and more creative—are also cited as the very reason many barriers exist to being taken seriously by management, trustees, and donors (McIlquham, 1978). These perceived strengths at the interpersonal level, however, are not, in the view of many men and women, directly transferable to advancing into management, where directing large campaign staffs at an impersonal level is a primary function of the CEO.

The new emphasis on short-term performance, the mercenary approach to mounting intensive capital campaigns that are also staff intensive, and the loss of long-term donor relationships due to the high turnover of fund raisers are also detrimental to women. These dynamics may be generating job opportunities, but too many are short-ended, where women are used to quickly fill slots in support roles, with limited visibility.

This carries into consulting as well, where the impact of women in fund raising is keenly felt. One midwestern development consultant acknowledged he has had to increase the number of women on his marketing staff because female fund raisers ask about the number of women he employs. But the final sales presentations, he noted, are still assigned to senior-level male consultants sent in to speak to what is usually a male-dominated board.

An additional paradox now evident is the recognition that volunteer work, still a female domain, has provided crucial experience to women and enabled many of them to enter and progress in paid fund-raising positions. Yet this type of preparation is not valued as highly as paid employment and is often used to justify paying women lower salaries (McIlquham, 1978).

The increasing professionalization of fund raising may construct additional hurdles for women who are bringing significant education and experience to the field. Often when occupations evolve to the status of professions, attempts are made to limit opportunity and restrict new recruits to preserve existing conditions. Boris, Daniels, and Odendahl (1985) note that artificial credentialism may appear and because of this, many who have benefited from accidental opportunity in one institution discover they cannot duplicate their experience elsewhere. Studies of women in science and social reform work have shown that women have more opportunity in fields that are open to gifted amateurs.

In spite of the gains women have made in numbers in fund raising in the last ten years, one stubborn issue remains to foil many who have ambitions to advance: the issue of mobility. Career advancement in fund raising, more than at any other time in its history, requires the willingness to relocate to achieve greater responsibilities. Women in hospital development, for example, flatly stated in 1987 (Bumgarner, Georges, and Luna, p. 17) that "women's lack of mobility not only limits their opportunities, but results in [their] being taken for granted." One female development vice president noted that "women are still less willing to relocate to move up, but in one lifetime there are only a few top positions in a given community. Without mobility you will have a nice career, but not a great one."

The Double Helix: The Future of Women in Fund Raising

For women in many careers, fund raising included, there are few linear paths to leadership positions and advancement. Like a double helix, women's experiences, personal and professional, wrap a central core comprising multiple roles. This ability to meet the demands of many constituencies ought to present an advantage to women in fund raising as the field develops more complexity and diversity. These strengths must also, ultimately, be recognized and rewarded by the institutions that employ women fund raisers, not used as convenient rationales to construct a two-tiered career system.

It is projected that by the twenty-first century, technological advances such as fiber optics, on-line packaging, telefaxes, and sophisticated survey research will significantly reshape the practice of fund raising (Warwick, 1990, p. 1). Successfully managing this information explosion and applying it in a myriad of ways to cultivate and sustain donor relationships is clearly the fund-raising challenge of the decades ahead. Warwick adds that "the lines among advertising, public relations, and fund raising will blur. All organizations, whether or not they are operated for profit, will be forced to take a holistic view of the ways they communicate with constituents" (Warwick, 1990, p. 2).

Likewise, to be effective, the work force of these organizations will have to reflect the wholeness of society, in gender, race, and age. To achieve this balance, action to circumvent feminization patterns and redress inequities is necessary now. Whether it is through the formation of a committee to study the way women negotiate for salaries, work responsibility, and job titles, such as the one created by the NAHD (Greene, 1990), or by the publication of a monograph on mentoring minorities and women in advancement, such as that sponsored by CASE ("CCAMW Receives CASE Partnership Grant . . .," 1990), strategies must be direct, issue oriented, and realistic.

Further, continued in-depth monitoring of the status of women in fund raising is critical to shape solutions and generate change. Studies must not be fragmented or intermittent. All three professional fund-raising associations should collaborate and share resources to develop a comprehensive picture of the role gender plays in the occupation, much like the Velvet Ghetto public relations study. Such self-examination does require risk, it is often controversial, and it is seldom easy. But without it, fund raising as an occupation may suffer a painful transition and be ill equipped to address the radical changes ahead.

References

Boris, E. "The Status of Women in Foundations." A report produced for *Women and Foundations/Corporate Philanthropy in 1988.* Washington, D.C.: Council on Foundations, 1988.

Boris, E. E., Daniels, A. K., and Odendahl, T. J. *Working in Foundations: Career Patterns of Men and Women.* New York: Foundation Center, 1985.

Brakeley Recruiting. *The Brakeley Compensation Report.* Stanford, Conn.: Brakeley, Jan Price Jones, 1988.

Broom, G. M., and Dozier, D. M. "Determinants and Consequences of Public Relations Roles." Paper presented to the Association for Education in Journalism and Mass Communication, Memphis, Tenn., 1985.

Bumgarner, S., Georges, A., and Luna, E. "Women on Women." *National Association of Hospital Development Journal,* Spring 1987, pp. 15–17.

Carbone, R. F. "A Professional Outlook." CASE *Currents,* Feb. 1988, p. 64.

Carbone, R. F. *Fund Raising as a Profession.* College Park, Md.: Clearinghouse for Research on Fund Raising, 1989.

"CCAMW Receives CASE Partnership Grant; Plans Monograph on Mentoring." *Advance,* Spring 1990, p. 3.

Cline, C. G. "The $1 Million Penalty for Being a Woman." In P. J. Creedon (ed.), *Women in Mass Communications.* Newbury Park, Calif.: Sage, 1989.

Cowan, A. "Women's Gains on the Job: Not Without a Heavy Toll." *New York Times,* Aug. 21, 1989, p. A14.

Creedon, P. J. "Public Relations and Women's Work: Toward a Feminist Analysis of Public Relations Roles." Unpublished paper presented at the International Association of Business Communicators, Dublin, Ireland, June 1990.

Davis, C., and Rosser, J. "Gendered Jobs in the Health Service: A Problem for Labour Process Analysis." In D. Knights and H. Willmott (eds.), *Gender and the Labour Process.* Brookfield, Vt.: Gower, 1986.

Desruisseaux, P. "Fund Raisers Weight Implications of Influx of Women into Field." *Chronicle of Higher Education,* July 29, 1987, p. 83.

Goss, K. "Woman Named to Top Post by Fund-Raising Group." *Chronicle of Philanthropy,* Mar. 7, 1989a, p. 11.

Goss, K. "Influx of Women into Fund Raising Poses Paradox: They're Effective, but Pay and Prestige Could Suffer." *Chronicle of Philanthropy.* Mar. 21, 1989b, pp. 1, 10–11.

Greene, E. "Women Fund Raisers for Hospitals Found to Earn Less Than Their Male Counterparts." *Chronicle of Philanthropy,* June 26, 1990, pp. 19, 22.

Grieco, M., and Whipp, R. "Women and the Workplace: Gender and Control in the Labour Process." In D. Knights and H. Willmott (eds.), *Gender and the Labour Process.* Brookfield, Vt.: Gower, 1986.

Gross, E. "The Sexual Structure of Occupations Over Time." Paper presented at American Sociological Association meeting, San Francisco, Aug. 1967.

Hartmann, H. "Capitalism, Patriarchy, and Job Segregation by Sex." In special supplement of *Signs* titled *Women and the Workplace: The Implication of Occupational Segregation, 11* (3) (Spring 1976), pp. 137–170.

Hymowitz, C., and Schellhardt, T. D. "The Glass Ceiling." *Wall Street Journal,* Mar. 24, 1986, Sect. 4, p. 1.

Koretz, G. "Big Bucks or Peanuts? The Growing Wage Gap Between Women." *Business Week,* Dec. 19, 1988, p. 22.

McIlquham, J. D. "Developing Women: Their Attitudes, Ambitions, Growth." *Fund Raising Management,* Mar./Apr. 1978, pp. 19–28.

Melillo, W. "Non-Profit Hospitals Raise $2.9 Billion in Year, 4 Pct. More Than in 1987." *Chronicle of Philanthropy,* May 30, 1989, pp. 1, 6.

"Mixed Results on Women in the Workforce." *Alaska Journal of Commerce,* Sept. 26, 1988, *12* (39), 8.

"The 1990 CASE-Ketchum Survey of Institutional Advancement." *CASE Currents,* Sept. 1990, *16* (8), p. 13.

"Pay Gap Widens Among Fund Raisers as Colleges Pursue High-Priced 'Stars.'" *Chronicle of Higher Education,* July 29, 1987, p. 22.

Phillips, A., and Taylor, B. "Sex and Skill: Notes Towards a Feminist Economics." *Feminist Review,* 1980, *6.*

Prial, F. J. "More Women Work at Traditional Male Jobs." *New York Times,* Nov. 15, 1982, *1,* C20.

"Profile 1988: NSFRE Career Survey." *NSFRE Journal,* Winter 1988, p. 22.

Reskin, B. F. "Bringing the Men Back In: Sex Differentiation and the Devaluation of Women's Work." *Gender and Society,* 1988, *2,* 58-77.

Rytina, N. F., and Bianchi, S. H. "Occupational Reclassification and Changes in Distribution by Gender." *Monthly Labor Review,* Mar. 1987, *107,* 11-17.

Strober, M., and Arnold, C. "The Dynamics of Occupational Segregation Among Bank Tellers." In *Gender and Society.* Washington, D.C.: Brookings Institution, 1987.

Toth, E. L., and Cline, C. (eds.). *Beyond the Velvet Ghetto.* San Francisco: International Association of Business Communications Foundation, 1989.

Touhey, J. C. "Effects of Additional Women Professionals on Ratings of Occupational Prestige and Desirability." *Journal of Personality and Social Psychology,* 1974, *29* (1), 85-90.

Turk, J. V. "The Changing Face of CASE." *Currents,* June 1986, *12* (6), pp. 18-20.

Warwick, M. "High Tech Fund Raising: What Does the Future Hold?" *Fund Raising Institute Monthly Portfolio,* June 1990, *29,* 1-2.

"Women in College Development Earn 20 Pct. Less Than Men." *Chronicle of Higher Education,* July 7, 1982, p. 12.

"Women's Group Blames Wage Gap on Occupational Segregation." *Daily Labor Report,* Oct. 7, 1988, p. A1.

PART FOUR

IMPROVING
FUND RAISING PRACTICE

Chapter 10

My Sixteen Rules
for a Successful Volunteer-Based
Capital Campaign

Alex Carroll

In 1971 the Indianapolis Symphony Orchestra not only lost a season due to a prolonged strike, but also, of necessity, undertook a complete reappraisal of its leadership, its status, and its goals. As part of that difficult but essential process, one of the country's oldest and best known fund-raising consulting firms was hired to conduct a feasibility study to help the ISO determine its potential support in Indianapolis, both financial and otherwise.

I'll never forget the evening the consultant's dramatic report was presented to the ISO board, of which I was a brand new member. He explained in a most sensitive way that he understood and sympathized with our very serious problems. Then he bluntly gave us his discouraging conclusions: His company would not take us as a client for a capital campaign because we just did not have sufficient support in the city to justify undertaking one at that time.

After we recovered from the initial shock, we all joined in a remarkably candid discussion under the consultant's leadership, which led to a plan of action to repair the damage and to embark on an organized program to revitalize the ISO. Since that time there has been nothing but optimism at the ISO, so that today we have one of the finest major symphonies in the country, one that is appropriately sized for our city. It is well managed and has come a long way toward that rare status of any large arts organization: financial health and stability.

Having learned from that experience and from many other capital campaigns, I have developed (under the tutelage of many different professional fund raisers) my sixteen rules. For those who find practical "rules" to be useful, I add one more conceptual thought that I consider to be fundamental. The task of organizing and the expectation of succeeding in any major fund-raising venture (especially if manned principally by volunteers) is a *process* and a discipline, every step of which is essential. To shortcut or eliminate any step is to court trouble and risk failure. It took me many years (and many failures) to learn that truth: There are no shortcuts.

My sixteen rules, in effect, lay out such a process and are as follows:

1. *Make your case exciting. Make sure your own house is in order first.*

Translation: Both contributors and solicitors prefer to support interesting, productive, and well-managed institutions. If your institution is in trouble, for whatever reasons, your prospects know it. It is far better to repair and improve the operation *first* before embarking on a capital fund drive. In fact, as in the case of the symphony, it may be difficult or impossible to mount a successful campaign unless your public image is a favorable one.

How can you be sure of that? The best way I know is to undertake a feasibility study, done by experienced professionals. Such studies provide invaluable information. Not only do they answer the fundamental question of whether it is feasible to expect to raise your goal, but they also help identify the best prospects for leaders, workers, and givers.

I finally decided, after many unfortunate experiences, that I would no longer succumb to persuasive recruiting efforts unless the organization is first and foremost an important undertaking (both to its community and to me) and, if possible, is well managed so that it will use the monies raised with good judgment. I have occasionally, as in the case of the symphony, helped an important cause change and improve its governance. But I no longer have any desire to help keep someone's favorite activity alive. Playing to preserve is a loser's game. Playing to excel is worth every effort.

2. *An organization's development director (working closely with the campaign director) must be the quarterback. His or her enthusiasm must be genuine and contagious.*

Translation: Although amateurs and volunteers can be counted on to raise meaningful dollars and to help reach challenging goals, the essential organizing both before and during any campaign requires effective and enthusiastic inside staff work. Asking volunteers to do the nitty gritty details is a waste of their time and talent and abuses the privilege of having their help.

In the real world the development director, while planning and coordinating a capital campaign, can be in a very difficult position in regard to his or her relationships with other staff. That is especially true with the organization's CEO and with the top volunteer leaders. It is important, in my opinion, that the development director be empowered to act for and to lead the way for the organization during a capital campaign. Otherwise, those who do not permit such authority are, in effect, assuming these responsibilities themselves. Unfortunately, such situations do happen (usually unwittingly) all too often.

3. *Top-level volunteer leadership is everything. BOTH a symbol of success and personal leadership are needed.*

Translation: Just as the best jockeys bring out the best efforts of their charges, so also do the owners of the best thoroughbreds pick the best riders for their steeds.

Selecting the best top volunteer leadership is probably the most important ingredient to ensure success of any capital campaign. The reputation and clout of top leaders is vital because other able volunteers, as well as potential supporters, know that such leaders not only endorse the cause but believe in achieving success in every effort in their own lives.

However, it is essential to keep in mind that the reputation of such leaders is not enough in itself. Be wary of those individuals who agree "to lend their names" to your cause. The proven leadership abilities of the best top volunteers are needed as well; absentee leadership is not acceptable.

It is important not to burden leaders with too many meetings or administrative duties, but it is essential to involve them in the most important decisions, such as goal setting, timetables, recruiting of other top leadership, selection of professional counsel, and inspirational personal messages at kick-off and other motivational meetings.

In short, the best campaign chairpersons combine both clout and personal leadership. Don't settle for less. One important sign of outstanding leadership is volunteers' early commitment to the cause by making their own pledges before asking anyone else for a commitment. I have learned that I am most effective when I voluntarily make my own pledge very quickly after accepting an assignment.

4. *Advance planning is worth the effort. Great things happen to those who plan every step of the campaign in advance.*

Translation: This is the part where the pros earn their fees many times over. No matter how much practice they may have had, no amateur capital fund raisers can hope to match the experience and training of the able and forceful professional development counselors.

I have been surprised many times by successful businessmen and women who stress planning in their own enterprises but do not apply the same dedication to capital fund campaigns. How often have you heard someone comment, "Why hire expensive professionals? We can do it ourselves. Just get the right people to ask the best prospects. Surely, we can do that."

Surely we can stumble, fumble, and fail, too—especially if we fail to realize how complicated it is to plan all the essential details and how long it takes to do the preliminary steps well.

5. *Recruit leadership in person. Don't count too much on the "back scratch" principle (who can your candidate not say "no" to?).*

Translation: When the campaign's top leader sets out to recruit campaign lieutenants, that leader enormously improves the success ratio by appearing in person, accompanied by a persuasive partner (ideally the president of the institution).

This step is too important to leave to a telephone call or

letter. It is too easy for the ideal candidates to say "no" when they are not in a face-to-face situation. Personal recruitment subconsciously improves results by building personal commitment. The top leader will help and back his or her lieutenants in every way; the lieutenants will make every effort to reach their goals.

It is especially important to avoid the temptation to recruit by asking those who "owe you one" in return for your helping them on their last project. That approach results in little or no commitment to success.

The single most successful recruiting effort I have ever experienced was when I, as chairman of the nominating committee of an important arts organization, went to call upon our very best candidate. Accompanied by the chairman of our board and the mayor of our city, I visited his office early in the morning, prior to his usual arrival time. It was almost impossible for our choice to say "no" under the circumstances, which is exactly what we had planned.

Pressure? Sure, in a way. But the choice was an ideal one and the results were all we could have hoped for. Everybody was happy, including the man recruited.

6. *Every organization has a natural constituency, so find those with a personal interest in your cause.*

Translation: There is tremendous competition for the philanthropic dollar and for effective volunteers. It is important for every organization to discover those people who are enthusiastic about its case and to involve them in a meaningful way to help raise money or otherwise provide support.

It is both naive and wasteful to spend too much time and effort on prospects who have no apparent connection with or interest in your project. In fact, it is a truism of raising financial support that the best gifts will come from those who already know and enjoy your services. Obviously, therefore, it is vital for every organization to find out who visits them often, who contributes regularly, and who is genuinely enthusiastic about their efforts. Surely from this group will come the best volunteers and financial supporters (if they are asked).

7. *Don't get the cart before the horse. Complete prospect selection, research, and evaluation in advance of solicitation.*

Translation: Perhaps the worst mistake in soliciting for large individual gifts is inadequate advance preparation. The unsophisticated believe it is just a question of finding the right person to ask the high-potential prospect. All too often such a simplistic approach leads to an easy but far too small pledge or to a quick refusal, leaving very little room for resolicitation.

The professionals have learned that it really pays to undertake extensive in-depth research (which may take weeks or even months) prior to actual solicitation. The purpose of the research is to discover the most successful solicitors and to develop information that will stimulate the potential donors to give generously. Often effective research uncovers information so helpful that it becomes the basis for requesting and justifying a much larger gift.

For example, one institution was successful in "creating" a very logical family gift. First, it uncovered the information that the original head of the institution had led it inspirationally for over three decades. Three generations of descendants were identified and persuaded to give enough to collectively memorialize the founding director by naming a new headquarters after him.

The preparation for each and every major gift prospect (individual or institutional) should be organized as a campaign in itself. No actual solicitation should be made until the best possible volunteer is armed with the most personal and persuasive arguments that extensive research has uncovered and trained to use them effectively. It is just that kind of preparation that generally makes the difference in accomplishing very challenging goals. Remember that 75 to 80 percent of the goal of the great majority of capital campaigns comes from a very small number of generous donors. Inability to attract a few large gifts all too often leads to the failure of campaigns.

8. *Set your goals high, but make sure good research justifies it. Don't confuse hope with pragmatic reality.*

Translation: Most successful capital campaigns identify *in advance* not only the specific sources of a majority of the gifts but the amounts expected and received.

In fact, part of the preparation for a capital campaign should be (1) to prepare a table of the size and number of gifts needed to succeed and (2) to identify at least three prospects for each of the large gifts that are so essential to success. Unless the staff head and the volunteer leaders can develop such lists, and unless the feasibility step can verify their realism, it is difficult, if not impossible, to establish a goal that they can reasonably expect to reach.

The worst possible way to set a campaign goal is by adding up the needs and simplistically accepting that amount as possible to achieve. That may be a first step, but unless it is verified to be realistic by careful and pragmatic research, it is both foolish and naive to go ahead based on hopes and needs alone. Hope is not a valid strategy.

All well-managed campaigns will provide the dollar amount to ask for each prospect. This rating will be set by knowledgeable people at a level appropriate with the financial capabilities of the prospect and in line with amounts being asked of others of similar means.

Many years ago when I was a team captain in a United Way campaign, a volunteer solicitor was assigned to me. His name was Bob Boone. I will never forget him because he helped me develop Carroll's three steps of effective solicitation.

Bob said to me as he left the breakfast kick-off meeting, "I'm a commission salesman. Time is money to me. I'm going to try to complete my assignments this morning." In less than two hours he was back with all three pledge cards signed, two with nice increases.

When I asked him how he did it, his answer was wonderfully simple. "All I did," he said, "was to insist on seeing the boss in person, act enthusiastic, tell him how busy he is, so why not make this important decision *right now*. Then before he could react or stall, I said, 'Last year you gave $100. The goal is up 15 percent this year; why not pledge $125 and be a hero? Sign here, please!' "

So now, thanks to Bob Boone, my advice to all solicitors is (1) Go *now*, (2) go *in person*, and (3) ask for a *specific amount*. It works!

9. *Meetings are important—or are they? Professional consultants like meetings better than workers do. Subrule: Keep them few, short, fun, and organized.*

Translation: The pros consider meetings to be the principal opportunities to inform and inspire workers. But the top volunteers (that is, the busiest people) consider them necessary evils at best.

The pros use progress meetings as deadlines to try to stimulate workers to make their contacts early, but volunteers tend to show up only when they have positive results to report. Many pros feel personally successful at meetings because they are in action "doing their thing," but volunteers feel pressured by too many meetings.

What is the answer? Plan as few meetings as possible. Keep them short (under an hour is best), and try to make them fun. I especially remember a campaign where four very amateur slapstick comics pretended to be erecting a scaffold. They were so corny and so hilarious that meeting attendance was extraordinary. So was the campaign's progress. As unimportant as it may seem, anything to make meetings different is worth the extra effort. It is also very important to start and finish all meetings on schedule. Attendance will be better if you do.

10. *Make it sound simple and easy for the workers, but then expect a lot from them.*

Translation: The ultimate accomplishment in any capital fund drive is to have each worker say to himself or herself, in effect, "This is a good campaign. I'm enthusiastic about the cause. I like the leaders. It is well organized. I know exactly what is expected of me. I accept the time schedule. The amounts I'm expected to ask for are appropriate. I'm going to do my very best to accomplish my assignments and on time."

After many experiences trying to create that kind of atmosphere, I have learned to be very direct and to say, "Your responsibility as a key solicitor in this campaign is *not* just to make your calls on time and to try to be persuasive; you should also accept the challenge of successfully completing the job by meeting the specific goals set for your prospects."

11. *Teach effective solicitation. Oversimplifying is better than overwhelming.* (It is worth repeating the three basic steps of effective solicitation: Go *in person,* go *now,* and ask for a *specific amount.*)

Translation: Most people have heard the tongue-in-cheek sales adage KISS: Keep it simple, stupid. Believe that, because it is very sound advice. Solicitation only becomes difficult when we try to improvise, to oversell, to talk incessantly about the cause and its importance.

A simple script like this when said face to face with your prospect will fit virtually all causes. "Good morning, Mr. Jones. I'm Alex Carroll, a volunteer for the _____ capital campaign. It's a cause that I believe in strongly. I'll be delighted to answer any questions you may have about the organization and the campaign. My job is to ask you to please consider a gift or pledge of $100,000."

At that moment the best advice for any salesperson is to *stop talking*. Answer questions, sure. Provide information, sure. But do not talk yourself out of a decision.

12. *Carroll's unproven truism: The best results come from the calls made earliest and vice versa.*

Translation: The moment of maximum enthusiasm in any campaign comes at the end of an effective kick-off meeting. Calls made immediately thereafter are bound to be the most effective. The longer a solicitor delays doing an assignment, the lower the effectiveness level. Postponement until the last days of a campaign inevitably means lower enthusiasm and poorer results, sometimes even no solicitation at all.

One of the most effective campaigns I ever worked on included a unique system to maximize early contacts with prospects. As the twenty-five solicitors left a breakfast kick-off meeting, they were met by twenty-five taxis (contributed by the owner). Each solicitor was driven to the door of his or her corporate prospect, who had been advised in advance that a gift was to be hand delivered that morning. Result: over 80 percent of the first solicitation calls were made and completed that very morning. The campaign exceeded its goal by over 50 percent!

13. *Progress reports stimulate. Don't forget to keep score. Let your workers know often what they have accomplished and even more important, what is left to do.*

Translation: Once a week is ideal for campaign workers to get a progress report on their division's and their own accomplishments to date. Nobody wants to look bad among his or her peers. Publicity is the best way to prevent lagging. Reports remind all workers that their job is not over until all calls have been made and all results are returned.

All too many campaigns start with a bang but end with a

whimper as workers are not involved enough or prodded often en
route.

14. *Everybody admires Boy Scouts and Girl Scouts. "Difficult cards" are opportunities for heroism.*

Translation: Every campaign has some major potential prospects that are considered to be very unlikely supporters and are
therefore "difficult cards." Rather than write them off as not worth
the effort, why not look upon them as especially promising, because
any gift from them would be pure gravy and symbolically very
exciting.

I learned this rule first hand from an early experience when
a chief executive refused to see me about a United Way corporate
pledge. An eager young volunteer, I decided not to give up easily,
so I appeared at his receptionist's desk every morning about 7:30 for
a week. After five days of that treatment, he finally came out, swore
at me, and said he was going to report me to headquarters for
harassment. Fortunately, when he did, the campaign chairman—
who happened to be his banker—called him, bawled him out, and
praised me for my perseverance. Result: the first corporate gift in
history from that company.

15. *Design your campaign and its meetings to have fun, because raising money, almost by definition, is not!*

Translation: Somehow, in every community, a few individuals are identified as "enjoying raising money." As a result, those
few are turned to time and again. Not only do they become worn
out with the burden but, as a result, a lot of very important and
worthy causes are underserved too.

The truth is that nobody, but nobody, likes to ask for contributions. It is important that leaders understand that.

A further truth is that those few who *seem* to enjoy it have
learned that properly organized capital campaigns can actually *be*
enjoyable (especially when they exceed their goals) and indeed *must*
include as much fun as possible in order to increase the potential
for success.

- It is fun to put together a cadre of leaders who work well together and who share high sights.

- It is fun to organize so well that nobody's assignment is burdensome.
- It is fun to create an atmosphere of optimism and success.
- It is fun to work to raise money for an organization that is widely, even universally, regarded as important and well managed.
- It is fun to share your own conviction and commitment with others capable of important support.

Unfortunately, not enough leaders who might otherwise be motivated have been exposed to campaigns that are fun precisely because they are well organized and well led. Success in any endeavor is fun, and capital campaigns need be no exception.

16. *Show appreciation. "You can accomplish miracles if you don't care who gets the credit."*

Translation: That last sentence is quoted from a book by the famous football coach and owner Paul Brown. I have practiced it because *it works*. It is wonderful how people respond to "thank you." We all want to be appreciated. We all appreciate being on the receiving end of thoughtful, personal, and individualized messages of thanks. Every capital campaign should have someone in charge of thanking contributors, ideally, with messages that are immediate and personalized.

I'll never forget the reaction of Bob Boone, referred to earlier, when I made a major case of his "do it now" United Way success. How he reacted to my appreciation taught me an invaluable lesson: A sincere thank you is flattery in the finest sense.

So think about this rule! It may be the ultimate ingredient of a good campaign, a secret of success, a way to accomplish miracles, when we are wise enough to put aside our own egos and heap our praise on others.

In that spirit, and with tongue only slightly in cheek, let me thank those who chose my chapter to try to help motivate more people to take fund raising seriously.

Chapter 11

Can We Throw Away
the Tin Cup?

Kay Sprinkel Grace

A striking trend in fund raising in the past decade is the perceptible shift away from a "begging" attitude. Increasingly, organizations are developing a sense of pride in their accomplishments and are emphasizing the community needs they are meeting. They are stressing the opportunities their programs provide for funders to help solve critical human and social needs. The organization positions public relations outreach and fund-raising materials to emphasize its ability to address community and global issues. Funding requirements are discussed not in terms of institutional objectives alone but in terms of progress toward solving community problems or meeting societal needs.

This attitudinal evolution has enabled many organizations to "throw away the tin cup" and approach fund raising as an opportunity for community investment in organizations that are capably serving recognized human and societal needs. The trend has sparked some new perceptions of the not-for-profit sector that have encouraging long-term promise.

Fund Raising as an Exchange Process

Fund raising is a dignified process, based on marketing principles and an exchange of values. In this voluntary exchange, the contributor offers a value to the organization without any expectation of a material return, apart from the tax deductibility authorized by the government. The nonmaterial reasons for making the gift are numerous: belonging, recognition, satisfaction in supporting a worthy cause, making a difference in the community, and a sense of ownership in a program dedicated to serving the public good. As such, fund raising is about relationships more than it is about money.

When the tin cup is used, this exchange process is damaged. The tin cup connotes begging, weakness, and an inability to support oneself. Its association with the not-for-profit sector still resides in the minds of many, including those within the sector who do not understand the joy of asking and giving. A tin cup approach thus diminishes the dignity of the exchange process and demeans the organization by conveying a sense of apology for asking.

In spite of an increasing application of the exchange principle in not-for-profit positioning, the tin cup lingers as a symbol and a "tool" of fund raising. As a *symbol* in the public mind, it reflects a historic bias that categorizes not-for-profit organizations as "needy." This belief is a misplacement of the concept of "need." The tin cup as a *tool* is still utilized by many nonprofit organizations and ultimately cripples their ability to build long-term relationships that can lead to financial stability and community recognition.

Because the needs emphasized in fund raising should be those of the community it is serving and not those of the organization, donor education and relationship building is required. Constituents must travel the distance from awareness, to understanding, to involvement, and, finally, to commitment, if they are to become stakeholders in community organizations. This maturation of the prospect- or donor-institution relationship depends on the organization's ability to recognize and encourage the linkages, ability, and interest of its donors and to present funding opportunities that are based on an exchange of values. This process requires diligence on the part of a not-for-profit organization and is one that may not be immediately rewarding financially.

The Impact of the Tin Cup. When the urgent is permitted to overpower the important, expediency is the result. Tin cup fund raising is usually based in crisis, when organizations resort to various appeals for raising money quickly. The need shifts away from the community and back to the organization. This misplacement of the concept of need has far-reaching effects within and outside the sector. Volunteers are reluctant to fund raise because they feel as though they are "begging" for money to cover the institution's financial problem. There is a sense of apology because asking is focused not on strength but on need. Staff members are also drawn into this attitude. They apologize not only for asking for money but for asking for help from volunteers in raising the money. And the public, to whom the volunteers and staff members turn, are conditioned to focus on the needs of the organization, rather than the needs of the community. Their gauge for giving is based not on an understanding of the programmatic impact of their gift but on the desperate need for funds. Where this is the emphasis, the potential for the size and number of gifts is diminished.

The legacy of the tin cup affects community attitudes not only toward fund raising but toward institutional operations as well. The public perceives that not-for-profit organizations, because they are needy (otherwise, why would they ask for money?), do not require certain basics to function effectively and maintain morale: decent office space, adequate salaries and benefits, professional-appearing publications. These trappings of prosperity seem, in the public mind, to negate the need for funds. If an organization is asking for money within the community, then it must look as though it needs it. This attitude toward needy organizations is reinforced by the heritage of America's work ethic/bootstraps culture in which organizations and individuals are expected to be self-sufficient. An accommodation of the needs of certain individuals—particularly the ill, elderly, children, or homeless—has occurred somewhat in this century, but the tough attitude toward organizations prevails: Survive on your own or go under. The issue is broad. The whole concept of not-for-profit, tax-exempt organizations is still distressing for some individuals who fail to understand the role of the sector in providing programs and services in communities.

Changing Attitudes About Fund Raising

To move American thought away from this confusion about the true basis of needs in fund raising and into an understanding of the role of the not-for-profit sector and its basis in meeting human and societal needs will require that many not-for-profits change their approach to fund raising. The residual ring of the tin cup is magnified and public attitudes are reinforced when organizations, out of ignorance or desperation, continue to emphasize their own, rather than the community needs they are meeting, as the rationale for community fund raising. Until the public can accept the dignity of this new concept of a fund-raising process, we will be unable to throw away the tin cup.

Thoughtful fund raising is based on relationships. Tin cup donors give impulsively. They respond and then walk on; it is unlikely they will circle back and put more money in the same cup. In the long term, this approach to fund raising fails, but in spite of this, organizations continue it. The reasons lie in the public's acceptance that this is a valid way to raise funds.

The tin cup mentality is encouraged by the media. *Newsweek*, in a September 5, 1988, article on prospect research entitled "Prospecting for Alumni Gold," added the subtitle, "America's Colleges Go Begging in High Style." The article explores the intensive efforts of prospect researchers at colleges and universities to find individuals of wealth to whom they can present institutional needs. The writer observes, "American universities have always been supplicants—ever since the Massachusetts Bay Colony sent three clergymen to England on a begging mission to secure an endowment for Harvard College in 1641." The article subtly positions fund raising as not only begging but *manipulative* begging (Harrison, Hutchison, and Leslie, 1988, pp. 66–67).

Another disturbing article was published in the March 6, 1990, issue of the *Chronicle of Philanthropy:* "What's the Difference Between a Beggar and a Fund Raiser?" The article, by Leslie Lenkowsky, summarized a recent court decision in New York state—

which was later reversed on appeal—in which a federal judge, Leonard B. Sand, ruled that begging was entitled to the same legal protection as fund raising. In the first portion of his decision, Judge Sand established that begging was not illegal under New York law and followed with a further ruling that begging was actually a form of raising money for charity. Judge Sand was quoted in the *Chronicle of Philanthropy:* "Both solicitors for organized charities and beggars approach passersby, request a donation, and perhaps explain why they want the money." He continued, "Distinguishing between charitable and noncharitable solicitations on the basis of the intent of the solicitor would lead to the anomalous situation where one homeless person could not solicit for himself, but two homeless people could solicit donations for each other." In commenting on the decision, Lenkowsky said, "In Judge Sand's world, the defining characteristics of a charity are not what it does and what it deserves, but what it needs and what it raises" (Lenkowsky, 1990, pp. 31-32).

Behind this decision is a concern about panhandling, particularly in cities like New York. But there is an obvious and deeper concern as well. How will "charities" be defined? Once before, such a case went to the United States Supreme Court. At that time, Chief Justice Rehnquist (*Village of Schaumberg* v. *Citizens for a Better Environment,* 1980) stated that there are differences between beggars and fund raisers. Had this case gone to the Supreme Court, Lenkowsky predicted, "with Judge Sand's decision (possibly) headed his way, the Chief Justice may soon get another chance to persuade his brethren that this view is correct, and that if beggars may often act like aggressive fund raisers, there is at least some difference between them" (Lenkowsky, 1990, pp. 31-32).

We cannot miss the irony in Lenkowsky's conclusion. Too often the public still thinks of fund raisers as aggressive beggars, in spite of increasing professionalism in fund raising and growing sophistication among askers and donors. If fund raising is to be taken seriously, this issue must be dealt with.

When people respond to appeals that are not translated into meeting community needs, they condone the beggar mentality. As long as the tin cup is filled, organizations will not throw it away. If public attitudes continue to be shaped by legal decisions that define fund raising and begging as related practices, what position should professionals and volunteers take?

Breaking the Begging Syndrome. The exchange principle requires organizations to express their missions in ways that invite funders to participate in programs that extend the donors' values and preserve their interests, while meeting their needs for recognition, belonging, and a feeling of making a difference. This kind of fund raising is conducted without a tin cup, and removes the beggar syndrome from the process. Institutional *needs* are presented as *opportunities* for donors to invest in programs that are solving community problems effectively, deploying human and financial resources in a way that leverages each gift.

Mission statements that answer the question "why" position the organization as it relates to the community need it is meeting. Such statements describe a globally understood condition and lead into a discussion of the ways in which those needs are being met. A mission statement that tells "why," followed by a purpose statement that tells "what" the organization is doing, establishes an image of strength and responsibility in the mind of the prospective donor. This strength does not negate the need for funds: It says, instead, that the organization is a good place for those who share common values and concerns to invest their charitable funds. It is a strength based on a relationship over time with the donor, one in which these values and concerns are shared, discussed, and accomplished.

The Trust for Hidden Villa, an educational organization in the San Francisco Bay Area, recently recast its materials to remove the last traces of the tin cup. This is from their Spring 1990 newsletter: "Our Mission Statement is as follows: We are challenged as never before in our history to reverse the environmental destruction and social injustices that are eroding our stability as a planet and a people. If we are to succeed, our actions must be directed by a profound appreciation of the interdependence of all living things and a bold commitment to support the dignity and diversity of all individuals. The Trust for Hidden Villa is meeting these challenges by engaging children and adults in hands-on, innovative programs promoting environmental awareness and humanitarian values. A 1,600 acre wilderness preserve with a teaching center and working farm, Hidden Villa demonstrates stewardship of the land, fosters cooperation between groups, and offers the community an incomparable natural, educational, historic and recreational resource."

Another powerful, but shorter, example was created by the Yale University School of Medicine for its capital campaign of a decade ago. "We are in the midst of one of the most profound intellectual revolutions of all time, the revolution in the biological sciences. Its implications for understanding life processes and combating disease are boundless. . . . Yale is in the forefront of this revolution" (Yale University, 1985).

This one was written during a basic course of the Fund Raising School by the executive director of a health care agency:

"Hands are a powerful expression of the human soul. We talk with them. We play with them. We work with them. We comfort and love with them. A serious disability to the hand affects every aspect of a person's life. Vector's Hand Center gives people back the use of their hands" (Vector Health Programs, Inc., Eureka, California). When the mission of an organization is expressed in an involving statement of a globally perceived need, the stage is set for the exchange process to begin. The asker is relieved of embarrassment and apology. The donor is more inclined to respond positively because of understanding the benefits to the community of making a gift and a willingness to be drawn into a relationship with the organization based on a sense of mutual accomplishment.

Organizations with this approach are consistently more successful and can throw away the tin cup.

Or can they?

When to Use the Tin Cup. In the prospect- or donor-institution relationship, there appears to be a delicate balance between confidence in the strength of the organization and a need to feel that the investment is truly needed—not just by the individuals being served but by the organization itself. Too much organizational success may put prospects off; too little success will discourage investment (people will not "put deck chairs on the Titanic"). In a highly competitive marketplace in which many worthy organizations are vying for the charitable dollar, will the donor still respond to the need of the

organization more readily than to the concept of exchange and investment based on the need of the community? The first kind of
giving is impulsive, the second thoughtful. The first can be done
quickly; the second takes time. The first is often based on perceived
crisis; the second is based on an understanding of long-term institutional plans and a shared commitment to certain community
needs.

Public television stations often resort to a tin cup style of
fund raising, appearing with banks of volunteers, guest commentators, an array of donor "perks," and ardent pleas to respond during the pledge break "to keep us on the air." During these
campaigns, the focus is on the station's finances and needs: The
benefit to the donor is not described in terms of meeting long-term
community needs but of providing the donor with a book or mug
or canvas tote bag in exchange for a modest gift. When a tangible
return of some value is offered, the values exchange is affected. The
meaning of the gift may thus be different from one that is based on
a commitment to the organization's mission statement. A quid pro
quo is evident, and the exchange is material, not values-based. In
the excitement and frenzy of pledge nights, the tin cup sounds.

Environmental organizations may be justified in resorting to
"last chance" messages as we confront increasing challenges to the
stability of our planet. However, balance is paramount here as well.
It is not necessarily a tin cup approach to talk about the fragile
health of Mother Earth, unless the focus is on the needs of the
organization rather than on the needs it is meeting. The institutional rationale may be this: to encourage people to become
thoughtful stewards of the environment will require education; education requires funding; and initial funding can be derived from
the impulsive gifts of those who share their immediate concerns. As
the numbers of environmentally aware people increase, we can almost certainly predict that they will be responsive to the critical
environmental needs: What we cannot ensure are gifts beyond that
first impulsive response. For that, a relationship based on shared
values must be developed. The organization itself is the means, not
the end.

If organizations occasionally forget that their mission should
be community focused, answering the question "why"—rather than

organizationally focused and answering the question "what"—a simple lesson from a corporate training program can be applied. Sales trainees at Black and Decker are reportedly asked, "Why do people buy Black and Decker drills?" The answer, invariably, is, "Because they need a drill." The correct answer is, "Because they need a hole." The values exchange emphasizes the hole; tin cup fund raising focuses on the drill.

Under what circumstances, then, do organizations find themselves resorting to the tin cup if fund raising based on values exchange and relationships has greater long-term results? Organizations that utilize the tin cup represent the full spectrum of the not-for-profit sector and include (1) those that never threw it away in the first place and (2) those that have implemented relationship-based fund raising but find themselves in a financial or community crisis that requires immediate response from a constituency beyond their stakeholders.

Organizations that routinely use tin cup fund raising are diminishing in number. Education about the benefits of the principles of the values exchange has eroded their dependence on the institution-focused methods of raising money. Training of professional and support staff in the dignity of the exchange process and the accomplishments of the organization, and orientation of board members and other volunteers to the joy of asking and giving, are on the increase. There are still pockets of the sector that position their needs statements on the institution, and these organizations must be coached in new marketing approaches if we are ever to change the public's perception of the entire sector.

The subtle use of the tin cup by institutions that usually base their fund raising on the exchange principle and relationship-building is based on a belief—and a hope—that people want to help out in times of trouble. As such, it taps into the historic and commendable response of our American society in times of need. It is the basis for the disaster fund raising carried out by the American Red Cross and the Salvation Army, and of recent outpouring of funds for institutions that serve those who suffer from AIDS and those who are homeless. In this kind of fund raising, the emphasis shifts to the needs of the institution, which have been intensified because of a crisis or unforeseen situation. Those who respond to these appeals may have no previous relationship with the organization and may have no further relationship until the next crisis or disaster. Unlike fund raising that is based on problems internal to the organization (meeting a budget deficit, making payroll), these appeals are based on widely understood crises, for which public sympathy is usually high. However, the giving is still impulsive and not likely to be repeated over a long period of time.

The Tin Cup Combines with the Exchange Process. Sometimes situations arise within strong institutions that require them to resort to appeals that may border on the tin cup approach. These special appeals, often for very large sums of money, are not extended just to those with which the organization has an existing relationship. Instead, they are based on the hope or belief that someone receiving the appeal may make an impulsive gift *to help resolve that particular situation.* Such gifts are not based on the long-term mission of the organization but on an immediate need that has emerged. These appeals are institution- rather than community-focused, and thus they transgress the boundaries of more traditional values exchange-based outreach.

Stanford University has been, for the past several years, the most successful among all major universities in raising funds. Its materials are inspiring, and its volunteers and staff are dedicated, well trained, committed, and hold no tin cup when fund raising. Its $1.1 billion centennial campaign (1987–1992) is built around the notion of "investment" and the theme of Stanford's role in shaping the twenty-first century. The focus in materials and outreach is on the global needs Stanford is meeting through its education of talented men and women. More than 2,500 volunteers are involved in fund raising, bearing witness to a belief in the importance of relationships.

Stanford's marketing approach was summarized in one particularly inspiring piece. The simple fold-over card showed a nova and a scattering of stars against a black sky, with the phrase: "In a world in which it seems our actions have little impact, there are some things that we can do that touch the future." On the inside, the nova has been transformed into a thumb print against the black sky and the text says, "Giving to Stanford is one of them."

In the campaign case materials, the essence of the campaign philosophy is carried in an open letter, entitled "Leading the Way," from Donald Kennedy, president of Stanford. In it, he speaks not of Stanford's needs but of the needs of the world that Stanford-educated men and women will be capable of meeting, citing the parallels between this era and others that have demanded special leadership, skills, and talents.

But even for Stanford sometimes, the tin cup looms, not in the attitudes of its professional staff or volunteers but in the expressed perceptions of its constituents. At the very outset of the campaign in 1987, Donald Kennedy gave a speech that was published and distributed to volunteers: "How Come We Look So Rich and Feel So Poor?" This speech was developed to respond to those who could not understand why Stanford needed to undertake this campaign. It was developed to help volunteers and others be more adept at explaining the global needs Stanford meets to those who would interpret fund raising as meeting institutional needs alone.

Only occasionally has Stanford had to turn to institutional needs-based fund raising. And then, it has done so creatively and effectively. One of the centennial campaign components is funding for a new area of the campus that will house science and engineering teaching and research, an area in which Stanford has been a pioneer. The case for support of this component was presented in campaign materials as follows:

> A significant amount of the basic scientific research on which American technology depends is done at Stanford, and a great many of our future scientists and engineers are trained here—in the same laboratories, in the course of performing that research. The University also collaborates with industry to an extraordinary degree on the next step—translating research findings into products and processes—in (various) campus programs. Stanford developed these capabilities following World War II by daring to undertake new ventures and create new alliances among disciplines. . . . The spirit of adventure is still strong here, but for the past fifteen years there has been virtually

no federal funding for new science facilities. That drought, coupled with dramatic increases in the sophistication and cost of scientific equipment, threatens to disrupt the cycle of innovation in American technology, not just at Stanford but at all research universities" [Stanford Mailor, 1989].

This excellent "why" statement formed the strong community-based rationale for support of this project. And yet, this objective has lagged behind in its goal. In a move unusual for Stanford, it "went public" with this problem.

In an article published in *Business Week*, December 4, 1989, entitled "Can Stanford Build Labs for the New Millennium?", the subtitle was extremely candid: "It's having trouble raising cash for a massive new research campus." The story summarized the difficulty, even though the building project addresses a critical *university* need (shared, according to the article, by universities across America): Their laboratories are rapidly aging. Without such facilities, it will be impossible to continue with leading-edge research. However, against a goal of $350 million, the article reported that just $78 million had been committed, $40 million of which came from a single donor, William R. Hewlett. If the project were on track, $120 million should have been raised by December 1989.

The article was clearly an appeal for awareness, understanding, and response. The article explained the research needs of universities and why such buildings are essential, but it was intended to appeal to those who respond to *Stanford's* need. The bulk of the final funding will come from those who are closest to the university, who have a relationship and share its vision for the future.

A second recent appeal from Stanford also creatively utilizes the tin cup. A booklet was prepared, printed in black and white with splashes of yellow (with a bright yellow remit envelope), that summarized the devastation Stanford suffered in the enormously destructive October 1989 Loma Prieta earthquake. Although no lives were lost, the damage to property amounted to $160 million. A new centennial campaign objective, earthquake recovery, was added. This piece, with its "safety yellow" highlights, gets right to the core of disaster-related appeals: "Stanford and its students and

faculty *urgently* need your help." Highly focused on the effects of
the earthquake on historic Stanford buildings, residences, and
classrooms, it is interspersed with messages highlighted in yellow,
such as, "October 17, 1993—because of Federal requirements there's
no time to waste. To qualify for FEMA (Federal Emergency Management Agency) funds for eligible buildings, Stanford must complete all repairs and submit invoices to Washington by October 17,
1993—just four years after the earthquake." Questions are asked,
"Will we save our historic buildings?" Pictures of the devastation
enhance the message, and entries from journals of students who
wrote about the earthquake alternate with quotations from survi-
vors of the 1906 earthquake.

It is not a handsome piece, but it gets the reader's attention.
What it lacks in subtlety, it makes up for in clarity. It is a call to
action, a shotgun approach that Stanford feels may just work. It has
raised money (including a $10,000 gift) from individuals who have
never given before. It has heightened alumni awareness of this particular challenge. At the same time, the earthquake recovery objective is also being presented in more traditional one-on-one requests
for funds. The combination of the two approaches is tailored to the
particular prospects being targeted: Those who respond to the emergency appeal will be encouraged into a relationship with the institution, perhaps because of its history.

Although there was some heartening and surprising response
to these two urgent and unusual appeals, the earthquake recovery
and Near West Campus objectives still lagged as Stanford entered
into the homestretch of the campaign. Its strategies for closing the
gaps have played down the tin cup. Instead, volunteers and staff are
returning to some initial investors for an additional commitment
and revisiting many whose solicitations are still pending and with
whom a relationship has been built. New donors are becoming involved—many as volunteers—in the true mission of the university.

Meanwhile, another issue emerged at Stanford, which many
speculated would have a serious impact on the success of the campaign. In late 1990 and early 1991, a government audit was conducted at Stanford to review indirect cost accounting for research
grants. Potential problems with the cost reimbursements were revealed, and Stanford received national publicity on the investiga-

tion. The issue is being resolved, but it is certain to have long-term effects on university policy and procedures. However, its effect on fund raising was surprisingly small. While there were questions and criticism from some alumni and friends, Stanford's posture and response were firm—particularly since the press coverage was initiated before the final government auditor's report had been made. What has become apparent is that those who have an investor relationship with the university are concerned about this issue but realize that it deals with the "what" of Stanford, not the "why": It is related to the *drill*, not the *hole*. The exchange relationship remains strong with those who understand and value Stanford's capacity to affect the future. New donors, however, who have no previous relationship with Stanford, may be wary of investing at this time. Urgent tin cup appeals could well fall on deaf ears until the audit situation is resolved.

Can We Throw Away the Tin Cup?

Thus we ask ourselves the question, "Can we throw away the tin cup?" There are several answers.

First, until donors are educated about the nonprofit sector—the way it operates, its needs, its position, and its potential—there will be an expectation of tin cup fund raising. Public television station KQED in San Francisco was the subject of a series of articles in the *San Francisco Chronicle* (Armstrong, 1990). Although enormously successful, KQED has come under fire because of its new building and other signs of success. Responding to the criticism, KQED president and chief executive officer for the past twelve years, Anthony S. Tiano, acknowledged that the station is more business minded now, but says that is both a necessity and a virtue. "Critics have the luxury of not having to meet a payroll," Tiano told the *Chronicle*. "Nobody seems to like a successful nonprofit. When you become successful, there is a loss of that lean and hungry look, and maybe that lean and hungry feeling."

To replace the notion of "needy" organizations with the idea of organizations that are meeting community needs will require diligence and patience on the part of those who are shaping our sector for the future. It will also require an increased sense of partnership with the media, with legislators, and with the court system, to help them become advocates for a basic truth: Fund raising is not begging.

A second consideration has to do with the education of those agencies and institutions that are habitual users of the tin cup. For them, counsel and training in the joys of giving and asking based on an exchange of values must continue and increase. Fund raising must be seen as relationship-building and as an opportunity for individuals and other funders to *invest* in the perpetuation of the values they treasure and the solutions they seek. Until then, we will not break the cycle of perceptions held by the public, the media, and other constituencies.

The third and final conclusion is that there *are* times when it is appropriate to use the tin cup. The lag in donor understanding of more sophisticated approaches, combined with compelling needs that arise within institutions, permit us to use the tin cup for situations where other approaches have not worked or there is no time to develop the relationship we might need.

If the tin cup is not thrown away immediately, organizations should at least keep it on the shelf for real emergencies. Until those times, they should focus on relationship-building, donor and community needs, and true investment and exchange.

References

Armstrong, D. "Evolution of a Multimedia Empire." *San Francisco Chronicle,* Sept. 1990.

Buderi, R. "Can Stanford Build Labs for the New Millennium?" *Business Week,* Dec. 4, 1989, pp. 115–116.

Harrison, J. N., Hutchison, S., Leslie, C., and others. "Prospecting for Alumni Gold: America's Colleges Go Begging in High Style." *Newsweek,* Sept. 5, 1988, pp. 66–67.

Lenkowsky, L. "What's the Difference Between a Beggar and a Fund Raiser?" *Chronicle of Philanthropy,* Mar. 6, 1990, pp. 31–32.

Stanford Mailer. Produced by Mark Williams. Stanford, Calif.:
   Stanford Development Publication, Jan. 1989.
Trust for Hidden Villa. *Newsletter.* Los Altos Hills, Calif.: Trust for
   Hidden Villa, 1990.
Yale University. School of Medicine Brochure. New Haven, Conn.:
   University Publications Department, 1985.

Chapter 12

What Fund Raisers
Should Know About the Law

Betsy Hills Bush

The current harsh regulatory climate of fund raising at the state level makes it imperative that fund-raising managers actively improve their knowledge of and information sources on regulation and legislation. At a time when state laws are undergoing fundamental change, fund-raising managers must play a role in developing fair legislation, but they must have the information necessary to offer advice and assistance to state regulators and legislators.

First, fund-raising managers need to be familiar with basic principles governing fund raising, as well as the forces currently shaping legislation. I hope, in this chapter, to spark discussion of these principles and encourage fund-raising managers to become involved in state discussions of fund-raising regulation. They must also persuade their trustees and chief executive officers of the importance of becoming involved in these issues.

Two factors are pulling new state laws and proposed legislation in opposite directions. On one side is the Supreme Court's *Riley* decision, demanding that states abandon decades-old provisions as infringements of free speech rights.

The other factor, however, is all too familiar to fund-raising managers who have worked hard to dispel the air of disrepute that still hangs over the profession: the rash of sweepstakes fund-raising efforts by a few fund raisers and nonprofits that has garnered so much media attention. These methods, while remaining just within legal limits, are regarded as misleading or as poor practice by conscientious fund-raising professionals. The number of fund raisers utilizing these methods is very small, but state officials tend to view the problem in larger terms, one in which fund raisers and nonprofits place their constitutional rights before the public's best interest. Negative media attention on these practices hurts the nonprofit sector as a whole and puts pressure on state officials to respond to constituent complaints.

Unfortunately, much of the regulatory debate is taking place in a vacuum, with a primary group—fund-raising managers and other nonprofit executives and trustees—largely absent. Most are unaware of the changing climate affecting fund-raising laws in their state and in the states in which their organizations solicit. Often it is difficult for nonprofit executives to make informed comments about legislation being considered, as information on the bills is sparse or nonexistent. And many fund-raising managers, for example, may not feel competent or comfortable commenting on bills, because it is not a subject widely addressed among fund raisers themselves. Consider the following (the views expressed here are based on the author's experience and do not necessarily represent formal American Association of Fund-Raising Counsel policy, which is still in formulation on this subject):

- There are no questions on fund-raising regulation on the Certified Fund Raising Executive examination, administered by the National Society of Fund Raising Executives (NSFRE).
- There are few articles on regulation in the fund-raising trade press, such as *NSFRE Journal* and *Fund Raising Management,* which are important educational vehicles for individuals new to the field. Attorney Bruce Hopkins's column on regulation in *Fund Raising Management* is an exception, although he tends to discuss federal and IRS initiatives more than state legislation.
- Fund-raising courses, such as those given in adult education

programs, rarely include as a topic laws that govern nonprofit
organizations and fund raising.

- Regulation has never been a topic for monthly luncheon sessions at the New York chapter of NSFRE, the largest chapter in
  the country.

This resistance or indifference toward acquiring (and making
available) basic knowledge of fund-raising regulation is supported
by the "pep talk" atmosphere of many fund-raising gatherings.
Many conference planners are concerned primarily with topics and
speakers that will draw an audience. There appears to be very little
consideration of what fund-raising executives "should" know versus
what they want to hear. Regulation was dropped as a topic for Fund
Raising Day in New York, the largest one-day conference of fund
raisers in the country, when the session attracted only thirty to forty
people out of 1,700 attendees.

There are good reasons why fund-raising managers should
know more about the laws governing their activities and should be
able to comment knowledgeably about the principles regulating
fund raising:

- In a precedent-setting case in February 1990, a New York State
  Supreme Court ruling ordered a charity to return $58,000 it had
  received in donations from state residents before its registration
  with the state was complete.
- As laws are being redrafted, in response to both the *Riley* decision and the spate of allegedly fraudulent fund-raising appeals,
  state officials are looking for guidance from practitioners with
  established, blue chip charities. Yet, in at least one case, fund-
  raising executives are so eager to be seen endorsing tough legislation designed to "crack down" on charity fraud that they
  rubber-stamp bills that could be detrimental to most nonprofits.
  A set of regulatory principles that puts forth fair and reasonable
  provisions is not available to these executives, nor are such principles discussed.
- Tougher penalties and more complex regulatory schemes may
  mean that laws governing fund raising are no longer "intuitive." Registration, filing, and disclosure requirements may

mean changes in fund-raising practices, and certainly they will increase the costs of those practices.

• As fund-raising managers move into executive positions, knowledge of the law is essential to brief boards and to set proper policies and operating procedures, not to mention avoiding embarrassing gaffes and bad publicity. A worst-case scenario could include fines, audits, and organizational oversight by regulators. It is a field that can no longer be left to staff accountants and attorneys.

But the lack of genuine participation of fund raisers in the regulatory debate may have other negative consequences. Those few groups that have been active in monitoring regulation have long maintained that the most effective form of regulation of the industry is in fact self-regulation—which is in the best interests of all nonprofits. However, if fund-raising managers remain ignorant of regulatory principles of charitable solicitation law and indifferent to legislative developments, two situations may occur: State officials are less likely to believe that self-regulation of the fund-raising field is a realistic alternative to increased state regulation, and they may feel that fund raisers do not have a place in the regulatory debate at all.

A brief overview of the recent history of state regulation of charitable solicitation will describe how both the Supreme Court decisions in cases involving fund raising and accusations of widespread charity fraud are pulling legislation (and state regulators) in different directions. Recent examples of legislation introduced (and sometimes enacted) will show how fund raisers can and should play an advisory role in shaping new laws and working with state legislators. Last, in hope of prompting further discussion among fundraising professionals, a list of regulatory principles will attempt to define the requirements that are reasonable for states to demand, the obligations nonprofits and fund raisers have toward the public, and the types of provisions that can be considered unreasonable and burdensome to nonprofits.

Riley and the Current Regulatory Mood

A series of recent Supreme Court decisions, culminating in the *Riley* decision in June 1988, has established the free speech rights of

nonprofit organizations in their fund-raising appeals. The North
Carolina Federation of the Blind challenged the constitutionality of
North Carolina's charitable solicitation law (and won) on three
basic points:

1. Limits were placed on excessive or unreasonable fund raisers'
    fees. The Court cited earlier decisions, *Schaumburg* and *Mun-
    son,* which ruled that limitations on the percentage of fund
    raisers' fees are not sufficiently narrowly tailored to the states'
    interest in preventing fraud. The Court noted several scenarios
    in which charities may well have fund-raising costs above the
    "reasonable" limits.
2. Point-of-solicitation disclosures of fund-raising costs were held
    by the court to violate free speech rights of charities. The ma-
    jority found the mandated disclosure unduly burdensome, as it
    would "almost certainly hamper the charities they represent"
    (Harris, Holley, and McCaffrey, 1989, p. 45).
3. Licensing procedures that included an unlimited delay in
    granting licenses to solicit were ruled unconstitutional because
    such a delay "compels the speaker's silence" (Harris, Holley,
    and McCaffrey, 1989, p. 47).

The Federation of the Blind was supported in its court case
by many of the nation's most prestigious nonprofits, represented by
INDEPENDENT SECTOR (IS). IS presented an amicus brief, with
the signatures of fifty-one nonprofits, supporting the position that
percentage limitations and forced disclosures of costs were infringements on the right of free speech. Limits on fund raisers' fees, to
make another point, were unfair to small, newly organized charities
or those supporting unpopular causes, as they would have higher
fund-raising costs than well-established nonprofits. And new charities, noted *Riley* supporters, may spend a high percentage on fund
raising in order to build up a donor base. IS "rejoice[d] in and
celebrate[d]" the *Riley* decision as a victory for the free speech rights
of nonprofits (Harris, Holley, and McCaffrey, 1989, p. 2).

The decision left twenty-three states (out of the forty that have
charitable solicitation statutes) with unenforceable provisions (Harris, Holley, and McCaffrey, 1989, p. 9). Several were already consid-

ering amending or substantially revising their fund-raising laws, and over the next eighteen months, thirteen states enacted changes to their statutes. To help guide them in their efforts, a Model Act for the Regulation of Charitable Solicitations had been developed a few years earlier by a coalition of state regulators (National Association of State Charities Officials—NASCO) under the aegis of the National Association of Attorneys General (NAAG), and a private sector advisory group, chaired by John J. Schwartz, then president of the American Association of Fund-Raising Counsel (AAFRC). The Model Act, which was presented to NAAG in 1986 after two and a half years of deliberation, met with only qualified enthusiasm. For regulators, the act did not go far enough in proscribing the activities of fund raisers, as it excluded most of the types of provisions later deemed unconstitutional in *Riley*. For nonprofits and their supporters, the act contained several objectionable provisions, one of which was a point-of-solicitation disclosure of fund-raising costs. State courts in North Carolina and Maine had at that time ruled similar provisions unconstitutional, which *Riley* then confirmed.

Despite these objections, both state officials and nonprofits applauded the spirit of cooperation fostered by the Model Act. However, events would determine that the spirit of cooperation would be short-lived.

In late 1987 and early 1988, officials in several states began to hear consumer complaints about sweepstakes mailings by several (largely unknown) charities under the aegis of a direct-mail consulting company in Alexandria, Virginia. The sweepstakes mailings, which had several variations, announced that the recipient was a "cash prize winner in the $5,000 sweepstakes" and that an accompanying form had to be returned in order to qualify for the next round of drawings. Although the statement that no contribution was necessary to qualify appeared in the letters several times, recipients were urged to send in money. As one of the letters put it, "since this is a 'charity' sweepstakes, we do hope that as a cash prize winner you will wish to contribute at least $5" (U.S. Congress, 1989a, p. 132). In fact, many of these people received "prizes" in amounts as little as ten cents.

Although the letters contained great detail about the sweepstakes and procedures for entering, little was said about the soliciting organization, its programs, history, staff, and governing board. In some cases, a box with "the warning signs of cancer" (or a similar message, depending on the group's cause) in fine print would appear in one corner of one page. This was dubbed a public education tool by the nonprofits and fund raisers involved, and state officials would later learn it was used to allocate some of the expenses for the fund-raising mailing to "program costs."

The fund-raising techniques of this firm have been the subject of two congressional hearings, one of which led to the introduction in February 1990 of House Bill 3964 that proposed to bring interstate fund raising under the jurisdiction of the Federal Trade Commission. In addition, the fund-raising firm has been sued by at least fifteen states in connection with its sweepstakes mailings.

To many state regulators, these sweepstakes fund-raising appeals seemed to flaunt fund raisers' newly affirmed constitutional rights before the less-than-canny donating public. Supporters of *Riley* said fund-raising costs of new organizations may well be high because of the need to establish a donor base, and the sweepstakes charities learned this lesson first hand: Some received 3 percent or less from their fund-raising campaigns (U.S. Congress, 1989a, p. 232). Ironically, it was the sweepstakes technique used to build donor files that prompted so many consumer complaints to state officials and the Federal Trade Commission, raising questions about the logic and efficacy of such a program. As George A. Brakeley III, then chairman of the AAFRC, testified in Congress, "A fund raising campaign that tricks people into sending in contributions will not build a roster of loyal contributors" (U.S. Congress, July 28, 1989).

Riley said states could not require certain disclosures—such as fund-raising costs—in the course of appeals; the sweepstakes mailings did not give donors such basic information as where the organization was located; its staff, trustees, organizational history; or a clear description of programs. In some cases, the organization's name appears to have been formulated for its fund-raising appeal. Two animal shelters, one in Cincinnati, Ohio, and the other in Tulsa, Oklahoma, raised funds under the name National Animal Protection Fund, with no address or telephone number on the letterhead.

On top of these perceived abuses of free speech rights, many of these organizations, in the view of the state officials, took advantage of a recently revised set of accounting standards for nonprofits. These standards, promulgated by the American Institute of Certified Public Accounting (AICPA), allow organizations to allocate some of the costs of producing direct-mail appeals to public education or program expenses, recognizing, as did the Supreme Court, that mail appeals can contain information that is educational and valuable to the public.

One example of the allocation of public education expenses can be found in the 1988 tax return for the Adopt-a-Pet animal shelter in Tulsa, Oklahoma, which raised funds under the name National Animal Protection Fund. Adopt-a-Pet's 1988 IRS 990 tax form, published in the congressional record of the hearings, shows that it received over $2.9 million dollars in direct public support. Professional fund-raising fees totaled $576,460, while $1,725,281 was paid for printing and publications. Although the shelter paid $4,500 for veterinary care and another $4,500 for animal food (the return lists a total of $126,321 spent on "animals recovered, treated, boarded, spayed, or neutered and placed for adoption"), the return states expenditures of $848,510 for "public education—information on pet care and humane treatment provided to the public" (U.S. Congress, 1989a, pp. 44–45). That information can be found in the sweepstakes letter—in print smaller than that of the body of the letter, taking up approximately one-eighth of total page space on the bottom half of the second page, between the signature of the executive director and the sweepstakes official rules. The "Pet Care Guidelines" for cats and dogs include these tips: "fresh food and water daily," "keep in house and use litter tray," and "keep free of fleas and other parasites" (U.S. Congress, 1989a, pp. 136–137).

In percentage terms, the addition of public education to program expenses makes a huge difference in the fund-raising-program-cost ratio. With the addition of the public education program, the services rendered amount to nearly $1 million, or 33 percent of all funds raised. Without the public education program, however, program services—that is, the direct costs of the animal shelter—account for only 4.3 percent of all money raised.

Many state officials are of the mind that the information

offered in this and other examples is not worthwhile to the public and should not be allowed to be counted as a program expense. However, most fund raisers agree that many nonprofits do offer a valuable service when providing information to the public, whether it concerns health issues, the environment, or a host of other topics. After the experience of the last several years, however, it may be difficult to convince state officials and legislators that public education is a legitimate program activity. Current legislation reflects a general suspicion of public education programs, and, as will be seen below, includes accounting and disclosure requirements designed to discourage their use.

State officials are also concerned with the fund-raising practices that generally take place outside the professional world of staff development officers, membership in professional societies like the AAFRC and the NSFRE, and the ethical codes they promulgate. These practices include those of telephone solicitors/event promoters, who use paid callers to sell tickets to an event, such as a circus or a magic show, and door-to-door solicitation and/or sale of products. Police and firefighter benevolent associations cause concern among state officials, and some states have statutes to deal with the fund-raising activities of these particular groups.

These cases are discussed here because these experiences inform state regulators and legislators and shape fund-raising regulation. Legislation is being written to "get" certain fund-raising firms, rather than to balance the public's interests with fair demands on the nonprofits.

State officials' knowledge of fund raising and the nonprofit sector is incomplete. The cases that come to their attention and occupy most of their time—such as the sweepstakes mailings, high-cost event promotions, and door-to-door solicitations—are in fact a very small portion of the fund-raising activities carried out in this country. Because hospitals and universities are exempt from registration in many states, officials do not come into contact with the institutions and development professionals raising hundreds of millions of dollars through board solicitation of peers and other means of acquiring major gifts.

Fund-raising statutes focus almost solely on the outmoded concept of door-to-door solicitation, which many nonprofits have long since left behind. State officials grappling with issues like disclosure, fair costs, and registration requirements need to be informed of how charities really raise money, of advances made in direct-mail and telephone solicitation, and how they can regulate these activities fairly. Development professionals can be of great assistance in helping to shape future legislation, if they can mesh the needs of the states with the realistic requirements of charities.

This involvement could have an important effect on the regulation of fund raising. The only alternatives to more burdensome requirements for all concerned are (1) education of the donor public, in the hope that manipulative or duplicitous appeals will go unanswered and (2) self-regulation of the fund-raising industry, whereby industry groups and associations will establish standards of fair practice. But to be able to gain the trust of state officials, fund raisers need to establish credibility by understanding the principles of fund raising regulation and need to present a united front when discussing legislation.

Current Trends in State Legislation

Newly formed charities face the overwhelming task of filing a variety of forms and paying registration fees in nearly forty states before they can begin any kind of nationwide solicitation drive. And established charities must keep up with annual filings, which can be a job in itself. New York city attorney Seth Perlman, who handles nonprofit clients, estimates the costs of keeping current annual state registrations—each of which has a different expiration date, different filing requirements, and different forms—to be around $15,000.

State registration requirements have undergone tremendous change since the *Riley* decision. Between January 1989 and January 1991, at least nineteen states (Arizona, California, Colorado, Florida, Hawaii, Iowa, Maine, Maryland, Massachusetts, Minnesota, North Carolina, Ohio, Pennsylvania, South Dakota, Tennessee, Utah, Vermont, Virginia, and West Virginia) amended existing or enacted new fund-raising laws, in response to both *Riley* and the sweepstakes mailings. Many more have introduced legislation still under consideration. Yet, rather than moving toward uniformity— provided by the Model Act—states are instead going it alone, trying

to come up with their own formulas that they hope will stop perceived fund-raising abuses. The result for nonprofits, if even a few
of the bills introduced recently are approved and made law, could
be chaotic.

As states move away from the Model Act as a guide for charitable solicitation legislation, and as older methods of regulation
have been rendered unenforceable, legislators and state officials
have been very creative in devising new provisions they hope will
"catch" fraudulent fund raisers. Here are a few of the highlights
from recent legislative sessions. Note that most are bills that have
not become law but contain ideas that may catch on in other states
or reappear at other times.

Public Education Program Accountability. As recounted above,
public education as a legitimate charitable activity has become increasingly suspect, and some states have attempted to discount the
joint allocation of costs to both fund-raising and program budgets
recognized in revised AICPA standards of 1987.

Standards of Accounting and Financial Reporting for Voluntary Health and Welfare Organizations, published by the National Health Council, United Way of America, and others, defines
the AICPA standards for the joint allocation of materials that may
include fund-raising appeals. Although most appeals include descriptions of the causes the organizations are involved in, the book
notes, only an appeal "designed to motivate its audience to action,
other than providing financial support" (National Health Council,
1988, p. 56) can have its costs allocated to both fund-raising and
program services budgets. Joint allocation may also be appropriate
when "[a]n organization whose purpose is to raise public awareness
alerts individuals to a social or community problem and urges their
action in seeking changes" (National Health Council, 1988, p. 56).
These standards are apparently disputed by some state officials, who
seem to question the inherent worth of an organization whose programs consist largely of public education.

New Jersey Senate Bill 1045, introduced in January 1990 (but
not approved), would have singled out organizations whose principal purpose is the "general dissemination of information, ideas
and opinions or the advocacy of causes" [Amendment to Section

4(a)(9)] by requiring solicitors to state this at the time of solicitation, as well as indicating the same on state registration forms. The bill required the organization's annual report to state the percentage spent on "direct costs of goods and services provided to the recipients of charity" and "all other costs, *including the costs of fund raising, administration, general dissemination of ideas and opinions, and the advocacy of causes*" (New Jersey, 1990) (emphasis added). The intention of the bill appeared to be the discrediting of public education efforts of nonprofits and the refutation of the accepted accounting standards for program costs, by requiring a separate tally that would not include public education costs in its fundraising–program-cost ratio.

The same approach was proposed in draft legislation (not introduced) in 1989 by Senator Howard Metzenbaum. In this case, each solicitation by a nonprofit would include an "Exempt Purpose Expenditure Percentage"—the cost of fund raising in which no allocation of public education costs would be allowed. The draft legislation specifically stated that "the cost of any solicitation shall include the entire cost of preparing and disseminating the written or printed form, television or radio advertisement, or telephone call of which it is a part" [draft, "A bill to amend the Internal Revenue Code of 1986 to require tax exempt organizations to disclose the purposes for which donations to the organization are used, and for other purposes." Amendment to Section 6115 (2)] (U.S. Congress, 1989b).

And in Illinois, Senate Bill 1514 addressed the issue of joint allocation at some length. The bill specified that a nonprofit intending to use more than 50 percent of its program service expenditures "for informing or educating the public" must inform donors that a primary use of funds will be for public education [version LRB8605464Tmcam10, Section 9(b)(5)]. Organizations whose mission is to "disseminate an educational message or materials to the public with or in the course of fund raising activities and allocates the costs between fund raising and education programs," the bill states, "shall prepare and maintain written worksheets of how the allocation is made and the reasoning behind such allocation" [Section 9(b)(2)]. Two subparagraphs later, it specifies that the "factors and considerations utilized [in making joint allocation of costs] must

be reduced to writing and the organization's trustees must approve
the allocation methodology . . . " [Section 9(b)(4)] (Illinois, 1990).

State Public Information Programs. States have also taken to heart
a comment in the *Riley* decision that states should consider public
information programs on fund-raising groups, methods, and results
to be within their jurisdictions. Several states have instituted public
education programs.

Maryland and Florida have new statutes that include public
information measures. Maryland has established a charitable giving
information program in the office of the secretary of state, providing a toll-free number for information on charities and for reporting alleged violations of the law. Florida's law calls for a public
information campaign, at the same time discontinuing registration
requirements for charities. In the spring of 1991, however, a bill
reinstating registration was introduced, and it appeared that political momentum would make approval likely. For the past several
years, Connecticut has compiled data on the costs and final net
results of telephone solicitations that sell tickets by phone to a circus or other performance produced by the soliciting company. Typically, the study found the high costs of the event result in an
average of 25 percent of receipts actually going to the nonprofit. In
1988, at least one program netted no funds for the charity at all (U.S.
Department of Consumer Protection . . . , 1989, p. 14). The report is
released to the press and in past years has garnered a lot of publicity.
Minnesota compiled a similar report but included the results from
telephone campaigns that did not involve events, which showed that
telephone solicitations alone can yield an impressive return for nonprofits. New laws in Pennsylvania and Hawaii direct state officials to
publish annual compilations of charities, professional fund raisers,
and their fund-raising campaigns registered in the state.

Some state officials have rejected some public education attempts as "charity-bashing." Indeed, judging from the coverage al-
lotted to the recent rash of scandals, the charity appeal gone sour
is a story the media cannot resist.

Required Disclosures. Although *Riley* deemed requirement of point-
of-solicitation disclosure of fund-raising costs as an infringement of

free speech, the Court noted that required disclosures of a solicitor's professional status are appropriate.

A few states now require a written disclosure on all mail appeals, which states that more information on the soliciting charity is available from the state's attorney general or secretary of state. New York has had this provision in effect for several years, and the Charities Registration Office with the secretary of state responds to some 28,000 inquiries annually. This type of provision should guarantee that soliciting organizations will register in states in which this type of disclosure could prompt inquiries with the state.

Many in the nonprofit sector agree that this is a reasonable, fair means by which donors can get relevant information, although there is some concern that more states will require this type of disclosure, forcing organizations to include the unwieldy list of state officials' addresses on their direct-mail letters.

Accounting Procedures. How a charity accounts for its receipts, and at what level a CPA audit is required, has also received attention from the states. As we have seen, nonprofits' methods of allocating costs for public education has undergone scrutiny in several states. Others have proposed that certified audits, with notes and opinion of a CPA (as opposed to the more informal review or report), be required of more charities, placing a financial burden on them.

Many states require full CPA audits only for larger nonprofit organizations. Current statutes, on average, require full audits for organizations with revenues in excess of $100,000, although this can go as low as $50,000 or as high as $250,000. Most states will accept a copy of the IRS 990 form in lieu of a separate financial report, which could save smaller organizations time and money.

Also of concern are reporting requirements like those in West Virginia, where charities must report the amount of funds raised and spent on charitable purposes. Such a provision raises a host of accounting problems and would be especially burdensome if similar terms were adopted by several other states.

Recovery of Funds. As mentioned above, a recent New York state supreme court ruling set a precedent in ordering the return of $58,000 in contributions sent to the Pacific West Cancer Fund before the nonprofit was fully registered in the state. Other states are considering similar methods to restore or recover funds solicited or spent by an organization under false or misleading circumstances. A new West Virginia law allows prosecuting attorneys to recover funds collected by organizations or fund raisers in violation of the act.

Illinois House Bill 1514 (which was not approved) included a provision that would result in the forfeiture of compensation for professional fund raisers violating the statute. The legislation would have created the Attorney General's Charitable Enforcement Fund, in which the forfeited fees would be placed. It would also have allowed the attorney general, under court proceedings, to collect the assets of charities not in compliance with registration and filing requirements (*not* fraudulent or misleading activities) and place them in the Charitable Enforcement Fund. These types of provisions appear to be unique among charitable solicitation statutes and legislation under consideration, but the example they could set is worrisome.

Basic Principles of Fund-Raising Regulation:
A Basis for Discussion

Every profession is guided by standards and ethics as well as knowledge of the laws governing that profession. Principles of regulation of fund-raising and charitable organizations should be part of every fund-raising executive's education from the very beginning. They should be discussed in fund-raising courses, in articles, and at fund-raising conferences.

To start discussion among fund-raising managers, I propose the following as basic principles of fund-raising regulation.

Registration. Registration of nonprofits and fund-raising professionals (counsel as well as solicitors) must be recognized as being in the public interest, despite the fact that state registration is becoming more burdensome every year. The right of states to know what activities are taking place within their jurisdictions is hard to dispute, particularly when it involves solicitation of the public or contracts between professional fund-raising firms and nonprofit organizations.

Also, as we have seen above, states are using information filed with their officials to compile reports on the fund-raising activities taking place in their states and to answer questions from consumers regarding particular groups. Certainly, in encouraging the public to become informed donors, the states play an important role in helping residents to make informed decisions.

But in approving the concept of registration, perhaps we can reopen the discussion on the traditional exemption for hospitals and universities found in nearly every state. Should these institutions, which raise by far the most money, be exempt from registration? Would not the regulatory discussion be elevated by the participation of university and hospital development staff, executive officers, and trustees? Why should smaller organizations, such as social service agencies and arts groups, bear the brunt of registration and filing requirements alone?

That said, however, there is clearly a need for a uniform registration form, one that could be filled out once, photocopied, and sent to the forty states, at least for initial registration. A committee of reputable nonprofits should take the initiative to work with state officials to create such a form. States have a great deal to gain by accepting such a form. It would boost compliance with registration requirements, which would give them a more realistic picture of the solicitation activities being carried out in their states. Also, a less costly registration would mean less money taken up by administration costs and (presumably) more available for program services. New York state, for example, made great strides toward reducing paperwork for nonprofits in 1989 when it introduced a joint registration form for the attorney general and the secretary of state's charitable registration offices.

Disclosure. States are limited as to what they can legally require nonprofits to tell prospective donors. The following information should be made *voluntarily* during an appeal so that donors can make informed decisions:

- *Specific program information.* "Cancer research" should include details, such as who is carrying out such research and where, length of program expenditures, areas of concentration, and so on.

- *Organization history.* When and how did the organization get its start? Who was involved?
- *List of board of directors and executive staff.* Board members are performing a civic duty by serving; they should be listed as vouching for the worthiness of the organization and as stewards of the public trust.
- *Inform the public.* Let the public know that detailed financial information—including fund-raising costs—is available from the organization's offices or from the appropriate state officials.

Reporting Requirements. States should accept copies of IRS 990 forms for annual reports, requiring no additional state forms or new formulations of the same numbers (see the discussion of public education cost allocating above). However, the states have a right to a CPA-audited report for organizations with incomes of $250,000 and above.

Nonprofits should be concerned with a possible proliferation of separate reporting standards in different states and the toll this would take on administrative overhead. Nonprofits should instead urge uniformity in accounting standards and figures, stressing that charities (and in turn, charitable recipients) should not be penalized for compliance.

Contracts Between Fund-raising Professionals and Nonprofits

The following list of principles touches on several important points and leaves others unaddressed, but perhaps it will be viewed as a starting point for fund raisers in their discussions with state officials and among themselves.

- Charities must approve—and be responsible for—all solicitations prepared by outside professionals.
- All funds should go directly to the charity, or to a cashiering firm under contract to the charity, rather than to the outside professional. Charities should then pay fund-raising costs and fees as they pay other periodic expenses.

- All fees and expenses should be clearly stated in the contract, including expenses for which the charity is responsible.

In considering what constitutes good and fair regulation, the bottom line seems to be that good fund-raising practices are compatible with fair, well-considered law. It is when we fund raisers lose sight of our obligations to our donors and the public at large that problems are most likely to occur. When fund raisers or non-profits feel their constitutional rights (or simply their right to exist) outweigh those of the public, then tax-exempt status and privileges are called into question by public officials, and charities—all charities—lose stature in the eyes of the public.

References

Harris, E., Holley, L. S., and McCaffrey, C. J. *Fundraising into the 1990's: State Regulation of Charitable Solicitation After 'Riley.'* New York: New York University, 1989.

Illinois. House. Amendments to Bill 1514, version LRB8605464-Tmcam10, 1990.

INDEPENDENT SECTOR. *Charitable Solicitation Disclosure by Nonprofit Organizations: The Supreme Court's Riley Decision. A Summary Report.* Washington, D.C.: INDEPENDENT SECTOR, 1988.

National Health Council. *Standards of Accounting and Financial Reporting for Voluntary Health and Welfare Organizations.* (3rd ed., rev.) Report of National Health Council, National Assembly of National Voluntary Health and Social Welfare Organizations, and United Way of America. New York, N.Y.: National Health Council, 1988.

New Jersey. Senate. Amendments to Senate Bill 1045, Jan. 1990.

U.S. Congress. House. Deceptive Fundraising by Charities: Hearing Before the Subcommittee on Transportation and Hazardous Materials of the Committee on Energy and Commerce, ser. no. 101–81. 101st Cong., 1st sess., 1989a.

U.S. Congress. "A bill to amend the Internal Revenue Code of 1986 to require tax-exempt organizations to disclose the purposes for which donations to the organization are used, and for other purposes." Draft of amendment to section 6115(2), Washington, D.C., 1989b.

U.S. Congress. House. Committee on Energy and Committee on Energy and Commerce. *Hearings Before the Subcommittee on Transportation and Hazardous Materials of the Committee on Energy and Commerce.* 101st Cong., 1st sess., July 28, 1989.

U.S. Department of Consumer Protection and the Office of the Attorney General. *Paid Telephone Soliciting in Connecticut During 1988 for Charitable, Civic, Police and Firefighter Organizations.* A report to Mary M. Heslin, commissioner of consumer protection, and Clarine Nardi Riddle, acting attorney general. Prepared by the Public Charities Unit, a joint program of the Department of Consumer Protection and the Office of the Attorney General, Apr. 10, 1989.

Chapter 13

Contemporary Trends in Black Philanthropy: Challenging the Myths

Emmett D. Carson

Over 150 years ago when Alexis de Tocqueville made his now-famous observation that "Americans of all ages, all stations of life, and all types of disposition are forever forming associations . . . ," organized black philanthropy was already fifty years old. Surprisingly, however, despite the frequency with which Tocqueville is quoted, until recently scholars studying the nonprofit sector have exhibited little interest in examining the philanthropic behavior and traditions of blacks or of other minority groups. There are at least three reasons for the lack of scholarly interest in studying black philanthropy.

One part of the explanation is the near-singular focus of the early nonprofit scholars on wealthy individuals capable of making large gifts, few of whom were members of the black community. Brian O'Connell mentions this in his book *Philanthropy in Action* (1987, p. viii). This focus, however, is not sufficient to explain the exclusion of wealthy black philanthropists, few of whom have been adequately recognized for their charitable efforts. For example, the philanthropic efforts of Prince Hall (1735-1807), fraternal leader;

Paul Cuffe (1759-1817), businessman and colonizer; William Still (1821-1902), conductor on the underground railroad; John Jones (1816-1879), businessman; and Madame C. J. Walker (1867-1919), businesswoman, among others, merit further scholarly attention.

Another reason is that much of the early charitable activity of blacks occurred through the black church, often in secrecy, so that few outside the community had direct knowledge of their philanthropic activities. At least one reason for this secrecy stems from the fact that, at one time, for blacks to engage in charitable activity was against the law in many states. For example, in 1835, several states including Virginia, Maryland, and North Carolina had laws that prevented blacks from having "lyceums, lodges, fire companies, or literary, dramatic, social, moral, or charitable societies" (Ebony, 1971, p. 183).

However, perhaps the most important factor in explaining the lack of research on black philanthropy is that, over the years, many of those studying philanthropy placed little value on researching what they believed did not exist. The fact that the study of black philanthropy is only now beginning in earnest makes Tocqueville's quote a powerful reminder of the narrow perspectives that have historically shaped much of the past scholarship on the nonprofit sector.

Few scholars would disagree that the "Reagan revolution" to reduce government social services by relying more heavily on the nonprofit sector to aid the poor was responsible for generating much of the current scholarly interest in philanthropy (Salamon, 1984, p. 261). The emerging interest in black philanthropy is due to both a desire to broaden the existing scholarship on philanthropy and the growing realization among those who solicit financial and volunteer support through the nonprofit sector that tomorrow's givers are going to be increasingly black, Hispanic, and Asian American.

The future demographic trends are clear. The Bureau of Labor Statistics reports that by the year 2000, the growth rate of the white labor force will be less than 15 percent, compared to a 29 percent increase in the black and a 74 percent increase in the Hispanic labor forces (Kutscher, 1987, p. 3). The potential impact of these future nonwhite givers on the nonprofit sector may be enormous. The

American Association of Fund-Raising Counsel (AAFRC) estimates that 84 percent ($96.43 billion) of the $114.70 billion in total giving that was contributed to the nonprofit sector in 1989 was given by individuals (American Association of Fund-Raising Counsel, 1990, p. 9). This suggests that the current mix of programs supported through charitable contributions may change radically, particularly if tomorrow's increasingly ethnic and minority givers have markedly different philanthropic traditions and giving patterns from today's predominantly white givers. (Many charitable organizations are already facing the challenges of a more diverse community of givers. See the Southern California Association for Philanthropy [SCAP] special report *Private Resources and Public Needs: Los Angeles in the 21st Century*, made to a community forum sponsored by SCAP and the Council on Foundations, April 12, 1988.)

This chapter examines a range of questions about black philanthropy using the 1988 Joint Center for Political and Economic Studies' (JCPES) annual survey. The survey, conducted by the Gallup Organization, contains detailed questions, asked in face-to-face personal interviews, on the charitable behavior of a nationally representative sample of 643 black and 695 white Americans. The survey has a sampling error of plus or minus 5 percent. Survey questions include: What are the socioeconomic characteristics of blacks who engage in philanthropy? How much do they contribute? What are black attitudes toward charitable giving? Why do blacks give? Such information will be useful to those discussing the feasibility of strategies aimed both at increasing the number of black philanthropists and strengthening and expanding the variety of black nonprofit institutions.

It should be noted at the outset that because there are few statistics on the charitable giving of either blacks or whites, as well as widespread misperceptions about the giving patterns of blacks relative to whites, comparative giving and attitudinal data on both groups will be presented. The comparative data should not, however, be interpreted as suggesting that the charitable behavior of either group represents the desired or ideal level of giving. In fact, to the extent that the experiences and traditions of blacks and whites are different, one might expect there to be differences in their charitable behavior. One should also note that it is not unreasonable to believe that each ethnic group exhibits a different pattern of charitable behavior. To the extent then that Jewish, Polish, and Italian Americans, among others, are all grouped into a single category labeled "white," a comparison of blacks and whites may reveal even less than first imagined.

Before examining the data in detail, it is important to first understand why the study of black philanthropy has important consequences that go beyond how the changing demographics of society may affect the nonprofit sector. The study also includes the larger issue of shaping public attitudes about whether poor blacks deserve to receive government-sponsored social services.

Black Philanthropy and the American Work Ethic

One of the most important values in American society is that individuals have an obligation to provide for and help themselves. If, however, an able-bodied individual is still in need of assistance after doing all he or she can, then society begins to consider that individual as deserving of help. In 1987, 33 percent of all black Americans (9.6 million people) lived in poverty (Center on Budget and Policy Priorities, 1988, p. 2). Because of the strong American belief in the work ethic, coupled with the disproportionate number of blacks who live in poverty, the suggestion that blacks do not engage in charitable activities to help themselves has led some to question whether poor blacks are deserving of broader public financial support (see Loury, 1984).

By allowing the unchallenged perpetuation of the myth that blacks are not engaged in efforts to help themselves, public attention has focused on whether the poorest members of the black community are deserving of assistance, rather than on the more salient issue of what resources are required to address the needs of poor blacks. Whether intentionally or not, the lack of scholarly interest in black philanthropy has helped to perpetuate these beliefs by signaling either that blacks have no philanthropic traditions worthy of study or that their participation in the nonprofit sector is negligible.

The public perception continues to persist that blacks are less likely to engage in charitable activities than whites. For example, when asked in the 1988 JCPES survey if "black people give the same, less, or more money than white people to charitable organizations," 50 percent of blacks and 45 percent of whites reported they thought that blacks gave less. When these respondents were asked if it was because blacks had less money or less interest, 71 percent of blacks and 49 percent of whites thought it was because of less money. A total of 26 percent of whites and 16 percent of blacks felt that blacks gave less money because they had less interest. As will be discussed later, neither of these views presents an accurate picture of the current charitable activities of American blacks.

The issue here is not whether there is a connection between philanthropy and government provision of services but rather what the appropriate way is to view that relationship. The role of individual philanthropy, as it has developed in the United States, has been for individuals to engage in private action when they are unable to gather the necessary public support for government-financed programs and new initiatives. The development of black philanthropy is no different, having been shaped by the desire of blacks to provide a network of social services that were denied to them by the larger society on the basis of race. It should be noted, however, that the basis of this hypothesis is far from generally accepted. For example, Julian Wolpert has suggested from his preliminary research that those who are willing to be taxed more will also be willing to contribute more to charity. However, rather than refuting the hypotheses proposed here, one could argue that these individuals have yet to see the desired level of services that they believe are required and therefore do not mind being taxed, nor do they limit their charitable giving because they are taxed (Wolpert, 1987, p. 12).

Today, the growing federal budget deficit has led many to call for a renewed voluntary spirit to replace government programs. Despite President Bush's frequent references to "a thousand points of light," there is little indication that the public is willing to further increase individual giving in the event that the federal government cuts back on social programs that aid the poor. Sixty-three percent of whites and 40 percent of blacks who responded to the 1988 JCPES survey reported that their giving to charity would not increase if the government reduced programs for the poor.

Clearly, no racial or ethnic community has the level of resources needed to provide all of the social services that are currently provided by the federal government. Furthermore, a reliance on philanthropy, rather than government provision of services, would very likely result in an unequal distribution of services to those in need. Rather than substituting private resources for federal resources to aid the poor, it would appear that any internal efforts by the black community aimed at helping poor blacks should be viewed as supplemental to government efforts.

Evolution of Black Philanthropy

Even a cursory review of the history of American blacks speaks volumes about their determination to engage in activities to aid their neediest members (Carson, 1989). Black philanthropy has been an indispensable mechanism for the socioeconomic survival of blacks as well as providing the resources to sustain black efforts to promote social change. The philanthropic activity of blacks prior to the 1960s can be described as philanthropy among friends. Most of the churches, mutual aid societies, and fraternal organizations that engaged in philanthropic activity primarily focused on aiding individuals in their own community. After the 1960s, however, blacks began to develop charitable organizations that practiced philanthropy among strangers; for example, the National Black United Fund. These later organizations had a greater capacity to raise money and dispense services from and to individuals who were not personally known to each other.

Beginning as far back as the late 1700s, blacks began to engage in organized philanthropic activity to provide for their own basic needs. The charitable efforts of blacks were usually conducted through the black church or organizations affiliated with the church. Today, the black church continues to be the primary institution through which blacks engage in philanthropy (Carson, 1990; Byrd, 1989). The accumulation of money from these activities was responsible, in part, for the first black schools, banks, and insurance companies (Harris, 1968, p. 46).

However, not all of blacks' philanthropic efforts were internally directed. For example, during the great plague that struck Philadelphia in 1793, the Free African Society provided critical nursing and burial services to all of the city's residents (Quarles, 1979). It is a grave misreading of history to think that these early black charitable organizations—churches, mutual aid societies, and fraternal organizations—operated only for the benefit of their members. Many black charitable organizations were at the forefront in addressing the major social issues that confronted the black community while simultaneously providing a wide range of services through charitable activity. It is also a mistake to assert that blacks developed mutual aid societies only because they were not permitted to join similar white organizations. As historian Robert Harris states: "the early black benevolent societies as voluntary associations were not mirror-images or exaggerated forms of similar white organizations. They grew simultaneously with white voluntary associations. Moreover, they served different functions because of distinctive needs of the free black populace, many of whom had recently emerged from slavery. Common historical experiences, shared African ancestry, cultural affinities, and similar grievances brought free blacks together into benevolent societies to provide a sense of security in their new status as freemen" (Harris, 1979, pp. 608–609).

Equally important, blacks have used their philanthropic resources to provide the crucial financial and manpower resources to help them initiate and support virtually every black social movement in history, including the Underground Railroad, the Garvey movement, and the civil rights movement. Such a large mobilization of charitable resources itself creates what has been termed public power: the ability of individuals involved in social movements to alter fundamental perspectives in society (Mathews, 1987).

Not since the mid-1970s has there been any concentrated effort to study the charitable giving patterns of American blacks. King E. Davis's book *Fund Raising in the Black Community* (1975) and two special issues on black philanthropy in *The Black Scholar* magazine (in 1976 and 1977) raised important conceptual questions about the need for blacks to develop and support their own nonprofit institutions. What is noteworthy about these pioneering efforts is that, without the benefit of any statistical data, they were able to provide much of the theoretical groundwork for the now-thriving black fund-raising organizations, for example, the Black United Fund, United Black Fund, and Associated Black Charities

(Carson, 1988). It is hoped that the current scholarship on black philanthropy will also yield information that will help further develop the philanthropic capabilities of blacks.

Socioeconomic Profile of Contributors

The socioeconomic profile of blacks and whites who made charitable contributions in 1987 are shown in Tables 13.1 and 13.2, respectively. A majority of both black men and black women (56 percent) reported making a contribution to a charitable organization. Not surprisingly, better educated and wealthier blacks were more likely to make contributions of $500 or more. For example, 41 percent of black college graduates and 47 percent of blacks with household incomes of $40,000 or more reported making contributions over $500. Professional blacks (36 percent) were far more likely to have contributed $500 or more to a charity than blacks in any other occupation (a range of 14 to 20 percent). A total of 50 percent of unmarried blacks (compared to 34 percent of married blacks) reported that they had not made any charitable contributions. In addition, married blacks are more likely than unmarried blacks to have made a contribution of $500 or more, 28 percent compared to 10 percent.

One of the most interesting findings is the relationship between giving and geographical location. Blacks who live in the South are far more likely to have made a charitable contribution than blacks who live in any other region of the country. Nearly 64 percent of blacks who reside in the South reported making contributions, compared to 49 percent who live in the East and the West and 46 percent who live in the Midwest. These statistics merit additional research.

Table 13.1 also shows the giving behavior of blacks who live in different types of places. Blacks who live in the central cities are more likely to have made no charitable contribution (55 percent) than blacks who live in the suburbs (33 percent) or those who live in rural areas (31 percent). What makes this latter finding significant is that it is reasonable to assume that those who live in central cities are more likely to encounter the kinds of social ills—for ex-

Table 13.1. Demographic Profile of Blacks Who Made a Charitable
Contribution in 1987.

	$50 or Less	$50–$99	$100–$499	Over $500	None
Gender					
Male	7.5%	8.3%	24.0%	16.0%	44.2%
Female	7.7	8.4	21.7	17.6	44.6
Last Grade Completed					
Less than high school	10.3	6.6	22.1	10.7	50.2
High school graduate	9.0	12.4	21.3	12.2	45.0
Some college	2.5	5.3	25.9	27.2	39.0
College graduate	1.5	4.3	25.3	40.9	28.0
Household Income					
Less than $12,000	10.0	7.7	23.2	11.9	47.3
$12,000–$25,000	5.7	10.0	28.6	14.9	40.8
$25,000–$40,000	0.0	12.4	27.0	28.3	32.3
Over $40,000	10.4	5.7	21.3	47.2	15.4
Occupation					
Professional	0.0	9.4	21.2	36.4	33.1
Clerical	6.1	11.4	22.3	13.8	46.5
Blue collar	9.4	8.1	30.7	17.9	33.8
Student/housewife	6.0	3.1	24.1	13.5	53.3
Retired	6.0	7.7	22.2	19.6	44.6
Unemployed	16.4	7.4	15.9	6.6	53.7
Marital Status					
Married	7.2	6.1	24.6	28.0	34.0
Not married	8.2	9.9	21.9	10.1	50.0
Religious Preference					
Protestant	7.7	8.2	23.5	17.7	42.9
Catholic	4.7	6.9	26.3	9.3	52.8
Age					
18–29	6.8	11.3	21.9	7.7	52.3
30–49	9.2	5.8	20.9	22.3	41.7
Over 50	6.4	8.5	26.1	19.5	39.6
Region					
East	6.7	7.9	18.5	16.3	50.6
Midwest	7.2	7.4	18.5	12.4	54.4
South	9.2	8.9	26.5	19.0	36.4
West	2.5	8.3	21.8	16.1	51.3
Type of Place					
Central city	5.9	6.8	21.3	11.2	54.8
Suburb	8.1	7.1	24.3	27.7	32.7
Rural	11.4	13.1	24.5	20.2	30.7

Table 13.2. Demographic Profile of Whites Who Made a Charitable Contribution in 1987.

	$50 or Less	$50– $99	$100– $499	Over $500	None
Gender					
Male	6.6%	6.3%	27.2%	27.6%	32.3%
Female	9.5	8.3	24.6	29.0	28.6
Last Grade Completed					
Less than high school	13.2	9.7	17.8	16.2	43.0
High school graduate	9.1	6.5	28.9	25.2	30.4
Some college	4.8	9.2	30.4	31.0	24.7
College graduate	2.9	5.0	25.0	45.8	21.3
Household Income					
Less than $12,000	12.0	10.1	20.1	15.4	42.4
$12,000–$25,000	11.4	11.0	21.1	22.9	33.6
$25,000–$40,000	10.0	8.6	32.1	35.6	13.6
Over $40,000	1.9	2.7	32.1	47.2	16.1
Occupation					
Professional	2.0	8.2	26.1	41.4	22.3
Clerical	11.5	9.3	32.2	24.6	22.3
Blue collar	11.1	4.4	29.2	21.3	34.0
Student/housewife	11.6	7.0	19.9	25.8	35.6
Retired	5.7	5.8	20.3	26.0	42.2
Unemployed	6.4	9.7	26.8	29.8	27.4
Marital Status					
Married	5.9	7.4	25.7	35.2	25.8
Not married	12.3	7.2	26.4	15.5	38.6
Religious Preference					
Protestant	10.1	6.4	23.5	30.0	30.0
Catholic	5.3	9.0	29.6	26.9	29.2
Age					
18–29	11.8	9.4	30.8	11.2	36.8
30–49	7.2	7.6	25.9	36.3	23.0
Over 50	6.7	6.0	23.6	31.2	32.5
Region					
East	6.4	7.1	29.8	24.2	32.5
Midwest	11.6	8.0	23.9	28.6	27.9
South	8.7	5.9	25.1	27.3	33.0
West	4.6	8.9	24.7	34.9	26.8
Type of Place					
Central city	10.6	11.3	26.6	20.2	31.2
Suburb	6.8	5.9	28.9	32.5	25.9
Rural	7.6	6.0	23.0	29.9	33.5

ample, homelessness—for which charitable contributions are often requested.

At least one explanation for the different giving behavior may be that those blacks who live in central cities are less able financially to make a charitable contribution. Another explanation may be that those who see the problems of homelessness and severe poverty every day soon become indifferent and callous to them. For example, former New York mayor Edward Koch created a public furor when he suggested that many of New York's panhandlers "just don't want to work for a living" and that money given to them is used to buy "booze and drugs." Similarly, the cover of a September 1988 *Time* magazine read, "To Give or Not to Give," and the ensuing article suggested that the growing poverty in American society may have outstripped our willingness and/or ability to give. More research is needed to discover if what sociologists refer to as anomie, the disconnectedness of individuals living in urban environments, is responsible for the fewer number of black givers living in the central cities.

A central issue in discussions on black self-help is the degree to which blacks and whites with the same level of household income make similar contributions to charity. For example, of blacks and whites with household incomes less than $12,000, 12 percent of blacks and 15 percent of whites gave over $500. Among blacks and whites with household incomes that exceed $40,000, 47 percent of both blacks and whites reported making charitable contributions of over $500. The most notable difference in the giving behavior of blacks and whites with similar levels of household income is that among those with incomes of $25,000 to $40,000, blacks were significantly more likely to have made no contribution than their white counterparts, 32 percent as compared to 14 percent. Furthermore, there were no blacks in the $25,000–$40,000 income category who reported having contributed $50 or less, compared to 10 percent of whites who made contributions in that range to health groups.

Compared to the Joint Center's 1986 and 1987 surveys, the 1988 JCPES survey showed the greatest disparity between giving behavior of blacks and whites with the same level of household income. Additional survey data will be required to determine whether the 1988 survey findings with regard to the differences in giving between blacks and whites with household incomes of $25,000 to $40,000 is a result of a one-time sampling bias or the beginning of a trend.

These similarities are remarkable when one considers that, according to statistics from the U.S. Census Bureau, the median net wealth (ownership of assets) of white households is nearly 15 times greater than that of black households—$49,135 for white households compared to $3,397 for black households (U.S. Department of Commerce and Bureau of the Census, 1986, p. 5). This suggests that giving may represent a much greater economic sacrifice for blacks than whites. Overall, these findings appear to dispel the myth that blacks are far less likely than whites to make charitable contributions.

The total giving data above give little indication of the support that blacks give to specific organizations. Information on the contributions of blacks and whites to selected charitable organizations is also revealing. A greater percentage of blacks and whites contribute more to their own respective churches than to any other type of charitable organization. In addition, the overall giving pattern of the two groups to their churches is similar. In the over-$500 category, 13 percent of blacks and 19 percent of whites made contributions to their own church. In comparison, none of the other selected charitable organizations in the study had more than 2 percent of either black or white respondents report that they had made contributions totaling $500 or more.

Although the giving behavior of blacks and whites to community, education, and international aid groups was similar, the two groups do exhibit significantly different giving patterns to health, social welfare, and youth groups. More specifically, nearly one-third more blacks (61 percent) than whites (42 percent) said that they did not make a charitable contribution to a health organization. Further, while neither group exhibited a propensity to make contributions over $500, far more whites than blacks—33 percent and 18 percent, respectively—reported making contributions of $100 or less.

The data on giving to youth and community groups are not significantly different from those on giving to health organizations. Given the enormous health problems that exist in the black community as well as the growing need in many black communities for more effective youth and community organizations to address issues of teenage pregnancy and drug abuse, these data suggest that efforts should be considered that would increase the proportion of total black giving directed to these groups.

A major concern of the 1970s literature on black philanthropy, which continues to provoke vigorous discussion today, is the extent to which blacks are willing to support black organizations (Davis, 1975, p. 145), a matter that lies at the heart of any discussion of the feasibility of supporting existing and future black nonprofit institutions. Nearly one-fourth of all blacks reported giving all or almost all of their charitable donations to black organizations. Similarly, 13 percent of blacks reported giving more than half of their charitable contributions to black organizations, while 19 percent of blacks reported giving about half of their total charitable donation to black organizations. Overall, a total of 57 percent of blacks reported that half or more of their total charitable contributions were given to black organizations or organizations that served the needs of black people. In comparison, only 5 percent of the total charitable contributions of whites were donated to black charitable organizations.

These statistics refute the twin myths that (1) blacks are unwilling to support black organizations and (2) individual white contributors are more active in supporting black organizations than blacks. However, as will be discussed in the next section, strong evidence suggests that a significant number of blacks would rather support multiracial than black-oriented charitable institutions.

Attitudes Toward Charitable Organizations

The knowledge that blacks are active givers and that a large percentage of their total contributions are donated to black organizations does little to explain the motivations underlying that behavior. Information on the philanthropic motivations underlying charitable contributions is critical to the formalization of strategies to channel the philanthropic resources of blacks in ways that will be readily accepted and acted upon by members of the black community. As King E. Davis noted: "Before Black fund raising organizations can achieve success in influencing a behavior as specific as giving, they

must answer several interrelated questions: Why does one person
give to Charity A rather than Charity B? Will Black people give to
a Black appeal? Will Whites give to Black causes?" (Davis, 1975,
p. 142).

For both blacks and whites, the most important factors for
making a charitable contribution are either the belief that the organization is successful (20 percent of blacks and 27 percent of
whites) or a belief in the goals of the organization (20 percent of
blacks and 27 percent of whites). These findings are important
when compared to the percentages of blacks and whites who have
reported that they made contributions chiefly because they had
some identification, racial or otherwise, with the charitable organization. A total of 8 percent of blacks and 6 percent of whites reported
that they made a charitable contribution because they identified
with the organization. This raises serious questions about the validity of statements that suggest that blacks are only responsive to
appeals that support what are thought to be black causes.

Another significant attitudinal issue is: Do blacks and whites
differ on the problems that they believe charitable organizations
should most try to solve? The findings indicate that blacks and
whites have similar views on this set of issues. Drug abuse is far and
away the most important issue that blacks and whites believe charitable organizations should try to solve—28 percent and 23 percent,
respectively. Perhaps the most distinct difference between the two
groups is that 12 percent of blacks compared to 7 percent of whites
feel that unemployment should be the primary issue. This is not
entirely surprising when one considers the disproportionate numbers of blacks who are without work and are unable to find it.
Similarly, blacks and whites differ on the importance of health
problems. A total of 18 percent of blacks compared to 11 percent of
whites believed that health problems were the critical issue.

Charitable organizations are often concerned over whether
donors are aware of how their contributions are used. This interest
is particularly felt by those that sponsor a wide range of programs
for which they solicit contributions. The conventional wisdom is
that donors who know how their money is spent are more likely to
continue to make contributions over time. Some charitable organizations—for example, United Way—have initiated programs that

give donors an increasingly greater voice in determining which specific programs their contributions will be used to support.

Givers appear to be divided into those who are always or often aware of how their contributions are used and those who are seldom or never aware. A total of 25 percent of blacks and 28 percent of whites reported that they are almost always aware. Similarly, 23 percent of blacks and 16 percent of whites never know this. More research is needed to determine if donors who are aware of this are more likely to contribute more to charity over time, but these data indicate that a significant number of donors continue to be unaware of how charitable organizations intend to use their contribution.

A long-standing concern of those who advocate the development of black charitable organizations has been the extent to which blacks will respond to efforts to support them. Although the previous section provided strong evidence that a large percentage of the total contributions of blacks are donated to black organizations, this does not address whether blacks think that giving to these organizations to aid poor blacks is preferable to giving to multiracial organizations that seek to aid the poor of all races.

The majority of both blacks and whites appear to agree that blacks should work through multiracial organizations, rather than focus their activities to help blacks through black ones. A larger percentage of whites than blacks (63 percent compared to 53 percent) reported that they felt that blacks should work through multiracial organizations to help the poor of all races. Alternatively, 23 percent of blacks and 16 percent of whites believe that blacks should focus their charitable activities on helping poor blacks through black organizations.

There is clearly a contradiction between the attitudes expressed by a majority of blacks that blacks should support multiracial organizations and the strong financial support that blacks disproportionately give to black-run organizations. At least one explanation that reconciles these findings is that calls for a color-blind society with regard to equal opportunity may also have influenced black and white perceptions about the desirability of color-blind institutions in general. If true, this may suggest that strategies for black self-help that exclude other ethnic or racial groups may be out of step with the attitudes of a majority of black givers. Another explanation may be that blacks are reluctant to express what might be perceived as militant or racist beliefs about the need to create and support black charitable organizations that focus on aiding poor blacks. Yet another answer may be that multiracial charitable organizations have not made enough of an effort to solicit black contributors and, as a result, blacks continue to support black organizations because they do make charitable appeals to the black community. Still another reason may be that multiracial organizations are not confronting the most important problems that blacks believe should be addressed, for example, unemployment. Whatever the answer, this issue has significant implications for existing black charitable organizations as well as for the feasibility of creating new black nonprofit institutions.

Conclusion

This chapter has presented compelling evidence that blacks are actively involved in supporting black organizations and, in general, have giving patterns and attitudes toward philanthropy that are not significantly different from those of whites. As stated earlier, the charitable giving of blacks has evolved over time in response to new challenges and new opportunities. From slavery through the era of Jim Crow, much of the charitable activity of blacks was almost exclusively channeled through the church or through organizations connected to the church.

In the period following the 1960s, blacks increasingly focused on developing less personal mechanisms for charitable giving. As Council on Foundations president James Joseph wrote in a 1977 article that appeared in *The Black Scholar:* "The most creative way to work together to develop the resources we [black Americans] need for the struggle ahead is through the development of a philanthropic infrastructure which is self-controlled and self-determined. In some communities, this may mean developing Black United Funds. In others, it may mean the development of a private foundation."

Although few of the private black foundations founded at that time have flourished, those black charitable organizations that solicit contributions through work-site payroll deductions have met with remarkable success. Through a series of court cases, the National Black United Fund gained access to the Combined Federal Campaign, thereby opening the campaign to non-United Way charities. By using work-site payroll deduction plans, black fund-raising organizations have been able to successfully raise money from an increasingly heterogeneous black community. In 1989, the Combined Federal Campaign, with over 4.9 million workers solicited, raised more than $187 million for charity, $118 million of which was pledged to non-United Way charities (National Committee for Responsive Philanthropy, 1990).

The exodus of many upwardly mobile blacks from urban inner cities has eroded the ability of blacks with different socioeconomic backgrounds to communicate with each other, thus exacerbating the class differences that have always existed. As a result, poor blacks are unable to see the support that wealthier blacks give to charitable organizations, just as wealthier blacks are unable to see the degree to which poor blacks support charitable causes to help themselves. Unfortunately, these communication problems among blacks are likely to worsen as greater numbers of blacks experience economic success while the socioeconomic problems confronting the poorest blacks become more severe.

The income gap between the poorest one-fifth of black families and the wealthiest top one-fifth of black families has increased dramatically. Adjusting for inflation, the Center on Budget and Policy Priorities found that between 1978 and 1987 the income of the poorest black families dropped 24 percent from $5,022 to $3,837. However, during the same period, the income of the top one-fifth of black families grew from $51,858 to $55,107 and the income of the top 5 percent of blacks increased by 12.5 percent, from $71,947 to $80,917 (Center on Budget and Policy Priorities, 1988, p. 24). These findings raise important questions about the kinds of nonprofit organizations that need to be established and supported in order to surmount the challenges that face the black community.

As a greater number of blacks join the ranks of America's affluent, there will be increasing opportunities for the black community to utilize more sophisticated methods to channel their philanthropic resources to benefit the black community. At least one type of nonprofit institution that has been underutilized by the black community is the community foundation. The establishment of black-supported community foundations may be the appropriate next step in further developing and diversifying the black nonprofit infrastructure. Community foundations have the advantage of allowing more affluent givers the prestige of establishing an endowment fund with a relatively small gift that addresses the specific problem that interests them. In addition, because a community foundation manages several trusts simultaneously, overhead costs are minimized, an aspect that may make them ideal institutions for reconciling the apparent desire of many blacks to give to multiracial organizations while continuing to support black interests. Community foundations receive funds from a multiplicity of sources yet allow givers to determine criteria under which grants can be made.

As the twenty-first century approaches, the future of black philanthropy looks secure. The well-publicized $20 million gift by entertainer Bill Cosby and his wife, Camille Cosby, to Atlanta's Spelman College (Johnson, 1989, p. 25) is an extraordinary example of the kinds of gifts that a growing number of blacks may be capable of making in future years. With such gifts, the development of large private foundations cannot be far behind. More research is needed on the philanthropic attitudes and giving patterns of wealthy blacks, who are excellent donor prospects because they are likely to have only recently acquired their wealth and are unlikely to have made long-term charitable commitments. The creation of a new cadre of black-supported community and private foundations, coupled with the continued charitable activities of black churches and black fund-raising organizations, will ensure that the black community continues to develop its charitable nonprofit infrastructure to meet the challenges ahead.

References

American Association of Fund-Raising Counsel. *Giving USA: The Annual Report on Philanthropy for the Year 1987*. New York: American Association of Fund-Raising Counsel, 1988.

American Association of Fund-Raising Counsel. *Giving USA: The Annual Report on Philanthropy for the Year 1989*. New York: American Association of Fund-Raising Counsel, 1990.

The Black Scholar: Journal of Black Studies and Research. Mar. 1976 and Dec. 1977 (entire issues).

Byrd, A. "The Philanthropy of the Black Church: Historical and Contemporary Perspectives." INDEPENDENT SECTOR Spring Research Forum Working Papers. Washington, D.C.: INDE-PENDENT SECTOR, 1989.

Carson, E. D. "The Attitudes, Accessibility, and Participation of Blacks and Whites in Work-Site Payroll Deduction." Durham, N.C.: Duke University Center for the Study of Philanthropy and Volunteerism, 1988.

Carson, E. D. "The Evolution of Black Philanthropy: Patterns of Giving and Voluntarism." In R. Magat (ed.), *Philanthropic Giving: Studies in Varieties and Goals.* New York: Oxford University Press, 1989.

Carson, E. D. "Patterns of Giving in Black Churches." In R. Wuthnow and V. A. Hodgkinson (eds.), *Faith and Philanthropy in America.* San Francisco: Jossey-Bass, 1990.

Center on Budget and Policy Priorities. *Still Far from the Dream: Recent Developments in Black Income, Employment and Poverty.* Washington, D.C.: Center on Budget and Policy Priorities, 1988.

Davis, K. E. *Fund Raising in the Black Community: History, Feasibility, and Conflict.* Metuchen, N.J.: Scarecrow Press, 1975.

Ebony. *Pictorial History of Black America.* Nashville, Tenn: South Western Co., 1971.

Gibbs, N. "Begging: To Give or Not to Give." *Time,* Sept. 5, 1988, pp. 68-74.

Harris, A. *The Negro as Capitalist.* College Park, Md.: McGrath, 1968.

Harris, R. L. "Early Black Benevolent Societies, 1780-1830." *Massachusetts Review,* 1979, *20* (3), 608-609.

Johnson, R. "Bill and Camille Cosby: First Family of Philanthropy." *Ebony,* May 1989, pp. 25-34.

Joseph, J. A. "Philanthropy and the Black Economic Condition." *The Black Scholar,* 1977, 7 (6), 9.

Kutscher, R. E. "Overview and Implications of the Projections to 2000." *Monthly Labor Review,* 1987, *110* (9), 3-9.

Loury, G. C. "Internally Directed Action for Black Community

Development: The Next Frontier for 'The Movement.'" *Review of Black Political Economy,* Summer/Fall 1984, *13,* 31–46.

Mathews, D. "The Independent Sector and the Political Responsibilities of the Public." An address to the INDEPENDENT SECTOR Spring Research Forum, New York, Mar. 19, 1987.

National Committee for Responsive Philanthropy. *Special Report on Workplace Giving Alternatives.* Washington, D.C.: National Committee for Responsive Philanthropy, 1990.

O'Connell, B. *Philanthropy in Action.* New York: Foundation Center, 1987.

Quarles, B. *The Negro in the Making of America.* New York: Collier Books, 1979.

Salamon, L. "Non-Profit Organizations: The Lost Opportunity." In J. L. Palmer and I. V. Sawhill (eds.), *The Reagan Record.* Cambridge, Mass.: Ballinger, 1984.

Southern California Association for Philanthropy. *Private Resources and Public Needs: Los Angeles in the 21st Century.* Special report to community forum sponsored by SCAP and the Council on Foundations, Los Angeles, Apr. 12, 1988.

U.S. Department of Commerce and Bureau of the Census. *Household Wealth and Asset Ownership; 1984,* ser. P-70, no. 7. Washington, D.C.: Household Economic Studies, July 1986.

Wolpert, J. "Philanthropy: A Research Agenda." In Center for the Study of Philanthropy and Voluntarism, Institute of Policy Sciences and Public Affairs (ed.), *Setting the Research Agenda in Philanthropy and Voluntarism: Eight Discussion Papers.* Durham, N.C.: Duke University, 1987.

Chapter 14

The Economics
of Fund Raising

Richard Steinberg

How can one tell whether a fund-raising campaign is successful? Regardless of how much is collected, unmet needs remain. A well-run campaign could fail to achieve overly optimistic campaign goals; a poorly run campaign could exceed unduly pessimistic campaign goals. In this chapter, I suggest principles for determining whether campaign budgeting is optimal in the practical sense—obtaining the best possible results given the level of competition from other fund drives. First, I analyze whether the fund-raising budget is split up correctly among alternative fund-raising techniques. Next, I analyze whether the right total amount of money is spent on fund raising. I follow with a discussion of fund raising from the donor perspective, arguing that donors should be uncon-

Note: This chapter summarizes four papers of mine appearing elsewhere. Numerous colleagues have contributed to the development of my ideas, as detailed in these other publications. Research has been supported by the Program on Non-Profit Organizations at Yale University and preparation of this manuscript by the Indiana University Center on Philanthropy.

cerned with the fund-raising share (that is, the ratio of solicitation expenditures to total donations).

In sum, I develop rules for determining whether a given campaign is optimal. However, these rules cannot be usefully applied without statistical analysis of results from previous and similar campaigns. I provide a nontechnical overview of these techniques and then discuss empirical results obtained by several studies. I conclude by suggesting that a simple rule of thumb can provide guidance to campaign managers when statistical analyses are infeasible or unavailable.

The key to optimality, both across techniques and in total budgetary decisions, is to consider *marginal productivity* (the additional donations resulting from incremental solicitation expenditures), rather than *average productivity* (total donations divided by total expenditures). Many fund-raising professionals intuitively choose to use average productivity to plan campaigns. This intuition is dead wrong. For example, faced with the choice between spending $1 to raise $2 or spending $10,000 to raise $15,000, an intuition based on average productivity might dictate choosing the former—a 200 percent rate of return seems more attractive than a 150 percent rate of return. Nonetheless, the latter choice brings in a $5,000 net return, clearly superior to the $1 net return of the former. I shall demonstrate below how rules based on marginal productivity will always lead to the correct decisions.

Optimality

Optimal for Whom? Quite a few parties care about the fund-raising process—donors (actual and prospective), the board of directors, staff, and external fund-raising counsel—and they often measure success in different ways. In this chapter, I will examine success as defined by the board of directors. If the sole goal of the campaign is to obtain money, then fund-raising is optimal if the net proceeds—the difference between contributions received and solicitation expenditures—are as large as they can be. This difference provides resources for accomplishing the organizational mission, and mission attainment requires maximal resources. When campaign goals are more complicated, including advocacy, education, or the attraction of new members and volunteers, optimal fund raising no longer consists of maximizing the net proceeds of the campaign. These complications are considered in turn below.

Each fund-raising campaign may be optimal, viewed from the boards' perspectives, and yet total expenditures may be excessive from the societal perspective. When one organization expands its campaign, competing organizations must spend more just to stay in the same place. In the limit, competing campaigns may cancel each other out in their entirety rather than expand the pool of total donations. This external effect of fund raising may justify coordinated campaigns (as with United Way) or some form of governmental regulation.

There are other reasons why privately optimal campaigns may be bad for society. For example, donors supporting the National Association for the Advancement of Colored People are generally made worse off when the Ku Klux Klan optimizes its fund-raising efforts. Alternatively, a fraudulent campaign may be quite successful in monetary terms even if no charitable services are supported by the campaign. Thus, while the decision rules in this chapter may help individual nonprofit organizations to better meet charitable needs, it is not always true that society as a whole benefits from their widespread implementation.

Optimality Across Techniques. No matter how much money a nonprofit chooses to spend on fund raising, it would like to get the biggest return for its bucks. Money can be spent on a variety of techniques, such as direct mail, media advertising, or telemarketing, and some are more productive than others. In this section, I show how to allocate a chosen sum of money across such techniques.

First, we will consider the simplest interesting situation, where there are only two available techniques, media and telemarketing, which can be employed alone or in any combination. All donations come in the form of money, and all returns are immediate—a campaign this year does not affect donations in any other year. (Multiple techniques, nonmonetary returns, and delayed effects will be considered later.)

Measures of average productivity will not help one decide.

On average, it is simply not true that a nonprofit firm can increase its net return by increasing the share of its budget spent on techniques that are highly productive. Marginal productivity is directly relevant, so we will define the marginal donative product of a technique (MDPT) as the *additional* donations expected if spending on that technique is increased by $1 from its starting level and spending on other techniques is held constant. I will use MDPm and MDPt to denote the marginal donative products of spending on media and on telemarketing, respectively.

MDPm depends upon the level of media spending—the value of spending an extra dollar when you have already spent $1,000 is typically different from the value of spending an extra dollar when you have already spent $1 million. Commonly, MDPT is relatively high for the first few dollars of expenditure, then it diminishes, although the exact rate at which it diminishes depends upon the technique used and the competitive environment. There may also be interactions between the techniques. Thus, MDPm, for example, may depend upon the level of telemarketing expenditure as well as the level of media spending: When telemarketing is high, the thousandth dollar spent on media may bring in little additional donations; when telemarketing is low, the thousandth dollar spent on media may be more productive.

The optimal decision rule is simple: Split your fund-raising budget so that it is entirely spent so that MDPm = MDPt. The reason is that if marginal products were not equal, there would be a way you could spend the same money and yet increase total donations. For example, suppose that you had $1,000 to spend, and you initially chose to spend $500 on media and $500 on telemarketing. Suppose that the 501st dollar spent on media would bring in an additional $4 in contributions (so that MDPm = $4), while the 500th dollar spent on telemarketing brought in an additional dollar (so that MDPt = $1). Marginal donative products are not equal, and a reallocation toward media (that is, spending $501 on media and $499 on telemarketing) would cause donations to first rise by $4, then fall by $1, resulting in a $3 net increase. Any time MDPTs are unequal, a similar reallocation will increase net donations, and one should continue to reallocate until diminishing returns set in and equality is obtained.

In some cases, a technique is simply not worth using at all. The logic of the optimization rule covers these cases as well. If, for example, MDPm exceeded MDPt for every way in which your budget could be split, the logic of the rule suggests progressively reallocating expenditures toward media until telemarketing expenditures are driven to zero.

The rule is easily extended to cases where three or more techniques are available. One should split the budget so that MDPTs are equal for all techniques that are worth using, and so that the MDPT for the first dollar spent on techniques not worth using is lower than the common MDPT for techniques that are used.

The rule can also be extended to cases where there are nonmonetary goals. Campaigns may directly accomplish the charitable mission as a side effect of fund raising. For example, political fund raising may also raise the candidate's profile, and fund drives for Mothers Against Drunk Driving (MADD) may educate the public about the dangers of drunk driving while also raising money. Another nonmonetary goal is to attract volunteers, and fund-raising campaigns often accomplish this goal as a side effect of raising money. In these cases, one should convert the side effect into its monetary equivalent, then calculate the MDPTs based on the resulting "adjusted" contributions. For example, if spending an additional dollar on a technique brings in a $1 cash donation plus additional volunteers worth $2, the MDPT for that technique is $3.

One caution: The conceptually proper monetary equivalent of side effects is the amount of money the organization would willingly forgo to obtain the side effect. This amount need not equal the cost of such services if purchased directly, and it would generally be lower. For example, the last dollar spent on solicitation may, as a side effect, attract an additional hour of volunteer time. To obtain this worker directly, they might have to pay a salary of $10 an hour, and at this price, the worker might not be worth hiring. If the nonprofit would be willing to pay $3 an hour to obtain equivalent services to those provided by the volunteer, this willingness to pay, and not the market wage, should be used to calculate adjusted contributions.

Finally, consider lagged effects. Many techniques are worthwhile because they are an investment in the future, rather than a currently productive activity. For example, direct mail may bring in few donations in the first year because the net must be cast widely. Yet, as a result of that "unproductive" expenditure, the mailing list can be pared down so that all future campaigns will be more productive. There are other reasons for lagged effects: An alumnus solicited this year may form a habit and continue to give without the necessity of future solicitation efforts, or a donor may spread her gift over time for tax reasons or convenience. In these cases, expected future returns should be converted into their equivalent current value using the technique known as discounting (see any finance textbook for more on this technique). Discounted future returns can then be added to current donations to produce "adjusted donations"; MDPT can then be calculated from adjusted donations and will properly incorporate all lagged effects.

Optimal Total Solicitation Budgets. The rules described above can be used to determine the best way to split up any possible total budget. From this, we can determine the "donative revenue function," which illustrates the maximum possible adjusted donations for each possible total expenditure level. The shape and properties of this relation will enable us to calculate the best total budget, so it is worthwhile to discuss these properties in greater detail.

Typically, some donations would accrue to the firm even if fund-raising expenditures were zero (because of the organization's reputation and word-of-mouth advertising), but donations would go up if the solicitation budget increased. As before, the key is marginal productivity. Define the marginal donative product of fund raising (MDPF) as the extra (adjusted) contributions that would result if an extra dollar were spent on solicitation in total. The first few dollars spent on a campaign are not very productive because of large start-up costs. Thus, MDPF is a small positive number for small fund-raising budgets. Once the start-up is arranged, incremental solicitation money can be effectively targeted, so MDPF rises. Past some point, the donor pool gets saturated, and further solicitation efforts bring in little additional money. Thus, MDPF falls, and may even go negative (if donors are so offended by excessive solicitation that they withdraw donations they otherwise would have made).

When the revenue function has this shape, the rule is simple: The optimal budget is the one that leads to MDPF = $1. The logic is also simple. If, at the current budget, MDPF = $5, by spending an additional dollar, we increase donations by $5 for a net return of $4. Indeed, any time MDPF exceeds $1, an increased solicitation budget would more than pay for itself, and one should increase the budget until diminishing returns set in and MDPF falls to $1.

There are two technical qualifications to this rule that are worth noting. First, it may be that there are two drastically different budgets that both lead to MDPF = $1. Very small campaigns may have this MDPF because they are mostly covering set-up costs, but once these costs are fully covered, MDPF rises above $1. At a vastly larger budget, diminishing returns set in and MDPF falls back to $1. The logic of the rule correctly guides us here: The small budget is not optimal because an increase of more than $1 in solicitation would more than pay for itself. The larger budget is optimal: Once diminishing returns set in to this extent, no increase in solicitation can pay for itself. Second, in rare cases, the net returns for a budget of zero can exceed the net returns from the budget that makes MDPF = $1. This occurs if the organization's reputation is strong and solicitation very costly. In these cases, one should not conduct a campaign until reputation fades by enough to reverse the situation.

Should Donors Care About Fund-Raising Share?

I have argued that fund raisers should ignore average productivity (contributions divided by solicitation) and hence, by implication, fund-raising share (solicitation divided by contributions). Instead, they should concentrate only on marginal productivity. My argument is subject to question, however, if donors prefer to avoid charities with high fund-raising shares. Clearly, if donors remain ignorant of fund-raising share, my earlier analysis is unaffected; if donors learn of fund-raising share, however, how should they respond?

I believe the correct answer is "not at all." If donors share the goals of the board of directors, to maximize provision of some charitable service, then they ought to support decision rules based on marginal productivity regardless of the resulting share. New char-

ities have higher shares simply because of their weaker reputation
and their inability to target solicitation efforts to the most likely
donors, and this high share does not indicate any managerial failing. Even established charities will have high shares if there is extensive competition between them for a fixed donor pool. But
donors who support these charities should know that the high share
is inherent in the environment and that their support is still necessary for service provision.

In a deeper sense, donors should ignore fund-raising share,
and, again, the argument hinges on the difference between averages
and marginals. An organization may have a high fund-raising
share, but what matters to an individual donor is how much additional can be accomplished if their donation is added to that of
others. We can then distinguish three situations.

First, the recipient organization might not respond to an
incremental donation, leaving its solicitation budget constant and
simply spending the donation on services. In this case, 100 percent
of marginal (additional) donations are devoted to services, regardless of the fund-raising share. By adding a donation to that made
by others, one lowers the fund-raising share, but the key is that one
increases service expenditures dollar-for-dollar.

Second, it could be that the recipient responds to incremental
donations by reducing its planned expenditures on solicitation (say,
because they figure they do not need to spend as much to reach their
campaign goal). In this case, an additional dollar of donations buys
more than a dollar of additional service expenditure, regardless of
the fund-raising share.

Finally, it could be that the recipient responds to incremental
donations by increasing its solicitation budget (say, to keep the
fund-raising share constant). In this case, an additional dollar
would be partly diverted from services, which might discourage
some donors. However, one has to account for the effect of induced
fund raising. If, prior to your donation, the organization had a
budget where MDPF was greater than $1, then the money diverted
to fund raising more than pays for itself, and marginal donations
result in more than corresponding service increments. Donors
should only be discouraged if MDPF was less than $1 prior to their
donation.

The first case (in which fund-raising budgets are not adjusted in response to incremental donations) is likely to be the most common one, for this type of behavior occurs whenever the organization follows the advice given earlier in this chapter. All such organizations are equally good "buys" for the donor, regardless of their relative fund-raising shares. In the second and third cases, some charities are better buys than others, but the value of any particular charity is essentially unrelated to fund-raising share, so donors *should* ignore share.

What of real-world donors, unschooled in the arcane theories discussed above? Clearly, there have been some scandals where donations have dried up following revelations of extremely high shares, but it is unclear whether this is a response to the share itself or to the attendant notoriety of scandal revelation. As a practical matter, donors rarely know shares, charities practice accounting tricks to artificially deflate their shares, and some donors recognize that circumstances may dictate a high share for a well-functioning charity. Two empirical studies, using data from nonprofit tax returns, attempted to determine whether high-share organizations had lower donations, all else equal. My 1986a study found no such effect, whereas a study by Weisbrod and Dominguez (1986) came to the opposite conclusion. The matter remains unsettled.

Regression Analysis—the Basic Statistical Tool

In order to apply these decision rules, the manager must know the shape of the revenue function and the marginal donative products of each combination of techniques—a rather hefty requirement, but not impossible. The key tool for estimating these functions is known as multiple regression analysis, which is available through many standard statistics software packages. However, there is no cookbook recipe for applying these techniques—art, judgment, and training are required. As a practical matter, fund-raising counsel may wish to hire an econometrician (one schooled in economics and statistics) to conduct the analysis. Here, I would like to provide an intuitive background so that you can understand some of the issues and the limitations of the techniques.

Unlike physical scientists, social scientists and fund-raising practitioners can rarely conduct controlled experiments, varying, say, fund-raising expenditures and nothing else and noticing how donors respond. Although one could test-market different fund-raising strategies in different cities at the same time or in the same city at different times, there are problems with this approach. First, test-marketing is expensive. Not only must the test be designed and implemented by expensive marketing consultants, but the regular campaign must be suspended during the test period. This may be feasible for large national charities, but smaller organizations could hardly afford it. Second, it is difficult to be certain that the various test sites are indeed equivalent so that any difference in donations can be properly attributed to the differences in techniques. Finally, it is difficult to generalize results, as there may be interactions between the control and experimental variables. For example, direct mail may seem to be an unproductive fund-raising technique if, in our experiment, we compare giving in two lower-middle-class towns, one with direct mail and the other without. However, if the same experiment were repeated in two wealthier communities, results might be drastically different. This problem could be solved in theory but not practically. You would have to test each technique, at each expenditure level, in each possible setting, a prohibitively expensive undertaking.

Alternatively, we could let several things vary at once between our test sites, reducing the cost of the marketing experiment. Cheaper still, we could use data from the real world, where no marketing test was conducted and everything varied at once. Then, we could use statistical techniques to analyze this joint variation and sort out the probable independent effects of each factor. Multiple regression analysis allows one to do this.

The method is not perfect. Since confounding effects are only held constant in a statistical sense (that is, on average), we can only estimate MDPTs or MDPF in that same sense. For example, we might analyze evidence on giving to a specified charity across many cities, focusing on two. The first city has high donor income and the charity also has a large solicitation budget in that city; the second city has lower income and solicitation. If we could properly account for the difference in giving that was due to the difference in income, we could attribute the remaining difference in donations to the difference in solicitation budgets and compute the MDPF for these expenditure levels. However, our estimate of the effect of income will be fuzzy, with a range of plus and minus, and this fuzziness will spill over to our estimate of the MDPF. This problem becomes less severe as the size of our data set increases.

Published Estimates

To estimate the marginal donative products of various techniques and determine the optimal combination, one would need data in which different combinations of techniques were employed at different times or places. Such data exist (although often kept confidential within large national charities), but I know of no published studies that apply regression analysis to estimate marginal products.

Several studies have employed data on total fund-raising budgets to estimate the entire revenue function for various nonprofit organizations. Others have more modestly estimated the MDPF of average organizations operating at their current fund-raising budget. With the former, one could compute the optimal budget; with the latter, one could only tell whether the existing budget is too high or too low. I summarize these latter studies as Table 14.1.

Most of the studies found that too little was spent on fund raising. For example, Boyle and Jacobs (1978) found that if the typical local chapter of United Way spent an additional dollar on solicitation, it would receive $16.40 in additional donations. The only exceptions came from the two studies of tax return data. In my 1986b analysis, I found that the typical health organization only obtained 13 cents from its last dollar of solicitation, reducing service expenditures by 87 cents. If this estimate is believed, it indicates that health organizations conducted excessively large campaigns, but my 1983 analysis of the same data (using a different statistical specification) indicated the reverse—that MDPF for health organizations was almost $17.

Weisbrod and Dominguez (1986) also obtained evidence that fund raising was excessive for all organizations studied. They distinguished the partial effect (the direct effect of fund raising on donations) from the total effect (which also includes an indirect

Table 14.1. Estimates of MDPF—The Additional Expected Donations if Solicitation Expenditure is Increased by One Dollar.

Study	Type of Data	Control Variables	Type of Organization	Estimated MDPF
Boyle and Jacobs (1978)	Cross-section of local or state chapters	Income, population, density, medical need	United Way American Heart Association American Cancer Society	$16.4 $3.6 $2.6
Boyle, Jacobs, and Reingen (1979)	Cross-section of county units or individual orchestras	"A variety of socio-economic and administrative variables"	March of Dimes Symphony Orchestras	$3.9 $4.2
Jacobs and Lee (1979)	Cross-section of stations		Public Broadcasting	$2.6
Weinberg (1980)	Time series for a single university	No. of alumni, special campaigns	Anonymous University	$9.8[a]
Steinberg (1983; 1986b)	Panel of IRS forms 990	Individual effects, administrative and service expenditures	Welfare Health Education Arts Research	$14.2[b], $1.2[c] $16.8[b], $0.1[c] $31.0[b], $1.6[c] $1.2[b], $2.1[c] $113.0[b], $7.6[c]
Weisbrod and Dominguez (1986)	Panel of IRS forms 990	'Price' (based on share), age of organization	Library Art, Zoo, & Museum Aid to Poor and Aged Hospital Aid to Handicapped Disease Research Schools	$78[d], −$39[e] $27[d], −$48[e] $18[d], −$34[e] $55[d], −$21[e] $13[d], −$14[e] $17[d], −$7[e] $21[d], −$10[e]
Luksetich, Jacobs, and Lange (1986)	Cross-section of museums	Not specified	Museums	$3.3
Posnett and Sandler (1989)[f]	Cross-section of UK Charities	'Price' (based on share), age of organization, legacies, grants, autonomous income	Full sample Health Overseas Religion Social Welfare	$6.0[d], $1.2[e] $4.2[d], $0.8[e] $6.7[d], $2.1[e] $18.8[d], $4.4[e] $4.7[d], $1.1[e]

Notes: [a] linear specification.
[b] log-log specification from 1983 paper.
[c] baseline (linear) specification from 1986 paper.
[d] partial effect—neglects impact of fund raising on 'price'.
[e] total effect—includes impact of fund raising on 'price'.
[f] all elasticities calculated from data in article, evaluated at means of contributions and fund raising.

"price" effect). Measured by the partial effect, fund raising appeared inadequate, with MDPFs ranging from $13 to $78. However, Weisbrod and Dominguez argued that donors are discouraged from giving when the fund-raising *share* becomes too large (the "price" effect) and estimated the independent influences of fund-raising share and fund-raising level. Including this latter effect, they found that fund raising was so excessive that MDPF was negative in all cases—the last dollar of solicitation appeared to *reduce* gross donations. Two caveats should be kept in mind, however. First, I argued above that the price variable does not belong in the statistical analysis, and I found support for this proposition in my 1986a study. Second, Weisbrod and Dominguez's results are very fuzzy in a statistical sense. I have reported the most likely values, but the plus or minus range is quite broad for these estimates.

One is struck by the disparate range of estimates. To some extent, this is simply because the studied organizations are different. There is no reason to suppose that the typical symphony orchestra conducts its campaign with the same efficiency as the typical soup kitchen, and there is no reason to suppose that organizations were as efficient in 1978 as in 1986. However, much of the difference is probably due to differences in statistical technique. I survey these factors below.

The Problems of Aggregation and Excluded Variables

Regression analysis requires a reasonably large number of observations to produce reliable results. Unfortunately, in most samples, it is unlikely that all the included observations were produced from the same donative revenue function. Harvard University spends a different amount on fund raising than Cape Cod Community College and also receives a different number of donations. However, these two observations could not be used to persuasively estimate a single donative revenue function because the two institutions operate in such different fund-raising environments. We cannot look at Cape Cod's performance and persuasively assert that if Harvard had the same solicitation budget, it would have the same donations. The two observations come from distinct donative revenue curves. If we pretended otherwise, our estimates would suffer from "aggregation bias."

If each available observation comes from a different revenue function, then none of these functions can be properly estimated. Thus, researchers look for data sets containing observations that are expected to come from (approximately) the same curve. For example, Weinberg (1980) looked at twenty-one observations from the same university, figuring that the shape of the revenue function does not vary greatly over time for a given university. Boyle and Jacobs (1978), Boyle, Jacobs, and Reingen (1979), and Jacobs and Lee (1979) looked at cross-sections of local units of a national organization, implicitly arguing that they share the same revenue function because they serve the same need. The other studies looked at distinct organizations within the same nonprofit "industry," arguing that this provides sufficient homogeneity.

To a large extent, aggregation bias is due to the absence of data on relevant control variables. For example, if the reason that Harvard's revenue function is different from Cape Cod's is that Harvard has a greater number of alumni and these alumni are wealthier, then a study which subtracted out statistical estimates of the effects of alumni numbers and average wealth would, in effect, put both institutions on the same curve, allowing proper estimation. If measures of every single factor affecting donations could be included in the study, there would be no problem of bias. Of course, it is impossible to obtain all these measures, but studies are generally more persuasive if they include some of the more important factors.

Although precision requires a complete set of control variables, some of these variables are unnecessary for obtaining unbiased estimates (that is, estimates just as likely to be too high as to be too low). Estimates of MDPF are unbiased if the variables excluded from analysis do not systematically vary together with fund-raising expenditures. If fund-raising expenditures are usually higher when community income is higher, it would be important to include a measure of income in our analysis to distinguish which is the cause of variations in giving.

Panel data sets study the same group of organizations over several years. This kind of data allows researchers to do a much better job of eliminating possible biases caused by excluded variables. In my 1986b study, I applied the statistical technique known as the individual effects model to a three-year panel. This technique relates the changes in giving at each organization to the changes in solicitation expenditures. Since these changes *within* cannot be due to unmeasured differences *across* organizations, this technique removes the confounding influences of any excluded variable that remains constant at each organization over time. A similar trick removes the effect of common trends across organizations due to variables that affect all organizations similarly in each year but vary from year to year. Many other more powerful techniques for analyzing panel data have recently become available, and future researchers should use these to the fullest.

Accounting Problems

Different organizations utilize different accounting standards. Expenses classified as administrative by one nonprofit may be classified as fund raising by another and as program expenditures by a third. In some cases, differences reflect honest uncertainties about the proper accounting technique (for example, if the purpose of the organization is advocacy, and solicitation literature is informative, it is not clear whether expenses are fund raising or program related); in others, differences reflect public relations attempts to minimize apparent fund-raising expenditures.

Statisticians have shown that when explanatory variables (fund-raising expenditures) are badly measured, estimates of their effects will generally be biased toward zero. Thus, true MDPFs are probably larger than the estimates reported here, and the conclusion that most nonprofits spend too little on fund raising is strengthened.

The individual effects model will reduce the impact of biases caused by these accounting problems. Likewise, some of the cross-sectional studies should have little problem because all units of a national organization presumably use the same accounting standards.

One type of accounting problem is more difficult to handle. Our decision rule requires that we use *adjusted* contributions to compute MDPF, but typically we can only measure actual contributions. If fund raising results in increased volunteering or accomplishes the organizational mission as a side effect, a substantial error might occur. A campaign that looked to be excessive using estimates from actual contributions might be ideal using the proper measure. No existing study has attempted to solve this problem.

Determining the Shape of the Revenue Function

It is one thing to estimate MDPF to determine whether an organization is spending too much or too little on fund raising. However, to compute the precise optimal level of fund raising, one needs to know the shape of the entire revenue function to determine how much one has to spend to obtain MDPF = $1. In econometrics, this is accomplished by specifying a "functional form," a general shape (S-shaped, parabola, and so on) and letting the computer determine the best estimate for that form. There are then statistical tests to determine which of the tested forms is most appropriate.

In my 1983 work, I found that the functional form mattered quite a lot (the chief difference between my 1983 and 1986 estimates reported here in Table 14.1 is the assumed functional form). Further, none of the functional forms clearly dominated, using the conventional statistical tests. This type of result is rare in econometrics, and further research seems necessary (it might just have been a peculiarity of the particular data set I used, or it might represent a more serious problem).

Without a clearly preferred functional form, it is impossible to persuasively calculate the optimal fund-raising budget. I tried to do so in 1983 and got ludicrous answers (including "The average welfare organization should increase its fund raising by $2.1 billion in order to increase its net receipts by $319 million.").

Some Advice

Although it is not impossible to estimate the revenue functions required for computing optimal budgets, it is difficult, and the analyst will need to be well trained in econometric techniques before persuasive estimates can be produced. Nonetheless, the rules for optimality produce useful insights without statistical analysis. Fund-raising professionals can (and should) use their experience to gain a feel for what works and what does not. The optimizing rules then provide insight in how to apply that experience—techniques that work well on *average* need not work well on the *margin,* and optimality requires the analyst to consider the marginal gains from incremental adjustments to the budget.

There is a relatively simple method for obtaining estimates of MDPF that I call the differencing technique. A nonprofit planning this year's campaign budget need only have data of expenditures and contributions in the last two years, adjusted for inflation. To estimate MDPF, simply take the change in donations over the previous two years and divide this by the change in fund-raising expenditures. If the resulting number is less than 1, the organization should reduce its campaign size from last year's. If the estimate is close to 1, the campaign size should be increased by the amount of expected inflation. If the number is greater than 1, the campaign expenditures should be increased by more than the inflation rate.

The differencing method has two problems. First, it only indicates the direction, and not the size, of the desirable change in fund-raising expenditures. Second, it will be inaccurate if some factor other than the change in fund raising caused the observed change in donations over the prior two years. Nonetheless, the method is so simple that it is a useful first step, if applied advisedly.

References

Boyle, S. E., and Jacobs, P. "The Economics of Charitable Fund Raising." *Philanthropy Monthly,* May 1978, pp. 21-27.

Boyle, S. E., Jacobs, P., and Reingen, P. "How You Can Raise Your Fund Raising Productivity." *National Society of Fund Raising Executives Journal,* 1979, *4* (1), 4-6.

Jacobs, P., and Lee, R. Y. "Public Broadcasting Fund Raising." *Philanthropy Monthly,* Sept. 1979, pp. 20-23.

Luksetich, W., Jacobs, P., and Lange, M. "Productivity in Museum Fund Raising: An Economic Analysis." *Philanthropy Monthly,* June 1986, pp. 20-23.

Steinberg, R. "Economic and Empiric Analysis of Fund Raising Behavior by Nonprofit Firms." Working Papers on Non-Profit

Organizations (PONPO), no. 76. New Haven, Conn.: Yale University Press, 1983.

Steinberg, R. "Optimal Fund Raising by Nonprofit Firms." In *Giving and Volunteering: New Frontiers of Knowledge,* conference volume. Washington, D.C.: INDEPENDENT SECTOR and United Way of America, 1985.

Steinberg, R. "Should Donors Care About Fund Raising?" In S. Rose-Ackerman (ed.), *The Economics of Nonprofit Institutions: Studies in Structure and Policy.* New York: Oxford University Press, 1986a.

Steinberg, R. "The Revealed Objective Functions of Nonprofit Firms." *Rand Journal of Economics,* 1986b, *17* (4), 508–526.

Weinberg, C. B. "Marketing Mix Decision Rules for Nonprofit Organizations." *Research in Marketing,* 1980, *3,* 191–234.

Weisbrod, B., and Dominguez, N. "Demand for Collective Goods in Private Nonprofit Markets: Can Fund Raising Expenditures Help Overcome Free-Rider Behavior?" *Journal of Public Economics,* 1986, *30,* 83–95.

Chapter 15

Investing More Money in Fund Raising—Wisely

Wilson C. Levis

There is general agreement that giving must increase at a faster rate if nonprofits are to provide urgently needed services. However, increasing giving at a faster rate of growth will require *wise* investment in fund raising at a faster rate. What is the current investment in fund raising? Using an industry estimate of 15 percent average fund-raising costs, the nonprofit sector spent $16 billion in 1988 to raise $104 billion and net $88 billion for programs. Was it worth $16 billion? If nonprofits had not invested $16 billion in fund raising in 1988, tens of millions of people, in fact all of us, would not have benefited from the $88 billion of net funds raised.

What if the sector had invested $25 billion in fund raising? Could it have raised $140 billion and netted $115 billion? Research indicates that there is a vast untapped potential for giving in this country. However, other research into the economics of charitable fund raising indicates that such an increase could not have been accomplished without first investing the additional money. The nonprofit sector urgently needs to realize this, set aside its negative attitudes toward fund-raising costs, and start taking the rate of growth of fund-raising budgets seriously.

Recommendation: An Ask-More Program

How can the nonprofit sector increase the annual rate of growth of giving from the current 10 percent to 12 percent or more? By increasing the rate of growth of fund-raising budgets from 10 percent to 12 percent or more—*wisely*. And how can the nonprofit sector do this? Individuals give primarily because they are *asked* to give. Therefore, it is recommended that "ask-more" programs be conducted around the country with a goal of increasing the annual rate of growth of fund-raising budgets to 12 percent. This will double the national fund-raising budget in six years from an estimated $19 billion in 1990 to $40 billion in 1996. The "ask-more" programs would encourage nonprofit boards, CEOs, and funders to invest *more* money in asking *more* donor/prospects to give *more* money.

The "ask-more" activities, while much more narrowly defined, would be compatible with and mutually supportive of INDEPENDENT SECTOR's Give-Five program.

Leadership for the "ask-more" programs could come from the fund raising profession and its professional societies and chapters. Implementation would be through collaborative efforts and partnerships among professional fund-raising groups, nonprofit umbrella groups, and resource-provider groups—for example, NSFRE chapters, nonprofit associations, and regional grant-maker associations.

However, translating giving potential into gifts cannot be accomplished simply by increasing fund-raising investments. Following the proposed guidelines for wise investment in fund raising is essential.

1. Set aside negative attitudes toward fund raising.
2. Match fund-raising costs with related revenue.
3. Recover fund-raising investments from related gifts.
4. Invest by appropriate categories of fund raising.
5. Give investors decision-useful information.
6. Keep fund-raising cost percentages reasonable.

7.   Do *not* try to lower bottom-line cost percentages.
8.   Test new fund-raising efforts.
9.   Learn from every fund-raising investment.

Increasing Giving at a Faster Rate of Growth

What is the current rate of growth in giving? According to *Giving USA,* published by American Association of Fund-Raising Counsel Trust for Philanthropy (1988, p. 10), Americans gave $104 billion in 1988. The rate of growth was 11 percent over giving in 1987. The 1987 rate of growth was 6.2 percent. The average rate of growth over the five-year period from 1984 to 1988 was 9.7 percent.

What could the rate of growth realistically be? In 1985, IN-DEPENDENT SECTOR's Measurable Growth Program set as its goal an annual rate of growth in giving of 12.2 percent, which would have doubled giving in six years from $80 billion in 1985 to $160 billion in 1991. (The Measurable Growth Program is now the Give-Five Program.) For its part in the Measurable Growth Program, in 1986 the United Way of America set a goal of 14.9 percent annual rate of growth for its Second Century Initiative in order to double giving to United Way in five years by 1991.

Research by these two organizations, and by the National Charities Information Bureau and the Program on Nonprofit Organizations at Yale University, indicates the great potential for individual giving in this country. Yet, it appears that the INDEPENDENT SECTOR's goal of 12 percent annual growth and the United Way of America's goal of 15 percent annual growth will not be met. Why? Because United Way and other nonprofits have not been investing 12 to 15 percent more money in the fund-raising capacity or the effort required to ask more individuals for 12 to 15 percent more in giving. Individuals give because they are asked to give, not because they have the potential to give or because nonprofits set goals for them.

Therefore, investment in fund raising at a faster rate is required. Effective asking costs money. It involves needs assessment, case development, market research and feasibility studies, prospect research, fund-raising planning and budgeting, volunteer solicitor recruitment and training, volunteer solicitation (*asking*), gift processing and acknowledgment, donor recognition, donor record keeping, results analysis, and fund-raising performance measurement and evaluation. Without the resources to conduct all these fund-raising activities with all the potential sources of funds, nonprofits cannot significantly increase the rate of growth of results. This conclusion is supported by research into the economics of charitable fund raising, showing that there is a direct relationship between fund-raising expenditures and results (Boyle and Jacobs, 1978).

Enter the Fund-Raising Investor

Who are the *fund-raising investors?* They include nonprofit board members and CEOs who make fund-raising budget decisions. Fund-raising investors also include donors who make fund-raising grants to broaden bases of support and to build organizations' capacity to raise money. Fund-raising managers, who do not make budget decisions, are not fund-raising investors; they recommend fund-raising investments and then spend the money that fund-raising investors invest.

Increasing investment at a faster rate will not automatically increase individual giving at a faster rate, but it is doubtful that giving can be increased substantially unless fund-raising investors make corresponding increases in fund-raising investments.

After they set challenging fund-raising goals, investing more money in fund raising *wisely*—in order to achieve those goals—will be the real challenge for fund-raising investors.

Guidelines for Investing in Fund-Raising—Wisely

It may seem that this chapter is encouraging nonprofits across the country to make significant increases in their fund-raising budgets in the belief that this will automatically increase results. This is not the case. Translating fund-raising potential into actual results cannot be accomplished simply by increasing budgets. The following nine rules are therefore proposed as a "first cut" at developing guidelines for investing more money in fund raising—wisely.

1. *Set aside negative attitudes toward fund raising and fund-raising costs.*

There are both legitimate concerns and uninformed negative attitudes toward fund-raising costs. Fund-raising investors cannot think clearly—wisely—about investing money in fund raising if their thoughts are filled with concerns or biased by negative attitudes.

One important example of a legitimate concern is that new-donor acquisition efforts usually cost 75 to 150 percent of what they raise. However, to be effective, fund-raising investors must accept that such performance is considered reasonable by virtually all members of the fund-raising profession and by most nonprofit executives. The reality is that this has been the practice for decades. Many of the most prestigious and successful charities have developed very efficient multimillion-dollar annual appeals and major donor programs with donors originally acquired at 100 percent fund-raising costs. Investing more money in new-donor acquisition—broadening bases of support—is absolutely essential to increasing giving at a faster rate of growth.

2. *Match fund-raising costs with related revenue.*

Budgeting and accounting systems should be set up to match expense and related revenue for each fund-raising effort. How can revenues be matched with related expenses? The concepts of assigning responsibility for, budgeting for, accounting for (matching), and evaluating fund-raising expenses and related results effort by effort may be new to nonprofits in general. These concepts fall into the general category of cost accounting; more specifically, responsibility accounting, profitability accounting, or activity accounting. They are not new to accounting. They are not new to nonprofit program services. They are not new to direct-mail fund raising. However, they are new to most other forms of fund raising.

How does this work for direct-mail fund raising? First, all new-donor acquisition mailings to cold prospects are categorized separately from renewal mailings to prior donors. Second, a return-on-investment code (ROI-code) is assigned to each fund-raising mailing. Sometimes a single mailing will have several ROI-codes identifying the different lists and appeal materials used. Budgeted and actual costs are allocated to each ROI-code based on the number of names assigned to it. Projected results plus actual receipts are

matched to related mailings by ROI-code. Sophisticated computer
analyses by ROI-code include but are not limited to

– Cost	*Renewal only:*
– Number solicited	
– Cost per solicitation	– Responses last year
– Number of responses	– Gifts last year
– Rate of response	– Average gift last year
– Amount of gifts	– Rate of growth/responses
– Net gifts raised	– Rate of growth/gifts
– Average gift size	– Rate of growth/size
– Cost per gift	
– Cost per dollar raised	

The cost data are most significant. Most fund-raising operations have sophisticated analyses for the revenue side of their other
fund-raising categories, but they include no cost data.

The information outlined above is far more detailed than the
information needed by fund-raising investors for reviewing and
evaluating fund-raising investment requests. But all the information they need is included.

If nonprofits are to invest more money in fund raising wisely,
they should adapt the budgeting and cost accounting techniques
now used for direct-mail fund raising and program services for all
of their fund-raising activities.

3. *Recover fund-raising investments from related gifts.*

Recovering investments in fund raising by deducting costs
from related gifts when they are received is an uncommon (or maybe
nonexistent) practice today. However, no accounting concept could
be potentially more important for the nonprofit sector. If there is
a vast untapped potential for individual giving and if costs can be
deducted directly from related gifts, there must be a vast untapped
source of funds to *spend* on fund raising.

Can fund-raising costs actually be deducted from gifts received? Yes. In fact, *all* fund-raising costs are deducted from some-
body's gift. Where else can they come from? United Way allocations?
Government grants? Program service fees? Bona fide membership
dues and assessments? Investment income? Unrelated business in-

come? No. At the end of a fiscal year, nonprofits in effect deduct all fund raising expenses from *unrestricted,* direct public support gifts. However, 70, 80, or 90 percent of these costs—depending on various circumstances—could be deducted directly from related gifts as they are received. If nonprofits are going to deduct fund-raising costs from gifts anyway, why not do so usefully—wisely.

Unfortunately, no examples have been found where a non-profit has actually deducted fund-raising costs from related receipts; however, here is an illustration of de facto deduction of fund-raising costs from related gifts. In 1974, a popular charity serving community problems in a major city invested $1,800 in a mailing to 8,000 randomly selected residents in the community (note that these are actual 1974 figures and would be two or three times greater today). The mailing produced over 200 new contributors and raised nearly $3,000. In January 1975, based on the successful $1,800 test mailing, the charity invested $13,000 in mailing to 100,000 demographically selected residents. Another 2,600 names were added to the donor list. The mailing generated more than $28,000. The charity invested in two more mailings in 1975 at a cost of $13,000 each. Their total investment in new-donor acquisition for 1975 was $39,000. They acquired 6,800 new donors and raised $78,000.

Whose money did the charity spend on fund raising? Where did (1) the initial $1,800 and (2) the $39,000 the charity spent on fund raising in 1975 come from? The donors, of course, who gave the initial $3,000 in 1974 and the $78,000 in 1975. If there had been a loss, it would have been deducted from the charity's reserve, which also came from contributors—*prior* contributors. In either case, the fund-raising costs would have been paid for with money from some group of contributors.

Exactly how did the charity have the donors pay for the fund-raising costs? In January 1975, based on the success of the initial test mailing, the charity placed orders for $13,000 worth of fund-raising materials and services. A mailing went out to 100,000 people, which resulted in a return of $28,000. *Then the suppliers were paid $13,000 of the $28,000 raised.* Thus, while the charity was at risk, it did not even need a working capital fund to finance its fund-raising investments; the 2,600 donors more than covered the fund-raising costs related to their gifts. Note that in 1975 the charity *spent* $39,000 on new-donor fund raising but only *invested* $13,000, which it rolled over three times during the year and fully recovered by year's end.

If nonprofits are to spend money on asking at a faster rate in order to increase giving at a faster rate, they need to take a bona fide investment approach to investing more money in fund raising. They need to start testing the overt deduction of the money they have invested in fund raising directly from the gifts their investment generates. In other words, nonprofit boards, CEOs, and grant makers should invest money in fund raising; fund-raising managers should submit requests for fund-raising investments and then *spend* the money approved. The accounting department should recover the funds invested by the fund-raising investors from related gifts as they are received. If direct-mail fund raising can be financed in this manner, other methods can be financed this way too.

If investors in fund raising can literally invest in rather than spend on fund raising, then what they will need is more working capital to invest, not to spend, and the amount of working capital needed to invest in fund raising will be a fraction of the total amount of money needed to spend. Nonprofit boards will be able to set up revolving-fund budgets for investing in fund raising. Grant makers will be able to provide interest-free loans, revolving-fund grants, and recoverable grants to enable grantees to expand their fund-raising efforts.

4. *Invest by appropriate categories of fund raising.*

Requests submitted to fund-raising investors (that is, budget or grant requests) should be presented by categories appropriate for making wise investment decisions. Separate investment decisions, including fund-raising grants, should be made for the following categories of activities related to fund raising.

a. Fund-raising investments in the *capacity-building* category are essential for long-term increases in the rate of growth of giving. However, capacity building produces no income and, therefore, cannot be evaluated in terms of return on investment. It includes:

> Assessing an organization's capacity to raise money
> Board recruitment and development

Development of a clear mission statement
Setting goals to achieve mission
Long-range strategic planning to achieve goals
Marketing programs and services
Accounting and financial reporting
Fund-raising market research
Major campaign feasibility studies
Setting up donor records systems
Setting up other fund-raising office systems

Since capacity building produces no income, investments in this category cannot be matched directly with specific gift receipts from which these investments can be deducted. Capacity-building investments are long-term investments that must be charged to the general operating fund and taken from reserves or funded through a capacity-building grant.

b. *New-donor acquisition* and related categories are intended to broaden a nonprofit's base of support from individuals. Through new-donor acquisition efforts, usually by direct mail, nonprofits build lists of several thousand donors that make small-to-medium-size gifts. Then nonprofits can identify several hundred prospective major donors from these lists of prior donors. Nonprofits can seldom start out soliciting a select group of several hundred individuals for major annual gifts and planned gifts.

New-donor acquisition efforts are income producing, but they are usually not expected or intended to produce *net* contributions. Most, if not all, direct, variable costs associated with new-donor acquisition can be deducted from related gifts as they are received.

c. *Individual donor renewal* is the category of fund-raising activity that produces net contributions from the second, third, and so on gifts from prior individual donors. Donor renewal is expected to be efficient and focuses on retention and upgrading of prior donors. It includes major individual annual gifts, special gifts, capital gifts, and gifts for endowment. Because of the large margin of "profit," all the costs associated with donor renewal can be deducted from related gifts as they are received.

d. *Individual planned giving* should be invested in separately from other donor renewal activities. Planned giving activities are directed toward those annual donors who respond to requests to consider making bequests or other deferred gifts. Planned giving has enormous potential for many nonprofits, and it can produce large sums of net contributions—eventually.

It should be invested in separately because, while it produces income, the related costs occur many years before the income is received. Therefore, it is not feasible to deduct related fund-raising costs from planned gifts received. However, once a planned giving program begins producing cash income, current-year planned giving costs can be deducted from unrelated cash planned gifts received.

e. *Grant seeking* from institutional sources such as corporations and foundations generally produces *net* income, even with the first grant. Because of the large margin of "profit," all the costs associated with grant seeking can usually be deducted from the unrestricted portion of related grants as they are received. However, there will be a shortfall if too many of the grants are restricted and the sum of the unrestricted grants does not equal all the grant-seeking costs.

5. *Give investors decision-useful information.* (See Illustrative Fund-Raising Investment Request Form, Exhibit 15.1).

For investing in all fund-raising activities except capacity building, fund-raising investors need information that will enable them to determine if each proposed investment is projected to have the desired rate of growth they want and to have a reasonable fund-raising cost percentage.

The fund-raising investment request for each activity should present expenses, projected results, and projected cost percentages. The request should show the net return for last year, the projected rate of growth, the projected number of gifts, and the average gift size. Each fund-raising investment should be assigned a return-on-investment code (ROI-code). The category or purpose for each should be specified—for example, new-donor acquisition, donor renewal, planned giving, grant-seeking (type code).

Exhibit 15.1 shows the projected net return on investment and the projected annual rate of growth that net return represents.

Exhibit 15.1. Illustrative Fund-Raising Investment Request Form.

Fund-Raising Activity	Type	Fund-Raising Investment Request (A)	Projected Results (B)	Net Return on Investment (B−A)	Projected Fund-Raising Cost Percentage (A/B)	ROI Code	Net Return Last Year (C)	Rate of Growth ((B−A−C)/C)	Projected Number of Gifts (D)	Projected Average Gift Size (B/D)
									Evaluation	

BEG. OF YEAR:

TOTAL:										

ADD-ONS DURING YEAR:

TOTAL:										

Instructions: 1. Enter fund-raising investment requests separately for each type of fund-raising activity and code as type a, b, c, d, or e.

    a. Capacity building (i.e., non-income producing).

    b. New Donor Acquisition, list building.

    c. Donor Renewal, major gifts, capital campaigns.

    d. Planned giving.

    e. Grant seeking, corporate and foundation.

    2. Submit progress reports with actual expenses and results in the same format as the investment request, completing all entries.

Fund-raising investors can see quickly if the sum of the projected net returns is equal to or greater than the goal for financing the program services planned for the following year. (The net funds raised this year should be the basis for the program budget for next year.) Fund-raising investors can also see if the projected overall rate of growth of net return on investment is equal to the goal of growth.

The accounting system should be set up to match and report the actual expense and related revenue for each fund-raising effort, in the same format as the budget (that is, the fund-raising budget request). Actual expenses and results can then be compared with the budgeted expenses and projected results so that more accurate budgets and projections can be made in the future.

6. *Keep fund-raising cost percentages reasonable.* (See Recommended Reasonable Fund-Raising Cost Percentages, Exhibit 15.2).

Projected fund raising cost percentages are included on the Fund-Raising Investment Request Form for each request. These should be reviewed during the budgeting process to assure that they are reasonable for each type of fund-raising activity.

Fund-raising investors should keep in mind that, if 80 percent of the money comes from the 20 percent who are major donors, then 90 percent of the net money comes from these donors. This is because the cost percentages for major donors are 5 to 15 percent, while gifts from the other 80 percent of the donors might cost 20 to 50 percent. But tomorrow's major donors are among today's 80 percent that are at the small-to-modest gift level, and $5 donors have their place in philanthropy—even at 50 percent fund-raising costs.

7. *Do not try to lower bottom-line cost percentages.*

Fund-raising investors should not pursue an investment policy of lowering overall annual fund-raising cost percentages by reducing efforts to broaden the base. In the long run, doing so significantly reduces the rate of growth of net contributions. In fact, nonprofits that do not invest in new-donor acquisition, for example, can experience a reduction in revenue and may even die.

Exhibit 2 does not include criteria for the reasonableness of overall fund-raising efficiency. This is because the efficiency of new-donor acquisition should be measured and evaluated separately from donor renewal using substantially different performance criteria. The efficiency of major gift fund raising should be measured

Exhibit 15.2. Recommended Reasonable Fund-Raising Cost Percentages
by Bill Levis (4-8-90).

Fund-Raising Cost Percentage (Efficiency):
Fund-raising expense as a percent of contributions.

Average Gift-Size Range (Contributions Divided by Number of Gifts	BROADENING BASE		RAISING NET DOLLARS	
	New Donor Acquisition, List Building, First Gifts, Special-Event Promotions		Donor Renewal, Major Gifts, Planned Giving, Capital Campaigns, Corporate and Foundation Support	
	Objective	Maximum	Objective	Maximum
$1,000,000 & Up	4.0%	10.0%	2.0%	5.0%
500,000–1,000,000	5.0%	10.0%	2.5%	5.0%
250,000–500,000	6.0%	12.0%	3.0%	6.0%
100,000–250,000	8.0%	14.0%	4.0%	7.0%
50,000–100,000	10.0%	16.0%	5.0%	8.0%
25,000–50,000	12.0%	20.0%	6.0%	10.0%
10,000–25,000	14.0%	24.0%	7.0%	12.0%
5,000–10,000	16.0%	30.0%	8.0%	14.0%
2,500–5,000	18.0%	40.0%	9.0%	16.0%
1,000–2,500	25.0%	50.0%	10.0%	18.0%
500–1,000	30.0%	75.0%	12.0%	20.0%
250–500	40.0%	100.0%	14.0%	22.0%
100–250	50.0%	100.0%	16.0%	25.0%
50–100	50.0%	100.0%	20.0%	30.0%
25–50	75.0%	125.0%	25.0%	40.0%
10–25	100.0%	150.0%	35.0%	50.0%
5–10	100.0%	150.0%	50.0%	75.0%
Under 5	100.0%	150.0%	50.0%	100.0%

Criteria for determining of fund-raising costs for each proposed fund-raising investment are reasonable, vary according to the following two dimensions.

1. The objective: (a) broadening the base of support (e.g., new donor acquisition) or (b) raising NET dollars (e.g., donor renewal). Broadening the base is not expected to produce significant NET gifts and costs of 100% or more can be reasonable. Raising net dollars, usually from prior donors, should cost less than 30% on average.

2. Projected average gift size. For example, reasonable donor renewal costs can vary from 2%–5% for a $1 million average gift size to 50%–100% for a $2.00 average gift size.

and evaluated separately from small-to-modest gift fund raising, also using substantially different performance criteria. Since capacity building produces no income at all, its cost percentage is infinite. There is no reliable performance criteria for determining the reasonableness of fund-raising efficiency when acquisition data are combined with renewal data, when major gift data are combined with small-to-modest gift data, or when capacity-building costs are included.

In this regard, legislators, regulators, and the media continue to focus on the bottom-line fund-raising cost percentage. Since negative attitudes on the part of fund-raising investors create resistance to increasing the rate of growth of wise investment in fund raising, charity legislators, regulators, review groups, and investigative reporters need to find ways to expose fund-raising abuses without at the same time creating and/or reinforcing negative attitudes about fund-raising costs. The bottom-line fund-raising cost percentage can be used as one tool for helping them identify potentially abusive situations that warrant further investigation. However, high cost percentages are not abuses, so other criteria must be applied in order to determine when an abuse has occurred.

8. *Test new fund-raising efforts.* To the extent possible, new fund-raising efforts should start with modest investments on a test basis.

New-donor acquisition efforts should start with a test of 5 to 10 percent of the names on each proposed mailing list. Further use of each list should be contingent on satisfactory test results. The criteria for satisfactory test results should be established before each test is approved. Fund-raising consultants can be used on a part-time basis to test such activities as major individual gifts, corporate and foundation grants, and/or planned giving.

9. *Learn from every fund-raising investment.*

Fund-raising investment requests should be accompanied by data about the results of previous fund-raising investments so that subsequent ones can be based on evaluations of the performance of previous efforts.

Funding Fund Raising Is the Key

More and more resource providers are helping their grantees increase giving from other sources. These resource providers include philanthropists, corporations and foundations, United Ways, and government agencies. They are in the best position to influence increased *wise* investment in fund raising for individual gifts. By making fund-raising grants wisely, funders will be showing fund-raising investors on the boards and staffs of their grantee organizations how to do it.

What could funders fund? (1) Grant makers could fund an initial fund-raising audit and then encourage grantees to periodically assess their fund-raising capacities and the effectiveness of their efforts. (2) Grant makers could fund projects to increase fund-raising capacities based on these assessments. (3) Grant makers could make revolving-fund grants or loans to grantees for investing more money in their fund-raising efforts that produce income. Direct grants are needed for categories 1 and 2, which produce no income, but revolving-fund grants or loans are more useful in the long run for fund-raising activities that produce income (category 3).

Once grantees implement these three types of fund-raising grants, their investors will quickly see that they can justify using their own funds for periodic assessments and capacity building. And they will also see that in applying the revolving-fund grant they have, in effect, set up a revolving-fund budget for investing in fund raising, to which they can add some of their own resources.

References

American Association of Fund-Raising Counsel. *Giving USA: The Annual Report on Philanthropy for the Year 1987.* New York: American Association of Fund-Raising Counsel, 1988.

Boyle, S. E., and Jacobs, P. "The Economics of Charitable Fund Raising." *Philanthropy Monthly,* May 1978, pp. 21–27.

Chapter 16

Taking Fund Raising Seriously: An Agenda

Robert L. Payton
Henry A. Rosso
Eugene R. Tempel

Philanthropy is universal; organized philanthropy appears in all civilized societies. No society, however, has put as much emphasis on organized voluntary action as has the United States. Understanding philanthropy is essential to understanding American society.

Andrew Carnegie began his essay "The Gospel of Wealth" with a short summary of his political and economic philosophy— what he called "individualism" (Carnegie, 1962). Underlying Carnegie's philosophy is an assumption that individuals are of central importance in a free society. His political and economic philosophy also assumes, however, an important role for the private market economy. The central debate of the modern era is about the extent to which individuals have freedom—and thus responsibility to look after themselves—and to what extent their freedom must be constrained to provide public goods (including the welfare of those who fail to or are otherwise unable to survive and prosper on their own initiative). There have been, as a result, continually shifting boundaries among the three sectors. At times the agenda of philanthropy is taken up by the marketplace in the form of welfare capitalism; at other times philanthropy becomes so dominated by government that we speak of the welfare state. Voluntary action expands and contracts in interaction with the other two sectors.

Assumptions

Fund Raising Assumes a Large Role for Individual Action. Fund raising not only assumes a role for individual action; it also assumes that the state will not be able, even under the best of circumstances, to provide for all the needs of the people. Fund raising also assumes that simple self-interest will fail to provide for the needs of many individuals and groups and for many of the needs of the society.

The United States Is a Three-Sector Society. The first sector in U.S. society is government, the rationale for which is the exclusive use of legitimate force; the second sector is the marketplace, the defining term of which is private property; the third sector is philanthropy, the defining term of which is morality in the form of voluntary action for the public good. Government pursues its fund raising primarily by taxation; the marketplace uses diverse forms of investment and venture capital. Fund raising in the third sector lacks the coercive power of government to tax and the promise of the marketplace of pecuniary or other material rewards. Third-sector organizations generate their resources and income from voluntary contributions of money, goods, and services—*and* from the sales of services and from government grants, as well as from activities sometimes only peripherally related to their mission or function.

The Three Sectors Intersect and Overlap. Each sector has its special characteristics, yet bears some of the characteristics of the other two. Business corporations and government agencies make grants for public purposes; volunteers work without compensation for political parties and government agencies; voluntary associations receive tax exemption from the government and sometimes compete directly with business corporations in the sales of services. There are great practical benefits in lowering the barriers among the sectors and in sharing the larger burdens of the society. At the same time the subordination of the core values of one sector to those of another leads to a serious distortion of the values of each sector as well as of the society as a whole. In the 1960s, for example, many organizations of the third sector received such increases in tax-related income that their basic practices changed and became increasingly determined by legislation, administrative action, and judicial decision. Some voluntary associations abandoned social service programs to government agencies. In more recent years, many voluntary associations have adopted the values as well as the practices of business corporations. For example, some voluntary hospitals originally established to serve the poor have rejected patients because of their inability to pay. The national social welfare agenda is shaped by continuing debates over the relative roles of individual responsibility, government programs, and voluntary giving and service.

As we mentioned earlier, we see fund raising as more than marketing. Fund raising as an aspect of philanthropy is different from for-profit business. The single-minded pursuit of self-interest is not enough to produce the public good—something more is required. The rationale for the third sector is increasingly subject to value contamination from the other two sectors, and the current concern is the seepage of business values into the different (if not always purer) waters of philanthropy.

The Third Sector Is Pluralistic. One would almost say, "Of course the third sector is pluralistic." The diversity of the sector is now greatly amplified by the demographic changes that bring cultural attitudes and values different from the western European values that have dominated philanthropy in the United States for three hundred years.

The Third Sector Is Goad, Critic, and Advocate. Even though voluntary associations are dependent on the government for protection and on the government and the marketplace for financial support, the third sector claims the right to speak and to be heard because of the moral force of its position. Voluntary associations express the plurality of views and preferences of the society; their pluralism also often threatens to disrupt social order and harmony. The debate over abortion is the most obvious example; foreign policy, environmental issues, and a wide range of human rights claims are equally familiar.

Philanthropy Often Requires Cooperation; in the United States Philanthropy Assumes Competition As Well. Voluntary associations sometimes work together to achieve common goals. At other times they compete directly for what are assumed to be limited resources. Many organizations are engaged in continuing philosophical conflict, attempting to weaken or to destroy the *cases* being made by other organizations. Some organizations deny the social and moral legitimacy of the very mission that other organizations exist to serve.

Fund Raising Is a Right. To organize a voluntary association for some public purpose is a right; to seek to raise money for it is a right guaranteed by the First Amendment of the Constitution. The right of voluntary associations to raise money to advocate social change and reform—as mentioned in a previous paragraph—is not a privilege casually given and taken away by government. On the other hand, fund raising is also a privilege, because there is no obligation for anyone to contribute. The right to ask for money includes the right to be refused.

Critiques and Criticism

We take "critique" to mean here an evaluation of the merits of the theory and "criticism" to mean a judgment that one is falling short of acceptable standards. There is a criticism of philanthropy, for example, that argues that voluntary action does not work; coercion is necessary to accomplish collective purposes on a large scale. A second criticism argues that philanthropy undermines individualism. A third says that voluntary giving eases the pressure on government to meet its responsibilities, by trying to provide what government should provide by taxation. Another criticism is that fund raising is economically inefficient.

   The most common criticism of all is that fund raising is demeaning; regardless of the form it takes, fund raising is begging. Such a definition puts the fund raiser in an inferior social as well as economic position. The notion that the fund raiser and donor can share equally in serving a cause is brushed aside as romantic nonsense. The complex psychological relationship that arises from fund raising for a philanthropic organization is different from selling products and services in the marketplace. There is a clarity of objective in the marketplace that is missing from fund raising. The resulting ambiguity makes many people uncomfortable, driving them out of fund raising altogether. Despite fund raising's importance, the field has not been the subject of extensive empirical research that would illuminate these psychological problems.

Almost all writing about fund raising is written for believers or for those who want to believe. Writing about fund raising by practitioners is about practice, but it usually gives answers only to a narrow list of questions; it avoids awkward and complicated questions. Perhaps that is why there is not yet a serious book on the ethics of fund raising—no book about the ethics of competence, the ethics of relationships, and certainly not about the ethics of rhetoric.

Fund raising is usually thought of as a *business*; fund raisers borrow most of their practices, language, and even their values from the marketplace. The philosophy of fund raising is often a crude form of pragmatism ("vulgar pragmatism," one might say)—opportunistic and manipulative. If it works, it's good (or good enough).

In general, theoretical critiques have addressed other aspects of philanthropy, while fund raising has been usually subjected to criticism for bad practice rather than for bad theory. In this chapter, we are less concerned with the distinctions between theory and practice and more interested in getting the issues on the table.

The Scholar's Agenda. Every concept and statement in what has gone before is admittedly subject to correction and modification. The theory and practice of fund raising have never enjoyed the benefit of close scholarly scrutiny and analysis. Fund raisers typically borrow whatever seems useful from professional schools— principally from schools of law, business, and public administration, but also from communication or journalism and occasionally schools of social work and education—schools which are themselves notorious borrowers from the more basic disciplines of the humanities and the social sciences. As a consequence, fund raising in particular, and philanthropy in general, skate on thinner intellectual ice than is prudent. *Our first recommendation is that fund raising be studied from the perspective of the liberal arts.*

Thus far, most involvement of the liberal arts in the study of fund raising has been from a social scientific perspective: economics, political science, and psychology. What is lacking in the study of fund raising is the disinterested, critical, historical, and interpretive analysis that characterizes the humanistic liberal arts at their best.

There are several areas where scholars could make an immediate and important contribution to understanding fund raising: in social psychology (questions of dominance and dependence and how they affect fund-raising relationships); in psychology (motivations for giving; the ways personality affects fund-raising performance); in anthropology (the cultural variations in fund raising and in giving attitudes and behavior); sociology (socialization of the young into giving and fund raising), and so on.

Historians, the most generous contributor of all the disciplines to philanthropic studies over the years, should be encouraged (financially as well as rhetorically) to look much more closely at fund-raising practices and how they have developed in the twentieth century. Public history, now on the rise, has much to offer. New archival collections of the papers of fund-raising consultants and others will make possible a higher quality of historical research than the field has yet seen. Oral history is a valuable tool to explore the world of practice, as students of politics have learned. Comparative studies of fund raising in diverse cultures and among diverse ethnic groups should attract the attention of anthropologists. The most disturbing omission from the literature is the inadequate treatment of fund raising in religious traditions, both within Western religious traditions and in comparative studies of the traditions of non-Western religions. In ancient Judaism the two most respected men of the community were asked to collect the tithe; in many oriental religions, begging is a sacred act.

The unresolved philosophical issues underlying this essay are of course fundamental to any "philosophy of fund raising." Long-standing debates about public goods, free riders, and interest-group behavior have important implications for fund raising and

other aspects of philanthropy. In our opinion, the theoretical understanding of scholars will remain deficient as long as it remains
at such a distance from the mundane evidence of practice. The
practice of the field, of course, will continue to make slow progress
by trial and error, by anecdote, and by rules of thumb.

Fund raising is a practice. The Fund Raising School has
become part of the Center on Philanthropy of Indiana University
because of the desire to make fund raising "more professional." The
links of fund raising to the study of business are manifold. Most
fund raisers talk about fund raising as if it were merely a business.
The field of public administration has declared a territorial interest
in nonprofit management (under which term fund raising is usually subsumed). Social work is a field of philanthropy, but in recent
years it has seldom shown an interest in fund raising as a discrete
activity. Fund raising seems to be thought of as a subordinate, not
very important subfield—a subsidiary of minor professions. Because
the professional schools are dominated by social scientific methods
and values, there is little attention to history, political and economic philosophy, and ethics in courses about fund raising.

We are convinced that fund raising must be understood in
context. We believe that the theory of fund raising should grow out
of practice, that each shapes the other dimension. The consequence
of ignoring fund raising has left the liberal arts without a persuasive
rationale even for themselves. The liberal arts lack an answer to the
fund-raising questions: *Why do you exist? Why should anyone give
you money?* We believe that the liberal arts would be stronger and
more influential both within the university and outside it if philosophers, historians, and sociologists were more immediately engaged
in fund raising, more attentive to their mission and their case.

The Practitioner's Agenda. We offer eight topics for consideration
(and with some opinions):

1. *Commercialization.* Fund raising leads philanthropy more
deeply into the commercialization of its techniques—and perhaps of
its values as well. But philanthropy is not commerce, and some
commercial techniques are unsuitable.

2. *Volunteers.* We believe that voluntary service is the lifeblood of philanthropy. Volunteers are an essential but diminishing

force. The denigration of the role of volunteers by professionals and other staff may be weakening the general public's will to volunteer. Volunteers are philanthropy's most credible voice; they legitimate the voice of the professional.

3. *Professionalism.* We believe that a professional is more than a technician. Fund-raising practitioners without a strong ethical sense and commitment tend to equate success with money raised—or, more precisely, with their own income.

4. *Bureaucratization.* As mentioned earlier, voluntary associations are subject to all the same organizational constraints and problems that plague government agencies and business corporations. Some philanthropic organizations are suffering from problems of scale: alienation from donors (and sometimes from employees); failures of communication; and top-heavy administration.

5. *Accountability and regulation.* Too many organizations have failed to take accountability seriously, which has encouraged new regulatory initiatives by the states. Limits on fund-raising costs are the most familiar. A second form of regulation seeks to control unwanted solicitation in public places and intrusions into the privacy of the home. The new regulatory initiatives often clash with rights of free speech and assembly—rights that include the right to raise money. These issues must be addressed in the context of the right to raise money for unpopular causes. Fund raisers have tended to leave such discussions to others when it falls beyond their own organizational self-interest.

6. *Education and training.* In simplest terms, fund raising has been about training, not education; that is, there is an overemphasis on the "how-to" to the neglect of the "why." There is no consensus among fund-raising professionals about the general education of the fund raiser. Until recently, the leading associations concerned with fund raising have failed to make educational issues important; the overwhelming emphasis is on technique, with little more than lip service to ethics, values, history, and philosophy. (One way to think about the question is to ask what is the difference between a trade association and a professional association.) As a result, fund raisers rarely have a working rationale for the existence of the third sector.

7. *Rhetoric.* Philanthropy may soon go the way of patrio-

tism—a valuable concept sacrificed to cheap emotional exploitation. Borrowing marketing and advertising techniques from business is one part of the problem. Mr. Gresham's Law applies to fund raising as it does to money: bad money drives out good money. It becomes increasingly difficult for donors to discriminate among the flood of appeals. Quantity drives out quality. "Donor fatigue" results from strain on the psyche as well as on the eyes and ears. Following the lead of advertising and mass marketing, fund raisers exalt the simple forms of expression. Blunt ideas are driven home in short sentences built with small words, inadvertently sacrificing complexity and ambiguity—and often credibility as well.

8. *Demography*. Behind this innocent technical word lies the profound cultural changes of the modern age: the profile of "Americans" is changing rapidly and profoundly and will continue to change. The changes include those of values and attitudes: the expectations of women, racial and ethnic minorities, and age groups, and the shifting dependencies across the generations.

Fund raising and fund raisers are as subject to such forces as everyone else. Solid demographic knowledge is now part of the required general education of the fund raiser.

Conclusion

Fund raising would not be necessary in a perfect society. Given the imperfections of this democratic society from the beginning and into the most distant future, however, fund raising and fund raisers will always be with us.

This is a profoundly democratic lesson: We should attend to the reasons why fund raisers exist and persuade others as well as ourselves of the merits of the case for fund raising. American philanthropy is also inclusive: The philosophy of voluntary action assumes that there is a role for everyone, capitalist and socialist, the poorest and the richest, the most saintly and the most mean spirited.

Thinking of fund raising as a First Amendment right is a reminder that fund raising is an exercise in voluntary association and free speech. If there is merit in that view, fund raising is ennobled by it. Bringing fund raising into the university is simple recognition of the importance of fund raising as a form of voluntary action.

Our hope is that fund raising will be taken seriously.

Reference

Carnegie, A. "The Gospel of Wealth." In E. C. Kirkland (ed.), *The Gospel of Wealth and Other Timely Essays.* Cambridge, Mass.: Harvard University Press, 1962.

Index

A

Abbott, A., 110, 111, 116, 117, 121
Accountability: issue of, 279; and philosophy of fund raising, 7, 8–9; for public education costs, 206, 207–208, 210–212; for results, and conflicts of interest, 95–96
Accounting: in economics of fund raising, 253–254; regulation of, 213, 216
Addams, J., 20
Adopt-a-Pet, 207
Allen, W. H., 21, 36
American Association of Fund-Raising Counsel (AAFRC): and evolution of profession, 18, 26, 27, 30; and individual giving, 221, 236; and investment in fund raising, 259, 271; and professionalization, 104; and regulation, 201, 205, 206, 208; survey by, 49, 50; and women, 146

American Cancer Society, 250
American City Bureau, 26
American Heart Association, 250
American Institute of Certified Public Accounting, 207, 210
Amos, 58
Andreasan, A. R., 6, 15, 16
Anheuser-Busch, 83
Appreciation, in capital campaign, 183
Aquinas, T., 67, 72
Argument, as war, 41
Arizona, regulation in, 209
Armstrong, D., 197, 198
Arnold, C., 148, 169
Ask-more programs, investment in, 258–259
Associated Black Charities, 225
Ast, S., 18–19

B

Barber, F. C., 23
Barber and Associates, in pioneer generation, 23, 25

Barn raising, fund raising related
  to, 39
Beauchamp, T., 86-87, 98
Beaver, H., 25
Beggars, fund raisers distinct from,
  187-189. *See also* Tin cup
Bianchi, S. H., 147, 169
Black and Decker, and exchange
  values, 192
Black philanthropy: aspects of,
  219-238; attitudes toward, 231-
  234; background on, 219-222; in
  churches, 220, 224-225, 230; con-
  clusion on, 234-236; devalued,
  220; evolution of, 219-220, 224-
  226; future of, 236; socioeco-
  nomic profile of, 226-231; by the
  wealthy, 219-220, 226, 235, 236;
  and work ethic, 222-224
Black United Fund, 225, 234
Bloland, H. G., 103, 121
Bloland, P. A., 119, 121
Boone, B., 179, 183
Boris, E. E., 162, 163, 165, 167
Bornstein, R., 103, 121
Borsos, J., 18
Bowen and Gurin, Inc., in second
  generation, 30
Bowie, N., 87, 98
Bowyer, J. B., 15, 16
Boyle, S. E., 249, 250, 252, 255, 260,
  271
Brakeley, G. A., Jr., 27, 28, 32
Brakeley, G. A., Sr., 25
Brakeley, G. A., III, 206
Brakeley Recruiting, 146, 154-155,
  156, 167
Bremner, R. H., 21, 36, 84, 98
Brewer, M., 27, 31
Briscoe, M. G., 18
Broom, G. M., 161, 167
Brown, P., 183
Buderi, R., 198
Bumgarner, S., 146, 158-159, 165,
  167
Bureaucratization, issue of, 279
Bush, B. H., 200
Bush, G., 223
Business: aspects of practices from,

124-143; background on, 124-
  125; conclusion on, 142; and
  ethical issues, 140-142; fund
  raising distinct from, 129; practices of, in fund raising, 129-140
Byrd, A., 224, 237
Byrne, J. P., 141, 143

C

California, regulation in, 209
Campaign: capital, 173-183; as mil-
  itary metaphor, 44-45
Campaign method, development
  of, 21-22
Capacity-building fund raising,
  264-265
Cape Cod Community College, and
  aggregation issues, 251-252
Carbone, R. F., 117, 121, 140-141,
  143, 147, 153, 159, 160, 162, 167
Carlson, D., 34
Carnegie, A., 16, 20, 272, 281
Carroll, A., 173
Carson, E. D., 219, 224, 226, 237
Case making, and philosophy, 6-7
Cause, and philosophy, 8
Center on Budget and Policy Prior-
  ities, 222, 235, 237
Certified Fund Raising Executive,
  201
Chamberlain, R., 32
Charitable Enforcement Fund, 214
Charitable organizations, attitudes
  toward, 231-234
Charities Registration Office, 213
Chatterjeo, P., 144n
Cheating, deception by, 76-77
Chewning, P. B., 115, 116, 122
Chief development officer, role of,
  132
Civil rights movement, 225
Clary, E. G., 56, 72
Cline, C. G., 149, 160, 161, 162, 167,
  169
Colorado, regulation in, 209
Combined Federal Campaign, 235
Commercialization, issue of, 278
Commissions, in evolution of pro-

fessional fund raisers, 18–19, 23, 26, 32

Committee on Public Information, 24

Community, and religious fund raising, 56, 57, 58–60, 64, 65, 71

Community foundations, for black philanthropy, 236

Community needs, fund raising focus on, 184, 185, 186, 187, 189, 191, 194, 197–198

Competence: and philosophy of fund raising, 10, 14; and professionalization, 114

Conflict: and argument as war, 41; of goods and rights, 5–6; of loyalty, 105–106

Conflicts of interest: and accountability for results, 95–96; analysis of, 83–99; background on, 83–84; conclusions on, 97–98; defined, 85; and degree of control, 93–94; and dependence on corporate support, 96–97; and disclosure of funding sources, 97–98; discussion on, 93–97; and ethical theory, 85–87; and goals, 94; and guidelines, 96; idealism-pragmatism spectrum in, 86–87, 88–93, 97; interviews on, 87–93; and member reactions, 94–95; perspective on, 84–85; and wholeheartedness, 12

Connecticut, regulation in, 212

Conry, J. C., 144

Consent, as justification for deception, 77

Constantine, 65

Constituency, natural, for capital campaign, 177

Contracts, between fund raisers and nonprofits, 216–217

Control, and skill development, 115

Cook, F., 33

Corporate donors, conflicts of interest between nonprofits and, 83–99

Cosby, B., 236

Cosby, C., 236

Costs: managing, and business practices, 136–137; reasonable percentages of, 268–270; revenues matched with, 261–262

Council for the Advancement and Support of Education (CASE): and cost management, 136; and ethics, 79–80, 82; Greenbrier II Colloquium on Professionalism of, 114; network of, 27; and professionalization, 104, 114, 116; and women, 144, 147, 151, 153, 154, 166

Council on Foundations, 221, 234

Covenant House, governance of, 7

Cowan, A., 145, 149, 151, 152, 167

Creedon, P. J., 144n, 148, 155, 161, 167

Cuffe, P., 220

Cullen, F. T., 141, 143

Culture, in development, 105–107

Culver, C., 82

Cutlip, S. M., 19–20, 21, 22, 23, 24, 25, 36

D

Dahl, R., 112, 121

Daniels, A. K., 163, 165, 167

Dartmouth College, education at, 21

Davis, C., 168

Davis, K. E., 225, 231–232, 237

Deception: analysis of, 73–82; background on, 73–74; examples of, 77–82; and justification, 77, 81–82; nature of, 74–77; by withholding, 75–77

DeGeorge, R., 86, 98

Demography: issue of, 280; trends in, 220–221

Desruisseaux, P., 146, 149, 168

Development. See Fund raising

Development director, for capital campaign, 175

Dewey, J., 6, 12, 16

Differencing technique, for economics of fund raising, 255

DiMaggio, P. J., 112, 121–122

Direct-mail fund raising, investing in, 261–262, 263, 270

Directors, board of. *See* Trustees

Disclosure: duty for, 80–81; and free speech rights, 204, 206–207, 212–213; regulation of, 212–213, 215–216

Dominguez, N., 247, 249, 250, 251, 256

Donors: acquiring new, 265; corporate, and conflicts of interest, 83–99; decision-useful information for, 266–268; fund raisers in relationship with, 73, 79–80, 81, 185–186, 187, 190, 198, 276; fund-raising share concerns of, 245–247; motivations of, 14, 56–57, 84, 127, 185, 231–234; planned giving by, 266; renewing, 265; socioeconomic profiles of, 226–231

Douglas, J., 69, 72

Dozier, D. M., 161, 167

Dreshman, C., 25

Drucker, P. F., 13, 16, 96, 98

Duncan, R. F., 25

Duronio, M. A., 124, 125, 143

Duty: failure to do, 77; professional, 78–80, 82

E

Ebbinghouse, C., 144*n*

Economics of fund raising: accounting problems in, 253–254; advice on, 254–255; analysis of, 239–256; background on, 239–240; differencing technique for, 255; and donor concerns about fund-raising share, 245–247; issues of aggregation and excluded variables in, 251–253; and lagged effects, 243–244; and optimality, 240–245; and published estimates, 249–251; and regression analysis, 247–249; and shape of revenue function, 254

Education, issue of, 279

Edwards, R. A., 115, 116, 122

Elliot, P., 109, 122

Elliott, D., 73, 82

Enters, C., 43–44, 50

Entrepreneurship, and business practices, 137–138

Environmental organizations, fund raising by, 189–190, 191

Ethics: and business, 140–142; and commissions, 18; and conflicts of interest, 85–87; deception issues in codes of, 79–80; elements of, 9–10; morals distinct from, 9; and philosophy of fund raising, 5–6, 9–10, 13; and regulation, 214–216

Exchange process: and deception issues, 81–82; fund raising as, 185–187, 189, 191, 192, 193–197, 198; motivation in, 127; and positive thinking, 14

Exxon, 83

F

Feasibility study, for capital campaign, 174–175

Federal Emergency Management Agency (FEMA), 196

Federal Trade Commission, 206

Federation of the Blind, and regulation case, 204

Fees, regulation of, 204

Feminization: aspects of, 144–169; background on, 144–147; future of, 166–167; implications of, 155–157; and metaphors, 45; paradoxes of, 163–165; paralleled in other fields, 160–163; phenomenon of, 147–165; and status issue, 153, 157–160, 161

Fisher, J. L., 104, 122

Florida, regulation in, 209, 212

Folbre, 152

Foundations: community, for black philanthropy, 236; feminization of grant making by, 162–163

Francis, N. C., 9

Free African Society, 224–225

Free speech rights, and disclosure, 204, 206–207, 212–213
Freeman, D. K., 127, 143
Freidson, E., 111, 122
Functional approach, to professionalization, 110–111
Fund raisers, professional: and ambivalence about money, 128; associations of, 104; background on, 18–20; beggars distinct from, 187–189; commissions for, 18–19, 23, 26, 32; concepts of, 38–40; as consultants, 30; contracts between nonprofits and, 216–217; education and training of, 279; evolution of professional, 18–36; as facilitators, 15, 30; firms of, 23, 25–26, 27; hero image of, 48–49; metaphors used by, 37–50; negative perceptions of, 28–29, 30, 126–127, 261; occupational commitments of, 106–107; over-sixty generation of, 27–32; pioneer generation of, 20–27; professional duty of, 78–80, 82; prototype of, 63; self-perceptions of, 162; under-sixty generation of, 32–36; women as, 34–35, 144–169
Fund raising: agenda for, 272–281; aspects of practice in, 171–281; assumptions of, 273–275; attitudes about, 187–197; by black philanthropies, 219–238; business distinct from, 129; business practices in, 124–143; as calling or career, 19, 31, 35–36; careers in, 107–108; and community needs, 184–187, 189, 191, 194, 197–198; competition and cooperation in, 275; conclusion on, 280–281; costs matched with revenues in, 261–262; critiques and criticism of, 275–280; culture in, 105–107; deception issues in, 73–82; default entry into, 19, 28, 33; economics of, 239–256; enjoying, 182–183; essentials in successful, 13–16; as exchange, 14, 81–82,

127, 185–187, 189, 191, 192, 193–197, 198; by federated agencies, 20; feminization of, 144–169; field of, 1–50; investing in, 257–271; liberal arts in study of, 277–278; moral dimensions of, 8–10, 51–99; negative views of, 28–29, 30, 126–127, 261; and nonmonetary goals, 243; philanthropy related to, 125–128; philosophy of, 3–17; practitioner's agenda for, 278–280; premise of, 5; principles of, 214–216; professionalization of, 101–169; regulation of, 200–218; relationships in, 73, 79–80, 81, 185–186, 187, 190, 198, 276; religious, 53–72; as a right, 275, 280; rules for, 173–183; scholar's agenda for, 276–278; share of, donor concern about, 245–247; standards of, 29; in third sector, 273–275; with tin cup, 184–199; values of, 31–32; work of, 105–108
Fund-raising investor, role of, 260
Fund Raising School, 190, 278

G

Gallup Organization, 221
Ganzfried, D., 144n
Garvey movement, 225
Gates, O., 25
Geever, J., 33
Georges, A., 158–159, 165, 167
Gert, B., 74, 75, 82
Ghetto, women in, 145, 149, 151, 155, 160, 161, 167
Gibbs, N., 237
Gibson, E. B., 27
Glass ceiling, for women, 149
Goals: and business practices, 132–134; for capital campaign, 178–179; and conflicts of interest, 94; nonmonetary, 243
Goodale, T., 33
Godde, J., 84, 98
Goss, K., 83, 98, 145, 146, 147, 158, 168

Governance, and philosophy, 7–8
Grace, K. S., 184
Grant seeking, investment in, 266
Gratitude, and religious fund raising, 56, 62, 64, 69, 71
Greed, and religious fund raising, 67–68
Greene, E., 153, 154, 159, 166, 168
Greenwood, E., 110, 122
Grenzebach, M., 27
Grieco, M., 148, 158, 168
Gross, E., 150, 168
Guilt, and religious fund raising, 56, 58, 63, 64, 68, 69, 71
Gurin, M., 27, 30
Guthrie, A., 43

H

Hall, P., 219
Hamilton, A., 8, 10, 16–17
Harrah-Conforth, J., 18
Harris, A., 224, 237
Harris, E., 204, 217
Harris, R. L., 225, 237
Harrison, J. N., 187, 198
Hartford, University of, sponsorship by, 9
Hartford Early Learning Program, curriculum of, 9
Hartmann, H., 148, 168
Harvard University: and aggregation issues, 251–252; campaigns by, 24, 30, 127; early fund raising for, 187; education at, 24, 25
Haskell, T., 26, 36
Hawaii, regulation in, 209, 212
Hawkes, T., 40, 50
Hedrick, B., 25
Hewlett, W. R., 195
Higher education: and aggregation issues, 251–252; business practices in fund raising for, 124–143; campaigns in, 24, 30, 127, 190, 193–197, 199; deception issues in, 73–82; gift to, 236; professionalization of development in, 103–123; supplicants in, 187; workplace assimilation in, 116

Holley, L. S., 204, 217
Hopkins, B., 201
House Bill 3964, 206
House of Morgan, 25
Hull House, 20
Human nature, theory of, 10–12
Hunter, F., 112, 122
Hutchinson, S., 187, 198
Hymowitz, C., 149, 168

I

Idealism-pragmatism spectrum, in conflicts of interest, 86–87, 88–93, 97
Illinois, regulation in, 211–212, 214, 217
INDEPENDENT SECTOR: and business practices, 126, 143; and investment in fund raising, 258, 259; and regulation, 204, 217; and values, 70
Indiana University, Center on Philanthropy at, 239n, 278
Indianapolis Symphony Orchestra, feasibility study for, 173–174
Institutional approach, to professionalization, 112–113
Internal Revenue Service (IRS): data from, 250; disclosure to, 76; and regulation, 201, 207, 211, 213, 216; requirements of, 9
International Association of Business Communicators (IABC), 160
Investment in fund raising: amounts of, 257; in ask-more programs, 258–259; aspects of, 257–271; background on, 257–258; by categories, 264–266; centrality of, 270–271; for faster rate of growth, 259–260; guidelines for, 260–270; recovered from related gifts, 262–264; testing and learning from, 270
Iowa, regulation in, 209
Isaiah, 60–61

J

Jacobs, P., 249, 250, 252, 255, 260, 271
Japan, and conflicts of interest, 84
Jeavons, T. H., 53
Jesus, 53, 61–63, 70
John, 62, 63
John Price Jones company, in pioneer generation, 25–26
Johnson, M., 37–38, 39, 41–42, 50
Johnson, R., 236, 237
Johnson, T. J., 111, 122
Joint Center for Political and Economic Studies (JCPES), 221, 223, 229
Jones, I., 46
Jones, J., 220
Jones, J. P., 22, 24, 25
Joseph, J. A., 234, 237
Judis, J., 84, 98
Justice, and religious fund raising, 56, 60, 61–62, 64, 66, 71
Justification, and deception, 77, 81–82

K

Kant, I., 87
Kennedy, D., 194
Kersting, D., 26, 27
Ketchum, C., 22
Ketchum, D., 27
Klegon, D., 113, 122
Knowledge base, for professionalization, 114–119
Koch, E., 229
Koretz, G., 152, 168
Ku Klux Klan, 241
Kutscher, R. E., 220, 237

L

Lakoff, G., 37–38, 39, 41–42, 50
Lamount, T., 25
Lange, M., 250, 255
Language. See Metaphors
Larson, M. S., 111, 122
Latessa, E. J., 141, 143

Law, deception by disobedience to, 76. See also Regulation
Lawson, C. E., 126, 143
Leadership: need for, 14; personally recruited, 176–177; volunteer, 175–176
Lee, R. Y., 250, 252, 255
Legislation, trends in, 209–214
Lenkowsky, L., 187–188, 198
Leslie, C., 187, 198
Levis, W. C., 257, 269
Liberal arts, contributions of, 277–278
Licensure, and regulation, 204
Lilly Endowment, 103n
Loessin, B. A., 124, 125, 143
Loma Prieta earthquake, 195–196
Lombardo, B. J., 83
Long-term benefits, and business practices, 139–140
Lord, J. G., 130, 143
Loury, G. C., 222, 237–238
Luke, 61
Luksetich, W., 250, 255
Luna, E., 158–159, 165, 167
Lundy, G., 25, 26
Lying, nonverbal equivalents to, 75. See also Deception

M

McCaffrey, C. J., 204, 217
McCann company, H. K., 24
McDonald, F., 12, 17
McGuire, J., 85, 98
McIlquham, J. D., 147, 164, 165, 168
Macklin, R., 85, 98
Madison, J., 16, 17
Maimonides, M., 66–67, 69, 70, 72
Maine, regulation in, 205, 209
Management, and business practices, 134–135
March of Dimes, 250
Marginal donative product of a technique (MDPT), 242–244, 248
Marginal donative product of fund raising (MDPF), 244–245, 246, 248, 249–251, 252, 253, 254, 255

Mark, 61
Marketing, and business practices, 130-131
Marts, A. C., 19, 21, 22, 23, 24, 25, 26, 36, 84, 98
Maryland: blacks constrained in, 220; regulation in, 209, 212
Massachusetts, regulation in, 209
Massachusetts Bay Colony, fund raising by, 187
Material things, and religious fund raising, 62, 72
Mathews, D., 225, 238
Matthew, 53, 62, 63
Meetings, for capital campaign, 179-180
Melillo, W., 19, 36, 154, 168
Mellon, A. W., 84
Metaphors: analysis of, 37-50; assumptions and aspirations in, 43; chivalric, 47-48; for donor-fund raiser relationship, 73; in "fund raising," 38-40; military, 44-45; mixed, 45-47; organic, 43-44; orientational, 42; spatial, 47; of tapping, 49; theological, 44; working of, 40-41
Metzenbaum, H., 211
Meyer, J. W., 112, 122
Micah, 58
Minnesota, regulation in, 209, 212
Minnesota, University of, education at, 22
Minorities: in demographic trends, 220-221; in fund raising, 35. See also Black philanthropy
Mission: and community needs, 189-190; importance of, 129, 131; and philosophy, 6
Mobility, and women, 165
Model Act for the Regulation of Charitable Solicitations, 205, 209-210
Money: ambivalence about, 128; time as, 42
Montague, W., 83, 84, 98-99
Moral dimensions: aspects of, 8-10, 51-99; of conflict of interest, 83-99; of deception, 73-82; ethics

distinct from, 9; of religious fund raising, 53-72; rules in, 75; teleological and deontological approaches to, 86-87
Mothers Against Drunk Driving, 243
Motivations: of donors, 14, 185, 231-234; for false charity, 84; in philanthropic exchange, 127; sacred and secular, 56-57
Munson case, 204
Murphy, M. K., 122

N

National Animal Protection Fund, 206, 207
National Association for the Advancement of Colored People, 241
National Association of Attorneys General, 205
National Association of College and University Business Officers, 136
National Association of Hospital Development (NAHD), 104, 146, 151, 153, 154, 166
National Association of State Charities Officials, 205
National Black United Fund, 224, 235
National Charities Information Bureau, 259
National Committee for Responsive Philanthropy, 235, 238
National Health Council, 210, 217
National Society of Fund Raising Executives (NSFRE): code of ethics of, 79-80; and evolution of profession, 18, 27, 35; and investment in fund raising, 258; and professionalization, 104; and regulation, 201, 202, 208; and women, 144, 146, 151, 152, 155, 156, 158
Neusner, J., 66, 72
New Jersey, regulation in, 210-211, 217

New York: begging and fund raising case in, 187–188; and regulation, 202, 213–214, 215
New York City, panhandlers in, 229
Niebuhr, H. R., 10, 17
Nonprofits: attitudes toward, 231–234; contracts between fund raisers and, 216–217; corporate donors in conflict of interest with, 83–99
North Carolina: blacks constrained in, 220; regulation in, 204, 205, 209
Norton, W. J., 20

O

O'Connell, B., 219, 238
Odendahl, T. J., 126, 143, 163, 165, 167
Ohio, regulation in, 209
O'Neill, M., 46–47, 50
Optimality: across techniques, 241–244; for total solicitation budgets, 244–245; for trustees, 240–241
Organization, need for, 13–14

P

Pacific West Cancer Fund, 213–214
Packard, V., 38, 50
Pasqual, P., 144n
Paton, G. J., 136, 143
Paul, 63–64
Payton, R. L., 3, 70, 72, 125, 143, 272
Penney, J. F., 119, 122
Pennsylvania, regulation in, 209, 212
Perlman, S., 209
Philadelphia, black philanthropy in, 224–225
Philanthropy: black, 219–238; concept of, 4; emergence of organized, 20; fund raising related to, 125–128; mission of, 6; motivations for, 56–57; premise of, 5;

principle of, 10; and relationships, 13; self-interest in, 126
Phillips, A., 149, 169
Phillips Exeter Academy, education at, 24, 25
Philosophy: aspects of, 3–17; background on, 3–5; described, 5–8; and fund raising as moral action, 8–10; and human nature, 10–12; and successful fund raising, 13–16
Pierce, L., 21, 22, 23, 24, 25, 36
Planning, in advance of capital campaign, 176
Playboy Foundation, 83
Pluralist approach, to professionalization, 111–112
Polo, M., 46
Positive thinking, need for, 14
Powell, W. W., 112, 121–122
Power approaches, to professionalization, 111–112
Pragmatism-idealism spectrum, in conflicts of interest, 86–87, 88–93, 97
Praise, impact of, 12
Prial, F. J., 151, 169
Productivity, marginal or average, 240
Products and advertising, and business practices, 130–131
Professionalization: aspects of, 101–169; attributes of, 103–123; background on, 103–104; barriers to, 159; and business practices, 124–143; costs of, 115–116, 118–119; definitions and usages in, 108–109; evolution of, 18–36; and feminization, 144–169; goals, strategies, and tactics for, 113–119; issue of, 279; in pioneer generation, 26–27; summary on, 119–121; theoretical views of, 109–113; and work of development, 105–108
Progress reports, for capital campaign, 181–182
Progressive Movement, 21

Promise, breaking, withholding by, 75–76

Prospects: advance preparation for, 177–178; difficult, 182. *See also* Donors

Public education accountability, regulation of, 206, 207–208, 210–212

Public information programs, regulation of, 212

Public relations: feminization of, 160–162; by pioneer fund raisers, 23, 24

Public television stations, fund raising by, 191, 197

Q

Quarles, B., 225, 238

R

Raley, N., 115, 116, 122
Rawls, 87
Reagan revolution, 220
Reality, in language, 40–41
Reciprocity, serial, 16
Recovery of funds, regulation of, 213–214
Red Cross, 25, 192
Registration, regulation of, 214–215
Regression analysis, use of, 247–249
Regulation: aspects of, 200–218; background on, 200–203; of contracts, 216–217; current mood for, 203–209; issue of, 279; legislative trends in, 209–214; and principles of fund raising, 214–216
Rehnquist, W. H., 188
Reinert, P. C., 35, 36
Reingen, P., 250, 252, 255
Religious fund raising: appropriate practice in, 54–56; aspects of, 53–72; background on, 53–54; biblical views of, 57–65; and black churches, 220, 224–225, 230; and Greco-Roman tradition, 65–66; inappropriate, 55–56, 67–68; in

Judeo-Christian tradition, 53–65, 69–72; in Middle Ages, 65–68; New Testament views of, 61–65; Old Testament views of, 57–61; overview of, 56–57; principles of, 64–65; recently, 68–70; in Reformation, 68; summary and lessons of, 70–72

Research base, for professionalization, 117–119

Reskin, B. F., 145, 148, 149, 150, 157, 169

Responsibility, need for, 16

Rhetoric, issue of, 279–280

Riley decision, 200, 202, 203–209, 212

Ritzer, G., 110, 122
Roberts, O., 136
Rockefeller, J. D., 23, 84
Rosser, J., 168
Rosso, H. A., 3, 272
Roth, J. A., 111, 122
Rowan, B., 112, 122
Rule of Thirds, 26
Ryan, J. P., 29–30, 32–33, 45, 50
Rytina, N. F., 147, 169

S

Sacralization, and secularization, 69–70
Salamon, L., 220, 238
Salk, J., 46
Salvation Army, 192
Sand, L. B., 188
Sasakawa, R., 84
Schaumberg case, 188, 204
Schellhardt, T. D., 149, 168
Schwartz, J. J., 27, 31, 205
Scott, W. R., 112, 122
Secularization, and sacralization, 69–70
Self-aggrandizement, and religious fund raising, 56, 60–61, 63, 64, 65, 67–68, 70, 71
Self-interest, and philosophy of fund raising, 8, 10–12, 15, 126
Self-regulation, 203, 209
Seymour, H. "S.," 25, 26

Shoemaker, D., 114, 123
Skill development, for professionalization, 114–117
Smith, J. P., 128, 143
Smith, T. L., 72
Snyder, G., 95, 99
Snyder, M., 56, 72
Social control systems, and women, 150
Socioeconomic profiles, of black and white donors, 226–231
Solicitation: door-to-door and telephone, 208–209, 212; earliest, 181; effective, 180–181; optimality of budgets for, 244–245
South Dakota, regulation in, 209
Southern California Association for Philanthropy, 221, 238
Southern Education Foundation, 9, 17
Spelman College, gift to, 236
Staff, managing, and business practices, 135–136
Stamatakos, L. C., 119, 123
Stanford University, centennial campaign of, 193–197
States, regulation by, 200–218
Statesmanship, and business practices, 138–139
Status issue, and feminization, 153, 157–160, 161
Steinberg, R., 239, 250, 255–256
Still, W., 220
Street, W. D., 19, 26, 36
Strober, M., 148, 169
Swaggart, J., 136
Sweepstakes fund raising, and regulation, 201, 205–206

T

Tamblyn, G., 25
Taylor, B., 149, 169
Teamwork, need for, 13
Technology: in fund-raising evolution, 33; and future, 166
Tempel, E. R., 3, 272
Tennessee, regulation in, 209

Theory base, for professionalization, 117–118
Third sector, fund raising in, 273–275
Thomas, D., 29
Thomas, E. G., 108, 123
Tiano, A. S., 197
Time, as money, 42
Timothy, 62
Tin cup: attributes of, 184–199; breaking syndrome of, 189–190; conclusions on, 197–198; exchange process combined with, 193–197; impact of, 186–187; as symbol and tool, 185; using, 190–193
Tithing, and religious fund raising, 59, 64–65, 67
Tocqueville, A. de, 219, 220
Toth, E. L., 149, 160, 169
Touhey, J. C., 150, 169
Training, issue of, 279
Travelers, The, sponsorship by, 9
Treash, H., 31, 32
Trust, and philosophy of fund raising, 7–8, 13
Trust for Hidden Villa, 189–190, 199
Trustees: optimality for, 240–241; professional duty of, 79–80; stewardship by, 7–8
Truthfulness, need for, 15
Tucker, C. E., 25
Tufts, J. H., 12, 16
Turk, J. V., 153, 161, 169
Turner, R. C., 37

U

Underground Railroad, 220, 225
United Black Fund, 225
U.S. Bureau of Labor Statistics, 220
U.S. Bureau of the Census, 230, 238
U.S. Congress, 205, 206, 207, 211, 217–218
U.S. Department of Commerce, 230, 238
U.S. Department of Consumer Protection, 212, 218

U.S. Supreme Court, 188, 200, 203, 207, 213
United Way of America: and black philanthropy, 232, 235; in capital campaign, 179, 182, 183; and economics of fund raising, 241, 249, 250; and investment in fund raising, 259, 262, 271; and philosophy of fund raising, 10, 12, 17; and regulation, 210
Utah, regulation in, 209

V

Valdez Principles, 96
Values, in fund raising, 31-32
Vector Health Programs, 190
Velvet ghetto, women in, 145, 149, 151, 155, 160, 161, 167
Vermont, regulation in, 209
Vigeland, C. A., 127, 143
Village of Schaumberg v. *Citizens for a Better Environment*, 188, 204
Virginia: blacks constrained in, 220; regulation in, 209
Virtue, characteristics of, 12
Volunteers: in capital campaign, 173-183; expectations for, 180; and leadership, 175-176; motivations of, 56-57; need for, 15, 278-279

W

Wagman, 152
Walker, Madame C. J., 220
Walzcek, D., 110, 122
War, argument as, 41
Ward, C. S., 21, 22-23, 24, 25
Ward, Hill, Pierce & Wells, in pioneer generation, 25

Ward & Hill, in pioneer generation, 25
Warwick, M., 166, 169
Washington, G., 12
Weinberg, C. B., 250, 252, 256
Weisbrod, B., 247, 249, 250, 251, 256
West Virginia, regulation in, 209, 213, 214
Whipp, R., 148, 158, 168
Wilensky, H., 110, 123
Wisconsin, University of, documents at, 23
Withholding: deception by, 75-77; of positive information, 81
Wolpert, J., 223, 238
Women: as consultants, 165; devalued, 148-149, 158; earnings gap for, 152-155, 161, 162-163; future of, 166-167; in ghetto, 145, 149, 151, 155, 160, 161, 167; limited progress of, 151-155; numbers and percentages of, 144, 146-147, 151, 160, 162; roles of, 145-147; status of, 153, 157-160, 161; in third generation, 34-35. *See also* Feminization
Work ethic, and black philanthropy, 222-224

Y

Yale University: Program on Non-Profit Organizations at, 239*n*, 259; School of Medicine campaign at, 190, 199
Young, D. R., 134-135, 137-138, 143
Young Men's Christian Association (YMCA), and pioneer fund raisers, 21-23, 24, 25, 26

Z

Zucker, L., 112, 123